FOR FLUX SAKE

FOR FLUX SAKE

PUBLISHING

BEER, FAGS AND OPPOSITE-LOCK

Ian Flux with Matt James

Foreword by Tiff Needell

To Coral and William

Published in June 2023

ISBN 978-1-910505-69-4

Published by Evro Publishing
Westrow House, Holwell, Sherborne,
Dorset DT9 5LF, UK

Printed and bound in Malta by Gutenberg Press

www.evropublishing.com

CONTENTS

Foreword 7

1 Beginnings 11
2 The spark ignites amid dark times 20
3 Life as a grease monkey 32
4 Learning from the master 48
5 Grabbing the Formula 3 chances 63
6 Slow boat to New Zealand 89
7 South Africa and back 107
8 Gun for hire 115
9 A spot of Beaujolais 126
10 The Flux empire expands 138
11 Turning to tin-tops 163
12 Moving on up in a Big Cat 174
13 Murray knows my name 185
14 Taming the Beast of Blackpool 193
15 The Texan connection 203
16 After the ladders, the snakes appear 212
17 Newspaper assignments 220
18 A Radical revolution 253
19 Should I wear a blazer? 263
20 Racing past my half century 272
21 Some endings, some beginnings 283

Photo credits 296
Index 297

FOREWORD
BY TIFF NEEDELL

Welcome to a story that should have been told a long time ago. Ian Flux is one of the most charismatic drivers to have taken to the race tracks and his story is one of perseverance against the odds.

It is also the story of a lot of beer.

It was a special day for both Fluxie and me at the end of 1975 when we both headed to Goodwood to test the Safir Formula 3 car. We had just won championships at lower levels, he in Formula Vee and me in Formula Ford, and we both hoped we were destined for greatness.

That was the first time we met and, not living too far apart, we soon struck up a friendship that lasts to this day. He seemed like an innocent sort of bloke at the time, but little did I know how he would be the proverbial Dr Jekyll who could quickly turn into Mr Hyde!

Our paths in the sport may have gone in different directions, as I managed to climb the ladder to grand prix racing while he became a prolific winner on the national scene, but we remained very good pals and would often meet up socially.

Social life for Fluxie, however, would mean downing as many bottles of Pilsner lager as he could and heading to the punk clubs of West London to pogo up and down doing more damage to his hearing than driving racing cars ever did.

My then girlfriend, now wife, Patsy had a bedsit in Kew and, more often than not, we would end up with Fluxie asleep in the corner after one of our nights out when he had failed to make it home once again. Little did we know of his extra-curricular activities at that time...

He was one of the fastest drivers out there back then but his money ran out at Formula 3 level and things became much harder after that. His driving skills were worthy of an international career and, by rights, should have been appreciated by a much bigger audience.

Fluxie won so many races at the national level and his speed never diminished despite the lifestyle that he undoubtedly embraced so keenly. That enjoyment of life was maybe one of the things that stopped him advancing any further towards the highest levels of motorsport, something he recognises in this book.

I am also proud to have had a hand in the title of this fabulous tome, as I had the first 'For Flux's Sake' visor stickers printed when I was out racing in Malaysia, and I am delighted that my old mate has his chance to tell his story under that heading.

It is a colourful ride from the travails of an up-and-coming racing driver through to the story of a man desperately trying to spin the plates to keep a professional career going. But Fluxie's career is perhaps not an example to be followed by the ambitious young karters of today.

Despite all of that, all of the ups and downs, Fluxie's character and resolve remained strong, which is what makes this such an interesting tale. And, when you have finished reading his book, make sure you raise a glass to my mate — so long as it is a Pilsner lager, of course.

CHAPTER 1
BEGINNINGS

Contrary to popular belief, I didn't enter the world on full opposite-lock. And nor did I have a cigarette in one hand and a pint in the other.

I was born on 11th May 1956 at St Luke's Hospital in Guildford and remarkably it's still standing, although it's now called the Mount Alvernia Hospital. My mum and dad, Eileen and John, were both farmers. They had Norwood Farm in Cobham, Surrey. They had moved there with my grandparents in 1955. Dad's parents had farmed in Cranleigh, Surrey, right next to where the *Top Gear* test track is now in Dunsfold. Mum's parents' place was a poultry farm about four or five miles away on the other side of Cranleigh. They met at a young farmers' do. Dad could drive, just, so he was 17 when they met and went from there.

When they got married, they lived on my grandparents' newly rented farm, which was also in Cobham. Then dad started a plant-hire business with mum, and it was based out of that yard in 1959. I was three years old when we went there. That same year, on 12th May, my little sister Carolyn arrived.

We were on that farm until I was 12. It was 250 acres. We had loads of cows and there was milking every morning. We even had an electric milking machine, which was pretty advanced in those days. But ours, even though it was the latest thing, used to fuse. My grandad, Harold, was a right bodger and I remember him ramming a nail into it, bashing it with a hammer and turning around and saying "all fixed!" with a big smile on his face. The electricity never went off again.

Along with the livestock, the farm was arable too, so we had all sorts of machines like tractors and combine harvesters. There were about five or six blokes working on the farm along with my grandad, while mum and dad ran the plant-hire firm. By the time my grandad eventually moved out of the farm, when it was purely arable, dad could run the place single-handedly with the development in all the equipment you could use then. By 1968, things had moved on so far that we only really needed a couple of contractors and him.

Growing up on a farm was brilliant. I was free to roam anywhere I wanted, really. The farm had some tied cottages for the workers so there were plenty of people around. We had a semi-detached house in the middle of a field and adjoining us were dad's brother and his wife and kids. In all, there were about eight of us kids knocking about so there was always someone to play with.

Because mum and dad were busy with their business, which was separate, I spent hours with my grandad. Right from my first memories, I would go out with him if he was ploughing or using a combine harvester. There were no cabs on the tractors in those days and I would clamber up and perch on the bodywork above one of the back wheels. I guess a degree of interest in machinery came from that to begin with.

My sixth birthday was a massive turning point. I had no idea that I was going to get a go-kart as a present.

Mum and dad are the eldest in both their families and both had two younger siblings. The eldest in those days was expected to work on the land and follow their parents. Dad's younger brother, Mervyn, was allowed to go and buy an MGA twin-cam and he raced it three times at Goodwood — which was something dad wasn't allowed to. Dad was earning £8 a week for an 80-hour week while Mervyn was off enjoying himself.

Dad had always said — according to my mum, anyway — that if he were to have a son, he was going to make sure his boy could enjoy all the things he'd missed out on. He wanted to make sure it was all good for me and I would have a different kind of upbringing to his.

Dad had wanted to go racing. He had done the Motor Racing Stables course at Brands Hatch in a 500cc Cooper Formula 3 car. He spent about a fiver in 1959 and got 10 laps or so, but that was it. Mum said he really enjoyed it, but dad never spoke to me about it because I don't think he wanted to bring up that missed opportunity. But I think Mervyn having the MGA was the straw that broke the camel's back. He could see his spoilt younger brother doing everything he wanted.

On the morning of that birthday in 1962, I had gone to school and mum said that I would have my presents when I returned home. When I got back, they somehow managed to distract me and when I finally got into the kitchen, mum said, "Look out of the window."

There it was: my kart. I was thrilled. The first time I drove it was around the garden. I loved it. We had a mile and a half of tarmac roads around the farm and I would pound up and down relentlessly. To start with, dad would have to follow me in his Volkswagen Beetle because there wasn't enough steering lock on the kart for me to turn round at the end of the road. Maybe by the second or third day, I'd worked out how to turn the kart round on my own and I was up and down bombing around.

We had a field adjoining the house and, after harvest that year, dad decided to map out a little track using rollers. It looked similar to the shape of the Brands Hatch short circuit. It was a bit bumpy but not too bad. I needed a little cushion in the seat behind me so I could reach the pedals. I went around that field thousands of times. Dad would get the stopwatch out and he could tell I was getting better.

We couldn't run the kart in the wet because it would cut up the field too much. When it got drier again, Dad would get the rollers out again, so the course was always as close to smooth as he could get it. I remember Mervyn and dad used to stand at an apex — although I don't ever think they referred to it as an apex, it was just called the middle of the corner — and they would get so close that I would nearly run over their toes.

They would be making sure I was on the right line and giving me all sorts of encouragement and advice.

At that stage, dad would keep the kart up and running for me by wielding the spanners. All I did was just get in and drive. The kart was made by the same people that had built the Trojan Formula 5000 cars in Croydon and this little thing was called a Tro-Kart. All it needed was petrol and away you went. I knew nothing at all about karting at that stage.

Dad could see, in his wisdom, that I was getting good on the circuit he had made for me and I was able to go flat out everywhere. He thought I needed a bigger engine to provide more of a challenge. I was nearly eight years old by that stage. He got a Villiers 210cc, which I think he got out of someone else's kart. I went from having about 10 horsepower with a two-stroke Clinton engine to probably about 15 horsepower. These engines weren't cheap: a brand-new Clinton cost about £45 and at that time dad was only earning about £10 a week from the plant-hire firm.

Dad had an engineer who worked with him, a guy called Norman Currie. Norman had built his own Lotus 7, as you could do back in those days. He used to do that in the evenings when he wasn't working with dad's plant-hire firm. He could weld and things like that and dad encouraged him to help out with the upgrading of the kart.

They modified the back of it to take the 210cc engine. They got the engine in, got it all sorted and connected up the throttle, but they didn't have time to do anything with the brakes. They just thought it would be all right.

When you came out of the farmyard, there was a sharp left corner, not quite 90 degrees, but nearly. Dad decided to have a test run in the upgraded kart. His brother and I were standing there waiting for dad to come round this corner. When he braked, he lost control and smashed straight into a four-inch post. There was barbed wire either side and, somehow, he missed all of that. He hit this post, flipped up in the air and the kart landed on top of him.

We went from laughing about it and being so excited about this new super-powered kart to suddenly being very concerned because dad didn't move for a bit. He'd been knocked out and had a massive gouge in his foot.

That was what put me off. I didn't drive the kart after that.

They straightened out the chassis over the next couple of weeks and sorted the braking. It was a drum brake, just one on the rear axle. Dad went out in it and made sure it was OK. But I just didn't want to drive it again. I kept remembering the noise of that crash. I didn't touch that kart again until I was 12. I was scared and lost all interest.

But there were plenty of other ways for me to keep myself occupied. I suppose you could say my education was a roller-coaster ride. My first school was a kindergarten. Straight away, I knew I was always going to be in trouble at school. A big memory was the last day of the first term. There was a sports day with some races for parents. My folks came along.

In those days, little kids at school used to get free milk. The milkman would drop the bottles off at about five o'clock in the morning. On a warm day, the milk would go off by the time we were given it at the eleven o'clock break. That happened on the morning of the sports day. I caused a right fuss about this and refused to drink it. As a punishment for being so naughty, I was locked in a classroom. In the afternoon, all the mums and dads turned up for the sports day. I heaved open the window and escaped, just in time for the start of the mums' egg-and-spoon race.

As the mums started running, I knocked all the eggs off their spoons — except my own mum's of course! I think she got disqualified. It was my last day at that school.

After that, I went to Moleside in Cobham. It was a private school and cost about £20 per term. Mum drove me there on my first day. As I went to go in, I suddenly decided that I didn't want to go to that school and did a runner. The teacher ran after me up the road and coaxed me back inside. It was one of my first brushes with authority.

I was happy there after a while, once I got used to it. I didn't like school because I never liked being told what to do. I was disruptive because I loved being with my grandad on his tractor. I couldn't wait to get out of school, get home and put my farm clothes on, and get back into the fields. I just wanted to find my grandad and be with him.

To give you an example of what I was like, the last birthday party my mum ever held for me was on my seventh birthday. We sent around a load of cards to invite these other kids to my party, and I think about seven or eight — all boys — replied and said "yes". It was a Cowboys & Indians party and they all turned up in the requisite gear. I was a cowboy, naturally.

Outside the farm was a ditch. It was where all the sewerage went from all the houses. Bath water, dirty water, the lot. Mum assembled us all and told the crowd of excited youngsters that they could go anywhere they wanted — apart from the ditch. Within 10 minutes, everyone was in the ditch and, of course, it stunk.

Mum had to distract us somehow. She had a shed at the side of the house that she used as an office. She put us all in there and went outside to create a treasure hunt. There was a window in the shed and we watched her set it all up thoughtfully and carefully. We saw where she hid everything. When the game was ready, after about ten minutes, we all came charging out and completed it in about 30 seconds. Then we went back to mucking about in the ditch. She was in tears.

When dad got home, she told him he had to sort us out. He decided we should all play cricket. When he was around, because he was the male figure, everyone calmed down a bit. Afterwards, mum said there weren't going to be any more birthday parties. Now I'm well into my 60s, that has proven to be true.

We still had the kart, but it wasn't getting much use. I finally got back into it after we moved. We went five miles away from grandad's place to Fetcham in Leatherhead but the kart stayed at the farm.

One time, Dad had a go on the kart and asked me if I wanted to have a try again. He was great. He realised how shaken-up I'd been about the accident and never pushed me to get back in the driving seat. He left it up to me. But I did get back in. We had our new next-door neighbour with us, David Bragg, a kid about my age, and I wanted to show him what I could do. I'd been on about driving and motorsport and I think he thought I was just all hot air. I drove the kart that day and realised I'd got over the fear.

It reawakened all those feelings in me. I told dad that I wasn't going to go around the corner where he'd had the accident and instead used a bush right in the middle of the farmyard as part of my track. It was probably 400 yards in total. Within five minutes of getting back in the kart, I realised I loved it all over again.

CHAPTER 2
THE SPARK IGNITES AMID DARK TIMES

I had been going on about motorsport to my friend David Bragg because I'd firmly caught the bug — and I remember clearly where and when it happened.

It was in 1965. We went to Brands Hatch for the Guards Trophy and watched from South Bank. Jim Clark was my hero. We were at the bend that's now called Surtees and I remember Clark coming through there. I turned to dad and told him I wanted to be a racing driver.

It wasn't the first time I'd been motor racing but this time it certainly made a huge impact on me and I knew it was a path I wanted to follow.

In fact, my first recollection of what I saw at a race track had nothing to do with what was happening in front of us. We were at Goodwood in 1962 the day Stirling Moss had his accident, but I was only five and had no idea who he was. We were in the grandstand. I don't remember anything about the racing that day but what comes back to me is the absolute hush that descended on the place when he crashed. The cars stopped going round and there had obviously been a big shunt. You could have heard a pin drop. Instead of the sound of engines and all the bustle of a race meeting, there was suddenly silence.

One time with dad, we saw Jack Brabham in a Ford Mustang in a touring car race at Brands Hatch. Connaught, a local plant-hire company like dad's, had a connection with this Mustang and invited us as their guests to the British Grand Prix at Silverstone in 1965. But this didn't include giving us tickets because they didn't have enough to go round. We went up there in a Connaught van, a Commer, and Dad and I hid in the middle of a stack of tyres in the back of it when we got to the gate so we couldn't be seen.

We also went with Connaught to Crystal Palace. Roy Pierpoint was racing the Mustang that time rather than Jack Brabham. Jim Clark's Lotus Cortina was parked next to it in the paddock. So there was my hero — and I actually met him. I was really shy but dad egged me on and told me to go over and ask for his signature. He literally pushed me in front of him. I got his autograph in my race programme and we exchanged a couple of words. I wish I still had that programme.

All the time while I was enjoying these racing trips, things didn't go so well when I returned home, particularly when it came to my education. The teachers at Moleside couldn't control me and suggested that the best thing for me would be a good stint at a boarding school. So I was sent to a boarding school at the age of nine.

My mum's brother had gone to a boarding school and mum

thought it would be a good thing for me too. Initially, I was sold a good story about what life would be like there so I didn't expect it to be too bad. It was Belmont School in Holmbury St Mary, not far away, just outside Dorking. Compared with what I'd been used to, it was a real culture shock.

To see mum and dad drive away, having dropped me off with my trunk and tuck box, was harsh and I won't forget that feeling. The school didn't like parents coming to visit for the first six weeks, so there I was stuck on my own. I was allowed to write letters home, which I would do on a Sunday after church, and that would be the only contact permitted.

The nice thing for me was that nine other new pupils started on the same day. We were all in the same dormitory at night and Matron had her own door into the sleeping quarters. All of us new boys were in the same boat, which gave us a bit of comfort.

The regime was very strict. You would have to get out of bed when a bell sounded, have a wash and then go down for breakfast. Once you'd eaten, you would go back, make your bed and then you would have a list of duties, be that sweeping, cleaning the place, washing something. And then school would start at 9am. You would have a break, more lessons, then lunch, afternoon lessons and then the best part of the day was games, which you would do every day.

We played football September to Christmas, then rugby after Christmas to Easter, then cricket. We would go and play other schools on a Saturday afternoon. I did get into the under-11s football team but otherwise I was pretty useless and never made the grade. I did get involved with the cricket team but only to keep the scorecard — I could never work up any interest in cricket.

On the day I started at Belmont, a new headmaster also took up his post. He had to shadow the old headmaster for a term before he took over fully. The old headmaster was a proper nasty bastard. He looked aggressive and was aggressive. He loved caning people. But the new headmaster was much more a man of the times.

There was a football match to mark the old headmaster's retirement and my parents came along. I remember asking them what was number one in the charts. Was it Sonny and Cher's 'I Got You Babe' or The Rolling Stones with 'I Can't Get No (Satisfaction)'? Mum told me it was the Stones. The old headmaster, who was walking up and down the touchline at the match, overheard and came over to tell us that we shouldn't discuss that type of music in his school.

Once I'd been at Belmont for a year, I began to enjoy it, and found it really friendly. The old headmaster had long since gone and the camaraderie was good. After the first term and once we had learned the ropes, we then fitted in with the main timetable of the rest of the school.

That meant I had long weekends where my parents could come and pick me up after school on the Friday and I didn't have to go back until the Sunday night. We would have a whole two days at home. We would do that twice during a half-term and then we would have a week's break. Anyone who has gone through that only really realises afterwards what it has done to your relationship with your parents, the fact that you aren't with them so much. At the time, I didn't know any different and when I went home, they were pleased to have me back.

My behaviour improved. There were some nice teachers at Belmont. I got on really well with the history and geography teacher. He came from Kenya, and he was in his 50s, and I got to like those subjects because of him. He encouraged me and praised me. I did well at those subjects. That taught me how I liked to be treated and it's something that I've taken with me ever since, particularly when I coach young up-and-coming racing drivers.

Another thing I was good at — God knows how — was handwriting. My handwriting was excellent.

Nothing untoward happened to me at the school until late 1967, when I was 11, although I'd seen that some of the older boys did 'other' things. They had masturbation 'contests' in the bathrooms and things like that. As you got older, you became initiated in these things. But, in that environment, I just thought it was normal.

If you were brought up in isolation and didn't use a knife and fork, you would think it normal to eat with your fingers. It wouldn't be until you went somewhere else that you might think it wrong. The way boarding schools were in the sixties, boys fiddling with boys seemed quite normal.

But then something much worse happened. Whenever I hear The Bee Gees singing 'Massachusetts', which was number one in the charts at the time, it takes me back to the first time.

One of the masters woke me at two in the morning and asked if I fancied going up to his room for some cider. This man knew I liked motor racing and had taken me and a couple of mates, both called Simon, to Brands Hatch. Talk about proper grooming.

Anyhow, that night, when I got up to his room, one of the Simons was there already. We drank some Woodpecker cider, and it all started. That was the first night. He'd previously seen us having masturbation competitions. We hadn't known he was there but he'd obviously been watching us. He asked if we would like to have a masturbation contest in front of him. So we started — and he joined in.

Because of the environment we were in, this had all seemed normal enough when it was just between boys, but this didn't feel right. To this day I can never drink cider.

This went on for about 18 months. Very rarely would he ever do anything with only one of us there, maybe a couple of times, but invariably it would be two or three of us. I suppose he just liked seeing young boys doing it. But he never hurt us. It simply felt awkward. Things progressed and he liked to watch us having sex with each other. He would always suggest it. We kept it between the three of us — the two Simons and me — because he spoilt us and we had privileges as a result of it.

For example, I was in charge of the tuck shop in the morning and the afternoon. If one of my mates came in and was short of money, I soon figured I had one over on this master, who would be there overseeing things. I could help my friends out and slip them some free stuff, right in front of him. The master wouldn't ever say anything but would then put the shortfall in the cash register. I was never in trouble because the money always balanced. Through that, I became a very popular proprietor of the tuck shop.

The signs had been there of what a true monster he was. Two examples remain with me. I still have my old school reports and here's what he wrote about me in the Michaelmas report from 1968: 'Good progress. He approaches the subject with enthusiasm, and I think would welcome a large explosion.' He was just as disgusting in the report from Lent 1969: '[Ian] throws himself into the subject with gay abandon and thoroughly enjoys it.'

In 2013, I happened to be watching the news on Anglia TV when I heard the name Mervyn Rush. That was him. My ears pricked up to discover that he had been sentenced that very afternoon to 14 years for abusing young boys. I then searched online and found out that what he had done was exactly the same, but later on, at a different school in the early seventies. It had finally caught up with him. I felt justice had finally been done.

Regardless of that, I think I was popular anyway. If there was a joke to be had, I would be involved. I loved pranks. If I enjoyed the lessons and if the master was good, I was very involved — particularly history and geography — but it was hard to keep my attention on anything for too long if there was a prank to be pulled.

Maths was different. I didn't enjoy it and it was taught by

the headmaster. I persevered, though, because he taught me how to play snooker. There was a full-size snooker table at the school and that's how I learned about angles and how to add them up to make 90 degrees or 180 degrees and things like that, plus the scoring. I was good at table tennis too.

You had to leave Belmont when you were 13. I was meant to go on to St John's School in Leatherhead and had to pass the common entrance exam to do so. I failed. When that happened, I thought "Yes!" I could go to the local school. I badly wanted to get out of boarding school and go to the local school. I just wanted to be with friends. When you live on a farm, getting people to come and visit you has to be organised because you're in the middle of nowhere and someone has to drive. But when we moved to Leatherhead, suddenly I had mates just a few doors away.

I was terrible at exams. I wasn't aware of it at the time but I have a problem that makes exams difficult. If you put a paper in front of me, I know the answers, but my mind just goes completely blank. If it had been down to coursework, I would have been fine.

That summer of 1969 was certainly a turning point of my life as far as motorsport was concerned. Early in the school holidays, dad found out that there was to be a demonstration at Blackbushe kart track at Camberley of Formula 6 karts, fitted with Briggs & Stratton 250cc lawnmower engines. We went along. It helped that you could have a free test and I just flew around the track even though I'd never sat in anything like it before. All these other kids had been chugging around all day and I turned up and it felt so natural to me.

All that experience I'd gained on the farm turned out to stand me in good stead. There I was, doing really well, and it felt so easy and normal. I couldn't understand why but I was passing absolutely everyone. The kart at Blackbushe seemed slower than mine at home with the 210cc Villiers engine because it had bodywork and a steel chassis.

We bumped into a guy called Les Porter. He told dad he was part of the organisation and they were going up to Preston in Lancashire to do another demonstration event as a factory team. He asked dad if I would like to join them because I'd done so well at Blackbushe. Dad agreed.

Les lived in Cambridge. Mum put me on a train at Guildford, I went up to Cambridge and there was Les, ready to collect me off the train. He had two other boys with him, John and Desmond. Off we set in this maroon-coloured Ford Cortina Mk1 with a Formula 6 kart on a trailer behind.

We'd been going about half an hour when Les turned around and said, "Perhaps Ian would like to look at the magazines in the back." There was a bunch of pornographic magazines stashed away. All of a sudden, I noticed that Desmond, in the front seat, was masturbating Les as he was driving up the motorway.

John and I were in the back with all these magazines, *Penthouse* and *Playboy*, and of course it was interesting. We got to the kart circuit and put the tent up. The last peg was hardly in the ground before, bloody hell, Les was inside and undressed. One thing led to another and another — and he ended up abusing us all. As I had prior experience of this, it wasn't the shock to me that it might have been for some others.

After failing the common entrance exam, I went to Caterham School, another boarding establishment for boys that was even further from home. Mum and dad didn't want me to go to the local school, as I'd been craving, because they could see that I was probably going to slip back into my old ways. The only notable person from that school that I know of is Angus Deayton — and look what happened to him. If you're unfamiliar with British TV panel games, his role as smooth, suave presenter of the satirical show *Have I Got News For You* ended after a tabloid newspaper exposed his liking for cocaine and prostitutes. He was in my year. I used to sit next to him but only because we were put in alphabetical order.

I went to Caterham from the autumn of 1969 to the summer of 1972. The school was properly scary to me because there were much older boys there. We youngsters were tiny compared with the boys who were staying on through the sixth form.

I was in a dormitory on the second floor of an annexe. This was where they put all the troublemakers. There was the main school for the good pupils and this separate building for the rest. They put me there because I'd had to do an exam to get into the school but had failed miserably. All the same, the school wanted mum and dad's money and took me anyway — and automatically put me with the troublemakers.

A bloke called Ted was our dormitory captain. He was 17 or 18. He had his own bedroom at the end of the dorm but it was only behind a makeshift partition. I suppose there were about

13 or 14 of us sleeping on either side of the room and at the top there was Ted and his mate in this partitioned-off section.

On the first night, I remember we had to go to bed at eight o'clock and I think it was lights out at nine o'clock. Ted came striding in at nine o'clock to make sure we were all following the rules. We had been in bed for just five minutes when he came back and said: "Right, all you wankers, get out of bed and get up."

We all did what we were told and put on our dressing gowns. We followed Ted through the communal bathroom, down the fire escape, and into the woods nearby. Ted stopped us all, turned around and said: "Right, I don't want any trouble from any of you wankers" — and produced a shotgun. He fired two shots into the woods. Bang! Bang! He told us all that if we misbehaved, we would be introduced to the business end of the gun.

The first two terms were all right. That Christmas, I got my own Formula 6 kart, a Barnard, and started racing. My first race was on 28th March 1970. I won it. Mum and dad would come and pick me up from school after breakfast on a Sunday and we would go racing. I just had to be back by eight o'clock that evening.

While this was great, it had repercussions at school and in my dormitory. A kid called Russell, a big lad for a 14-year-old, picked on me mercilessly just because I was going off to do all this racing. Maybe he was jealous. He used to tie me up and smack me about. He made my life a misery. But later, in June the following year, there was some karma.

LSD was very popular at school and you could get it from a pub called The Surrey. It was 50p for a dot. Everyone else was doing it but it never appealed to me. One Saturday, we were all in The Surrey listening to the school band, which actually sounded really cool. The bully must have had a bad trip because he was in quite a state and had to be taken out of school, never to be seen again. That was a small victory for me. My whole life changed.

CHAPTER 3
LIFE AS A GREASE MONKEY

During the end of my time at Caterham and while I was still racing in Formula 6, I got a part-time job at the local garage, Ashby's, an Austin Rover dealer. At first I worked on the petrol pumps at weekends, then it became a summer holiday position, then permanent. I loved it. Mum and dad's plant-hire business was only about 400 yards from the garage. During the summer, I was on £13 a week and I was earning £15 a week in tips. I would always want someone to come in and either have their oil or tyres checked. I knew I would be on for a tip then.

I was good at that role: I was never late in the mornings and if there was a job to be done after work I would stay on and do it. Initially my job was just to deal with the customers who came onto the forecourt but, when I started driving, I was allowed go out in the works van and drop off the mechanics who were going to collect customers' cars. Then the guys would deliver the cars back again in the evening and I would go round in the van to collect them.

Driving on the road came easily to me. I reckoned that first I would learn how to pass my test and then I would get on and learn how to drive properly. I was taught by Mr Green, the local instructor from Cobham, in his turquoise Hillman Imp. I passed my test on 1st June 1973, just three weeks after my 17th birthday.

Of course, I had driven around the farm and done my karting but grandad also had a Mini pick-up and I used to rag that around. Grandad always had me reversing trailers at the farm so parking wasn't a problem for me. I actually had to slow myself down when I got on the roads. The instructor was always hovering over the brake pedal on the dual controls. I just had to teach myself to obey the rules.

The first vehicle I could use was a Ford Escort van. This was my dad's and was used for delivering diesel around the plant-hire business. Otherwise it was mine for a while, from 5.30 in the evening to 8.30 the next morning. The first vehicle I bought myself was a Volkswagen Caravanette that I got in February 1974.

While I was working at the garage, I carried on competing in Formula 6. I stayed in the category all the way through to the early part of 1973 and we were having a ball. Whenever you go into a form of racing, you think you might be the best but there's always someone who turns up and spoils it all. In 1971 that chap was Andrew Musguin. I was winning, but he always gave me a challenge. Before I was off the hook of school, I missed a couple of rounds because they were too far away for us to get back in time for the cut-off on Sunday night. That meant Andrew beat me to the championship title.

Dad was the main man spannering the Formula 6 kart. He knew what he was doing, and I never had a cross word with him when we went racing. I was always in trouble when I was back home, mainly about smoking and drinking. As soon as we drove through the gates of the race track, all my misdemeanours from the previous week seemed to fade away and we just concentrated on a single aim, which was to win.

As well as winning races and getting my first job, things were progressing in other departments too. My first sex — well, with a girl — was when I was 17 years old. She was called Lynn. She had come over from America. Her parents had emigrated to the United States in the sixties but she came back in the summer of 1973 to see her grandparents. They lived in Cobham. Lynn brought a friend with her called Bonnie. I was driving through Cobham with my mate Phil one night and we saw these two girls who clearly weren't from the town. We knew all the local girls.

We pulled up and wound down the window and started chatting. The friendship struck up. I think we met them at the end of their first week here and they were over for six weeks. I took Lynn out in the diesel van, and we stopped off on this long driveway to a posh school called Notre Dame in Cobham and we had sex. Phil had sex with Bonnie too that same time in his Ford Cortina next door. They went back to America and that was it for Lynn and me, but Phil had fallen in love and emigrated out there to be with Bonnie.

What happened to me at boarding school made me realise that I could use sex to my advantage in some situations. Things like the tuck shop experience. That teacher's exchange was for good things, like taking us racing or taking us out for meals. I don't think it affected me, but I think, as I went through my life, I've realised it has maybe made me like a lot of things that perhaps I shouldn't like. Well, not what many people would regard as normal.

If you asked me to describe myself, I would say 'promiscuous'. I've only had about five or six relationships in my life, but I've had an awful lot of one-night stands and have gone to brothels. So my reputation for promiscuity when I was younger isn't one I would really be able to deny. It's just how I was.

I also have a reputation for drinking, and that started at an early age too. As I said, we had a band at school when I was 14. The older boys, because they were 18, could go to the off-licence and come back with bottles of lager. I loved the feeling of getting a beer. I still do.

The first time I got pissed was at school, but everyone there was off their head on something — mostly acid. Thankfully, drugs never appealed to me and I've never touched them. That's partly due to what I saw around me: just think back to the guy who used to bully me — I'd seen what happened to him. I was nearly going to go down a very bad route but that stopped me in my tracks. I would just drink until I threw up. I preferred that. At school, we would get pissed most weekends when the older boys brought back booze. They would charge us double what it had cost them in the shops.

We used to fund this by going shoplifting in Croydon. We would jump on the bus from Caterham to Croydon on a Wednesday afternoon, pocket the stuff and come back with our loot. I would go into C&A in Croydon — skinny old me — and, without any problem, come out looking like the Michelin man. I would take anything people wanted: shorts, trousers, jackets. At the time I had five shillings a week pocket money and that would buy me 20 Embassy cigarettes. It was a tough life, but I made it work through fair means and foul.

When I was at the garage, I got pissed more often. I would go out on Wednesday, Friday and Saturday nights. And then Sunday too. I enjoyed live music and started going to gigs. I just love the atmosphere of a gig. My first proper one was Hawkwind in The Greyhound in Croydon on a Sunday night. It was in early 1971, just before they had their hit 'Silver Machine' go into the charts in 1972. That record has stayed with me.

I remember 1972 very well because that was the year I won my first championship title, in Formula 6 karting. Even after winning that, I wasn't thinking of motorsport in terms of making any career out of it, but I began to realise I was pretty good at it and there was always the thought of seeing how far I could go. Once I had won in karting, I needed to move into cars.

This was the next big step for me. Formula 6 had been run by the Rochester Motor Club and the club secretary there was a guy called Peter Ingram-Monk. He was dedicated to racing, a genuinely good bloke. When I was coming up to 17 years old, he asked my dad what he thought I was going to do when I transferred to cars.

The initial idea was to do Formula Ford, which had been going for five seasons. Peter told my dad and I that in Formula Ford, because it was so popular, we could be one of more than 40 entries. They then get divided into two sessions for practice and then if you didn't qualify, you didn't get a race. Peter pointed out that what I needed at that time was experience and mileage. The more I could race, the better it would be for my education as a driver. So we looked at Formula Vee.

The added bonus of Formula Vee, which used the air-cooled Volkswagen Beetle engine, was that VW was involved as a factory and you would get £200 per race win. There were also bonuses from firms like Bosch and Bilstein. If I got pole position, fastest lap and won the race, I could make £300 — and, take into account, the entry fee for a race was only £7. In Formula Ford, a driver would have been lucky to make £50 for a win and needed to be very, very good to achieve that.

We bought my first Formula Vee car, a white Scarab, for the 1973 season. The Scarab came from a guy called Keith. We turned up and had no clue what we were looking at. Keith wanted £650 for it but we managed to beat him down to £550. We had sold the Formula 6 kart and dad's plant-hire firm helped pay for the rest. Dad took it home and painted it yellow to match all the plant-hire vehicles. It had 'Flux Plant' plastered on the side and off we bowled.

I never thought I would immediately go out there and blow

the doors off everyone. We didn't have a clue about it but at that time there were loads of people like us. Even someone like Tiff Needell used to turn up with his Formula Ford car on a trailer and it was just him and his girlfriend as the entire crew. There was an innocence to it all, I suppose.

My first run in the Scarab was an afternoon's testing on Silverstone club circuit. We got to Silverstone early and went for a sandwich in The Royal Oak on the main road through Silverstone village. The first bloke we ever met to do with Formula Vee was Brian Henton and he'd been the champion in 1971. Now he was full of himself and in Formula 3.

The test session started at 2.00 in the afternoon. I remember Graham McRae's Formula 5000 car was there and I reckon he did two laps for every one lap that I managed. He came past me so often it was unbelievable. I could literally feel the ground shake each time he went by.

My first race was at Lydden Hill. I'd never been to Lydden. I qualified third but crashed on the last lap of practice at Paddock bend and went straight into the earth bank. It was my fault. I was using a dark visor and didn't see the oil that someone had dropped. It was a proper shunt: I bent the car significantly and we had to go home. Dad was OK about it because I had got myself on the front row — it was a three-by-two grid in those days — and I obviously had some pace.

The first time I competed in an actual race was at Snetterton on the old long circuit with the Norwich hairpin at the far end. I'd never been there either but after the Lydden accident I was totally over-cautious. I got spooked by every bend coming up. I think I qualified about second to last. I went a little bit better in the race, but I finished something like 16th.

We went to Mallory Park and I didn't do quite so badly there. Olly Hollamby won the race and Bruce Venn was second. Apparently they'd had a good race, but all I remember was that I didn't get lapped and I was happy with that. The driving bit came quite naturally to me from that point onwards.

Brands Hatch was next and I'd raced there in Formula 6 so I had a rough idea of where it went. This is when I realised that our engine must have been straight out of a standard Beetle. People I'd been dicing with at Mallory Park just blew past me down the straight and I knew I had come out of Clearways bend all right. It was like I was standing still.

We got talking to Olly Hollamby and asked if his Volkspares firm could do us a motor. The last race was at Llandow. I finished sixth with Olly's engine and then I realised things were going to be much better in terms of performance.

The old Scarab looked shit and for 1974 we wanted something that seemed more modern and professional, so we gave it different bodywork and made it look like a Royale. Despite all the work in doing that, when the season began we had trouble with the engine, of all things. We had a persistent misfire and we couldn't trace it — and nor could Olly. We tried absolutely everything for three rounds.

Barry Triggs had prepared the engine for the guy leading the championship. He said he would do us an engine, which was very kind of him. It transformed the thing. We also had a man called Bert Pullen come on board and help us out working on the car in the evenings. Bert had been a mechanic with the Connaught Formula 1 team in the fifties. By this time just about the only original things on the Scarab were the two top chassis rails. We'd done that much to it.

With the Triggs engine, things started to go very well at the mid-point of 1974. Towards the end of the season I had a run of second places at Croft, Rufforth, Cadwell Park and Brands Hatch. I started to think, "Heck, yes, maybe I can win this championship." But I didn't quite manage it. At the end of the year I was runner-up.

Formula Vee was really strong on the continent and I took on the best of the European boys when they came over for their round at Silverstone. They were miles quicker than me and it was a real eye-opener, but I was the top Brit that day, in tenth place.

Even at this point, I still wasn't thinking about motorsport as a career, but I'd hit another speed bump in life earlier that year when Ashby's garage in Cobham sacked me from the job I loved.

They'd sent me to study mechanical engineering at college. This wasn't something I'd ever wanted to do but stupidly I'd been persuaded into agreeing. I was happy with what I'd been doing on the forecourt and running the mechanics around to pick up and drop off customers' cars, but the bosses at Ashby's suggested that I would love taking this course and it would help me make progress in the company. They told me it was only one day a week, but after all the problems I had with school, I really didn't want to go back to learning. Of course, it turned out that it wasn't one day a week at all, it was 'block release'. It was six weeks at a time — so just like being back in full-time education. I didn't want it. I wanted to go back on the petrol pumps and do some driving.

One of the guys with a financial interest in the garage was Tony Vlassopulos, who co-owned a new Formula 1 team, Token, that was building its own car. He was friends with Brian Woodfield, who owned the garage. Brian spoke to Tony and said that he had a kid working for him who loved racing and had done bit of race driving. He told him that unfortunately this kid couldn't stay with him in the garage business due to his unhappiness about the college course he was doing.

Tony said Token was looking for someone to be floor sweeper and do the odd jobs — which is how I ended up working for them at Walton-on-Thames. There I was, suddenly employed by a grand prix team. I started for them on 1st March 1974.

Token had been created out of the remains of Rondel Racing, a successful Formula 2 team run by ex-Brabham mechanics Ron Dennis and Neil Trundle. For 1974, Rondel Racing had planned to move up to Formula 1 with its own car designed by Ray Jessop, but the team folded when its main sponsor, Motul, pulled out because of the oil crisis. When it fell over, Tony Vlassopulos, who was in shipping, and Ken Grob, who was in shipping insurance, got together and out of it emerged Token, as in 'To' and 'Ken', with Jessop and Trundle staying on board. Ron Dennis used to come over for lunch quite regularly to see how things were going. I just remember him being very flash. I didn't know him from Adam because I'd never been involved at that level before.

Token was going to be running Tom Pryce in Jessop's car, which was now called the Token RJ02. Besides Jessop and Trundle, the only other full-time staff were a guy called Chris Lewis and me — that was the whole team. What a different world from today.

My third day there was my defining moment. I still didn't know what I wanted to do with my life. I was enjoying my racing in Formula Vee, but I was a bit aimless otherwise. But after that third day, this light switch went on in my mind and I knew I loved motorsport. I adored everything about it — including working late and knowing you got the job done. Suddenly I knew this was what I wanted to do. Being part of a Formula 1 team floated my boat. My whole interest ramped up from that point and I started reading the magazines, things like *Autosport*, because Neil Trundle always had a copy.

I was soon turning my hand to everything at Token. At a race weekend, I became the tyre man and would take the wheels to Firestone and get them fitted with the tyres. I was responsible for the petrol going in the car and coming out. I made sure the batteries were on charge.

When I arrived, Token didn't even have a transporter. One day in the pub in Cobham I bumped into a mate who did crash repairs and he told me that an ex-Pickfords furniture removal lorry had just come in. I told Neil the next day and we went to look at the truck. We measured it to make sure the Token would fit inside and did the deal. We bought the truck for £650. We gave it a quick green-and-yellow paint job and I kitted out the interior to hang boxes of tools and spares, made a tyre rack, all of it.

One thing I remember vividly was going up to Cosworth in Northampton one afternoon with a huge cheque from Titan Properties, Chris Meek's company that backed Tom Pryce's career, and returning with a DFV in the back of the team's Volkswagen van.

My first race with Token — and the team's first race — was the non-championship International Trophy at Silverstone. It didn't go well. Tom scraped onto the back of the grid, 15 seconds slower than anyone else, and dropped out of the race before the halfway mark. Then we went to Nivelles for the Belgian Grand Prix.

Neil Trundle was pretty much a workaholic. The night before the race, we had a problem and had to work until four in the morning to sort the thing. It was the night ABBA won the Eurovision song contest with 'Waterloo', and Waterloo is less than eight miles from Nivelles, where the race was being held — I must have heard that song 100 times blaring out everywhere over the course of the following week. Anyway, things went better for Token that weekend. Tom qualified quite well, up with some more experienced drivers, but again didn't finish.

We couldn't get an entry for Monaco, so Tom instead drove Vlassopulos's March 743 in the Formula 3 race — and won. Then Shadow came along to get Tom's signature. We were testing the Token at Goodwood and these Shadow people all arrived in their helicopters. It was a very different world from filling people's Ford Cortinas with a tank of four-star on Cobham high street, that's for sure.

Token missed a few races and then signed a deal with David Purley for the British Grand Prix at Brands Hatch. The entry was very over-subscribed and he just missed the cut, the best of the nine guys who didn't manage to qualify for the race.

Then we had Ian Ashley in the cockpit for the next two races, in Germany and Austria. Neil Trundle had left by this time, to go to the Tyrrell Formula 1 team, and now we had Jonathan Greaves working for us. His nickname was 'Wingnut'. The first time Wingnut came along was when we went to Goodwood for a test with Ashley before we went abroad for the two races. It all went reasonably well and Ashley came up with the money, something that was never assured in those days. So off we went on our continental adventure, the plan being to stay out there between the races.

The first night away we stayed somewhere in Belgium, Wingnut and me sharing a room. Mum had packed my suitcase very nicely for my two weeks away with the team. Like me, Wingnut loved a drink. We got on the beer and were encouraging each other, having a very merry time. Finally we went back to our hotel room — and I threw up all over my nice fresh clothes. On my first night away...

When we got to the Nürburgring, I found the people who ran the Hesketh motorhome and they showed me the way to Adenau, where there was a laundrette. Thank God for that.

Ian actually finished both races, one lap down at the

Nürburgring in 14th place, but so far back at the Osterreichring that he wasn't classified. After that, Token folded. I was out of a job again.

It was just by pure fluke that my own racing in Formula Vee that year happened to be on weekends when there wasn't a grand prix. Neil Trundle was very interested in what I was doing and was a great encouragement. When I raced at Croft, Neil was there and of course that was the point when he realised I really could drive a bit. Neil attended in connection with a sports car team that was also part of the Token set-up. This was KVG Racing, which Ken Grob had established for his son Ian to race a Chevron B23 that Chris Meek had bought as part of some business deal.

As I said, Token had been using Firestone tyres. Firestone's base wasn't far from us, quite close to Heathrow, at Colnbrook. Before we went off to Germany and Austria, Wingnut had sent me up there in the team's Volkswagen transporter van to get the tyres we would need. I had been there a couple of times and knew the roads and where I was going. When I whizzed into the yard, all of a sudden this big old guy started shouting at me, clearly not appreciating my deft touch of opposite-lock with squealing tyres. He came over and asked me what the hell I thought I was doing. "How dare you drive into the yard like that," he screamed.

He eventually asked me where I had come from and I said I was from Token. He told me which bay to go to and I saw this fitter called Mick, whom I knew from the races. Mick asked me what I'd done to upset Ernie. I didn't know the bloke's name, but it was Ernie Brawn, and he was the manager. While Mick fitted the new tyres, he told me that it might be a wise idea to go down to Ernie's office and apologise for my reckless behaviour. So I did. We became quite friendly and of course I had no idea then that I would cross paths with Ernie's son a few years later.

There was also a bit of luck associated with Ian Ashley joining the team. He was sponsored by ShellSport and the frontman there was a guy called Keith Kirby. When we got talking, I told Keith I was racing myself and he asked me to keep him informed of my results. At the end of the season I phoned him and said it had gone well. He told me he would sponsor me for £1,000 to continue in Formula Vee in 1975. That was pretty unbelievable.

Dad took his £550 that he'd paid for the Scarab in the first place and put that back into his company, so the car was ours. I'd set myself up as a limited company by now, so the Scarab became one of my assets.

I had another sponsor, Ockley, who put in £2,000. Ockley was a local construction firm that had effectively built Bracknell new town and had hired a lot of plant from mum and dad. My mum told people there that I was doing Formula Vee but couldn't continue due to lack of budget and was going to have to stop. They asked how I'd done and the upshot was that I went to see the boss and showed him my results. I told him I wanted to go out and win — and he handed over the money. Thank you, boss. Thank you, mum.

I didn't damage the car all year and I reckon the 1975 season cost £1,800. We didn't do any testing, but nor did anyone else. Two of the races were in the wet but I had some great Goodyear wet tyres and absolutely dominated. The whole season was almost a dream scenario. I won the title.

CHAPTER 4

LEARNING FROM THE MASTER

W ith Token, I'd glimpsed a life that I really wanted but it had been snatched away. Just before Token closed, however, Neil Trundle phoned the workshop. Ray Jessop's wife answered the phone and said he wanted to speak to me. Neil said he'd heard that Token was shutting. He said he would call Graham Hill's Formula 1 team on my behalf because he knew they were looking for a new van driver.

Neil put in a good word for me. I didn't even have to go for an interview. Neil just rang back and told me I would be starting at Embassy Hill the following Monday. The team was based in Feltham, in the old Rondel Racing workshops, as Graham had raced for Ron Dennis's team and then taken over the premises after Rondel's closure. Graham had set up the team in 1973, running a Shadow, then turned to Lola in 1974. Now he was starting to build his own car, the Lola-derived Hill GH1.

Ray Brimble was the team manager. When I arrived on the

Monday morning, he took me upstairs to introduce himself properly and told me I was there for one month's trial. My first task was to fill the team's Ford Transit with fuel and go to Earls Barton near Northampton where John Thompson's company TC Prototypes built the monocoque for the GH1.

Embassy Hill was a much bigger set-up than Token. It was a proper team. I think there were 19 of us rather than just the four we'd had at Token. Andy Smallman was in the drawing office upstairs, Alan Howell was on the engineering strength and Alan Turner was the chief mechanic. There was even a secretary.

When I went to Token in 1974, I was on £25 a week, but at Embassy Hill I stepped up to £30, so I knew I'd really made it in grand prix racing at that point.

The first time I went anywhere with the team was a test session with Graham at Goodwood. Three of us went down there and my job was to hang out the lapboard. Graham was sponsored by Firestone and used to get paid so much per mile, so his idea of a day's testing was to do as many laps as he possibly could — *ker-ching*! I think he was doing times around 1m 7s, something like that, and I was hanging them out every lap: '7.1s', '7.2s', '7.1s'. He just seemed to drive past without looking at my board so I began to feel like I was standing there for no good reason. I asked the other two if he ever actually took any notice of the times. They said they didn't think he did and suggested we should have a bit of a laugh.

In those days, you had loose letters and numbers that you attached to the board. They wanted to put a very rude word beginning with 'C' on the board for one lap but they didn't have a 'C'. So I hung out 'Gunt'. On the very next lap, Graham came in: "What the fuck was on that pit board?" We told him it was the lap time, but he knew it wasn't. I was standing there all innocently and he called me over. He said, "It's a good job I have a sense of humour… However, this is the first time I have ever met you and I don't expect to be called a 'Gunt' on my first acquaintance with a spotty 18-year-old."

The atmosphere in the team was always slightly different when Graham was present. A hush would go around the workshop: "Oh gosh, Graham's here." The Old Man — that's what we used to call him — could be hard work. Because I was just the dogsbody, it didn't really affect me, but the mechanics were wary of him.

We used to have a lot of meetings, and one time I remember him laying down the law to everyone. He pointed at me and said, "If Fluxie doesn't go and get the parts, you mechanics haven't got the parts on the car to fix — it is a team." I remember him picking me out in this meeting. It stuck with me, what Graham said, but at the time I just remember being delighted that he knew my name.

Anyway, at the end of the month's trial, Embassy Hill kept me on over the winter, and we worked harder than ever, flat out building the first brand-new Hill GH1 for the 1975 season. I think I only had Christmas Day and Boxing Day off.

One day Ray Brimble told me to go and pick up Graham from his solicitor's office in Soho and take him to Gatwick Airport. The solicitor was called Lewis Cutner and ten years later he got struck off for being bent. I asked Ray which car he wanted me to use and he just pointed at the Transit and said, "Take that." I said, "Are you sure?" I found Cutner's office down this narrow street in Soho. It was hard to park anywhere. I turned up at the door wearing my Embassy jacket. I told the secretary to let Graham know I was there and then returned to the van because I was worried I might have to move it. Graham came out, I shook his hand and he got into the van.

There we were, chatting away. I don't know why, but by this time I'd had some successes in my racing career and I was much more confident. Graham said, "I hear you do a bit of racing?" I told him that I competed in Formula Vee and said it was going well but I had yet to win a race. Then something clicked in me. I thought, "It's Hyde Park Corner, it's a bit damp and slippery — now's the time to show the boss what I can really do." I was yanking this old Transit around. It wasn't properly sideways, but I got it a bit out of shape.

I remember passing a taxi and seeing Graham wave out of the window to the cabbie. He had to do that because there was nowhere for him to hide: we were in a van with 'Graham Hill Racing Team' emblazoned down the side. He was not amused. He said something along the lines of, "I have a flight to catch and I don't want to be ill getting onto the plane."

I delivered him safely to Gatwick but as soon I got back to work, all the others were pointing at me and saying, "You're in trouble!" I had to go up to Ray's office and he said, "You've caused yourself some shit. I have had the Old Man on the phone and he wants me to sack you." I couldn't understand why. Then Ray added, "Mr Hill thought you drove like a complete lunatic." I apologised.

Ray explained to Graham that just two days before I'd driven all through the night on a great big round trip to Lola in Huntingdon, TC Prototypes in Earls Barton, Cosworth in Northampton and BS Fabrications in Luton, and that I was an asset. Ray said, "I persuaded him to keep you but there's one condition: he never ever wants to be driven by you again." And he wasn't...

My appetite for a party was still strong, but with my new employer there was no way I could get away with things like I had done at Token. It was a bit more serious. The first time I went away with Embassy Hill was the Race of Champions at Brands Hatch in March 1975. It was also the first time I had happened across the Embassy promotional girls. We were all staying in the same hotel somewhere on the A2. We were all there in the evening, including ten of these girls, and nobody seemed to be going to bed — and I wasn't going to suggest it. It was very much work hard, play hard in those days.

The next race I attended was the French Grand Prix. By this time Graham had retired from driving — he stopped after failing to qualify in Monaco — and I was needed at Paul Ricard because this was the first time the team was truly at full strength, with two GH1s for Tony Brise and Alan Jones plus a third as a proper T-car. My main job was to deal with the fuel, keeping all three cars filled and emptied as necessary. I did the trip in the transporter and made sure the cars were topped up for the return journey so that we could siphon out the fuel when we got back and share it around the mechanics. Thank you, Esso.

My only other race with Embassy Hill was the British Grand Prix at Silverstone, where my duties were the same. Graham got back in the cockpit there and did one lap in the T-car, waving to the crowd all the way round. Ray Brimble wanted me to go to the Osterreichring and Monza but they clashed with Formula Vee races and I'd said from the outset that my own racing would have to take priority.

I remember Tony Brise joining the team after Graham stopped. He had to come to Feltham for a seat fitting. He was due at 10am but it was 12.30 by the time he eventually turned up and he didn't really apologise for being so late. Anyway, we got on with the seat fitting, which involved putting two-part foam in a dustbin bag, sitting Tony stock still on it for half an hour, and letting the foam set around him to exactly the right shape. After that, you had to cut away the solidified foam that had spilled out around him so he could escape. But because Tony had been a bit of a prima donna and the job had gone into our lunch break, we just buggered off anyway and left him there for an hour.

Alan Jones had four races with us, starting at the French Grand Prix. What I remember most was his incredibly attractive wife. Bev was so easy to talk to and I adored being with her. I had some very pleasant dreams about her for a while.

Graham was always very closely involved with the team.

We used to see him whenever the truck came back from a race weekend and he would still be there after it had been unloaded, talking to us all about what had to be done. Then he would be out and about much of the time finding the funds but would usually be around when the truck was ready to leave for the next event. He was the backbone of the whole thing.

I was in awe of Graham, I really was. When I met Tom Pryce, he was a hero, but he was much younger, very laid back and had come up through the ranks like I was trying to do, so I felt a bit like him to a very small degree. But Graham had been a star for a long time. I would have seen him race at my very first meeting at Goodwood, when I was five, even though I couldn't remember it. Hill was a double World Champion and a BBC Sports Personality of the Year — a real celebrity.

On one occasion while I was working at Graham's, I got home to find police waiting for me in the front room. I wondered what was up. I thought one of the neighbours must have complained about my driving — again. The coppers asked me if I knew a guy called Les Porter. I said "yes" and told them he had taken me kart racing when I was 13. They asked if anything untoward had happened and I said "no". I couldn't bring myself to say anything about what had really gone on. Mum and dad were there, and I just didn't want to jeopardise anything. I didn't want to get involved.

I had a great job with Graham Hill. My own racing was going well and I was leading the Formula Vee Championship. Why would I want to put any of that on the line for this man? I thought, "Why do I need to bring anything up? He has obviously been caught." He'd been arrested after another boy complained to his parents. I thought that saying something wasn't going to bring me any benefit and anyway he was going to go to prison regardless. He did eventually serve time — so both of the men who had assaulted me ended up being jailed.

After I won my third Formula Vee race on the trot during that 1975 season, it suddenly struck me that this was something I could do for a living. It went from being fun to being something I seriously considered. Before that, I'd been quite happy doing my Formula 1 job, but it got to the point where I could do my own race driving almost without thinking. Everything I raced, I just got into it and won. But I still loved my job in Formula 1.

At the end of the season, after I'd won the Formula Vee Championship, all the Embassy Hill boys came down to watch me in the last race at Brands Hatch. I remember talking to the circuit commentator, Brian Jones, on the rostrum after the race and there were a load of Hill mechanics all there cheering. They were all there for me and they were all shaking my dad's hand and congratulating him on preparing the car.

When Graham found out that I'd taken the title, he asked if I would like a pair of his old overalls. I thought that was a lovely touch. They were silky-type Gold Leaf Team Lotus ones. I never used them because it didn't seem right and anyway I was getting free overalls from a supplier. I kept them for over 20 years and then put them in a Brooks auction and got £9,500. That paid for an extension to my house. We always called it the Graham Hill wing.

Tragedy struck at the end of the season, on Saturday 29th

November, when Graham was killed along with five members of the team — Tony Brise, Ray Brimble, Andy Smallman and mechanics Tony Alcock and Terry Richards — when flying back from a test at Paul Ricard in the South of France.

I was never going to be at that test. We were still trying to build one of the new cars for 1976, the GH2, so I was at the workshop. This was the second of two test sessions at Paul Ricard and the first hadn't gone well because the first GH2 was rubbish out of the box. This second test went better and I remember we received a telex in the office that Friday afternoon to say they had put the rear end of the original GH1 onto the tub of the GH2 and all of a sudden it went two seconds a lap faster. It was all looking good and the mood was upbeat. They said they were calling an end to the test and coming home early.

On the Saturday night, I went to see the band Queen at Guildford Technical College. Because bands were often booked well in advance, Queen had been lined up for this gig before they were famous. They rocked the place. That evening I met a girl called Carol Ives during the half-time interval. I convinced her I could run her back to her home in Cranleigh, just down the road, because that's where my gran lived.

There was a thick fog, extremely bad that night. It was a proper pea-souper and I was driving very slowly and carefully, making sure I got my precious cargo, my new best friend, to her home. We had Radio Luxembourg on in the car. The normal news bulletin came on at 11.00. It said there had been a light aircraft crash at Elstree aerodrome — and I just knew.

I knew the team was meant to be coming home that evening and my heart sank to the pit of my stomach. I panicked a bit.

I got Carol to her home. I explained to her that I thought the news report was probably about people from work and they were potentially my friends who'd been involved. I asked her if I could come inside and use her parents' phone. I rang 'Moby', Alan Turner, the chief mechanic, who hadn't gone to the test. He confirmed the worst and I asked if I could come round to his place. As I got there, at about midnight, he was getting in his car and about to drive off. He had to go and identify the bodies. He told me to go into his house and wait with his wife. When he came back, he said they were so badly burned that he could only identify them by their watches.

The plane crash was a seismic thing and so unnecessary. As it turned out, Graham's plane wasn't insured and it had the wrong altimeter, but besides all that, if only he had flown to Luton, as he had been told to do by Air Traffic Control, instead of chancing it at Elstree in the fog, then none of it would have happened.

But that was Graham. His outlook to anything was, "I'm doing it my way". His road car was at Elstree and he had a dinner party to go to that evening and I think he just didn't want the hassle of landing at Luton and not having his motor with him. He took risks, but this one had such a dreadful outcome.

It didn't put me off motorsport because it was just someone not doing what he was told. I actually felt far more affected when Tom Pryce died in the South African Grand Prix in 1977 because he was someone I knew as a racer. Tom couldn't avoid a marshal running across the track with a fire extinguisher and it hit his head and killed him. He had been in a racing car doing nothing wrong but the result was the same.

Alan Turner carried on at the team to sell all the assets and I stayed with him because I was the cheapest member of staff, so there were just the two of us. It took us about three months to effectively close the place down. We became quite friendly during that sad period.

Meanwhile, I was certainly moving forward in my racing career. After winning the Formula Vee title that year, I knew I had to progress and thankfully I was able to. Formula 3 had to be the target for 1976.

The people at Ockley were fantastic. After being in for £2,000 during that Formula Vee season, they stumped up £25,000. Amazing. Shell chucked in a couple of grand too.

Now, all of a sudden, we had our own Formula 3 team and we needed a mechanic. By the time Alan Turner had finished getting rid of all the Embassy Hill stuff, it was too late for him to find another post in Formula 1 and he was out of work. So I spoke to the guys at Ockley and told them the situation. I explained that Graham Hill's former chief mechanic didn't have a job and that he'd already done Formula 3 on his way to grand prix racing. I asked if we could offer the same money that he'd been on at Embassy Hill to do Formula 3 with me. He'd been on £85 a week and would never have considered coming aboard for less. Anyway, Ockley agreed, and Alan agreed. So, in a way, every cloud has a silver lining.

We were based in Camberley, at Ockley's head office. Alongside their HQ, they had this triple garage and we ran the car from there. We put all the benches in and painted the floor and made it look like a Formula 1 workshop. We used a Ralt RT1 for that first season after trying alternatives.

The first chassis I tested was the Safir, which was part of the Token group. Patrick Neve had raced it in 1975 and it had a Holbay twin-cam engine. I went to Goodwood that October to drive it and the engine was beset with a misfire, but despite that I did the same lap times as Tiff Needell, who was testing too.

Then, through the Token connection, I got invited to Silverstone by Nick Jordan to test the Modus alongside Rad Dougall and Kenny Gray. I really liked that car and felt at home in it straight away, but they were based in deepest Norfolk.

Geographically it made huge sense to go the Ralt route because everything was close by in our part of Surrey: Ralt was in Byfleet, Alan lived in Woking and the team was in Camberley. Ralt was quite a new manufacturer founded by Ron Tauranac, who had been with Jack Brabham right from the start of Brabham cars as engineer and designer, then briefly had taken charge of the team upon Jack's retirement before selling out to Bernie Ecclestone. Alan already knew Tauranac because he had been at Brabham before going to work for Graham Hill. And we knew the RT1 was a good product because Larry Perkins had used one to win the European Formula 3 Championship in 1975.

With Alan running me in 1976, the chassis was always spot-on because he knew what he was doing. There was either a tiny bit of understeer or a tiny bit of oversteer. We would either pull the splitter out or stiffen the rear bar, and I was there in terms of lap times, right on the pace. At this time my technical knowledge about setting up a car was quite limited: I could spot a misfire but that was about it. I'd never had any real need to know more. Bert Pullen, the ex-Connaught man who had worked with me in Formula Vee, used to tell me that the most important thing was that when you turned the steering wheel, the car had to turn with you. If it wasn't doing that, I had to sort it until it did.

It was during these seasons that I really thought I might be able to make a career out of being a racing driver because it was all going my way. Having said that, at that point, I never had the dream of being a grand prix driver. All I wanted to do was get to the next weekend and race whatever was put in front of me. With the backers I had in Formula 3, I was able to pay myself £40 a week. I was 19, I had a wage, I was paying a mechanic. And before the end of that first season in 1976, Ockley had decided to weigh in for 1977 too — now to the tune of £30,000.

I got a couple of second places and a couple of thirds in 1976. I tried hard but I honestly don't think I was as good as Bruno Giacomelli, who did most of the winning that year. Giacomelli was the only one that season I couldn't match. I finished ahead of Rupert Keegan, Geoff Lees, Stephen South, Tiff Needell in individual races, but just couldn't beat Bruno in his March 763. There were two British championships, run separately by the BARC and the BRDC, and Giacomelli won one and Keegan the other.

Monaco was part of the British Formula 3 season that year. Because it was so soon after Graham Hill's death, and the scene of so much triumph for him, it was difficult there. Bette Hill, his widow, did the timing for me and Jackie Stewart spent a while in my pit. It was my first trip to Monaco and I will never forget Jackie's advice before I went out: "Give yourself two inches of gap everywhere." I finished eighth in my heat and eleventh in the final. I went to Monaco three more times after that, but my first visit brought the best result.

At the end of 1976, Ron Tauranac was keen to improve the Ralt RT1's bodywork but didn't want to spend anything. With Ockley's continuing support, I already had a budget for the coming season so Ron put the new bodywork on my car and I went out and did lap after lap of Goodwood refining it. Over that winter I got to know Ron really well and learned more in that period than at any other point in my career. All the testing taught me a lot about set-up and other ways to make a car go quickly.

I've always thought that I had a good intuitive mechanical feel for a car and most of the seeds were sowed by that time. But Ron told me that I had to learn from him and I was more than happy to do so. He said that any question I might ask would never be too silly. He said I could ask anything because he knew what the car should be doing and I didn't. He said that if the lap time got slower after a change, he needed to understand why, and I was the only one who could tell him.

I must have spent about 20 days at Goodwood with Tauranac and that development Ralt. We were there in the frost and cold, and when it was pissing with rain, but that all helped me as well. I didn't really know it at the time, but my technical learning got so much better. It's all about your feel for a car.

CHAPTER 5

GRABBING THE FORMULA 3 CHANCES

In 1977, it all turned to shit. At the first race, on the full track at Silverstone on 6th March, I did all right but spun out. The second race was at Thruxton on 13th March and during practice I was going well in a drying session and had provisional pole position. The last time I went past the pitboard, it said 'P1 +0.2'.

I never came around again. I slid across the grass out at the back of the circuit and thought "no problem, I've got this" but the field on the outside of the track had just been ploughed. The car dug in and I went over and over. I think I went over four or five times. I smashed my right hand because I stupidly held on to the steering wheel.

That put me out for six weeks and I missed a couple of races. They got Paul Bernasconi, an Australian racer who had run out of money and was working for Ron Tauranac at the Ralt factory, to drive my car. I came back for Brands Hatch, which was a week before the showpiece Monaco Formula 3 race, and that went all right. However, because of those races I had missed, I wasn't at the top of my game for Monaco. I had done well there in 1976 but this time I failed to qualify and that was it. It did my head in a bit and then things got worse. I got glandular fever too, to add to everything.

After Monaco, it was the Queen's Silver Jubilee weekend. I raced at Silverstone on the Sunday and Donington Park on the Monday. I finished second to Geoff Brabham at Silverstone (in the BRDC Championship) and then qualified on pole at Donington (in the BARC Championship). I led for 19 and three-quarter laps. Then as I approached the chicane for the last time, I started to wonder if I would make the front page of that week's *Autosport*. I hit the brakes too early and that was my victory out of the window, beaten again by Geoff.

After that, the rest of my season was rubbish. Ockley decided enough was enough. I was in the shit with no prospects of an alternative drive. Alan Turner wanted to get back into Formula 1 and went off to work for Fittipaldi. Looking back, I realise that being on the piss so much of the time during that period certainly didn't help.

Dad stepped in massively for 1978. He bought a second-hand works March, a year-old 773 that had been raced by American driver James King. It cost him £8,000. Robin Herd was very helpful and did us a good deal on it because I think he wanted to get me away from Ralt. At least I had something to race, but not much money to race it with.

At Graham Hill's team I had worked with Alan Howell. He had set up his own operation, Cloud Engineering, and had

ABOVE Here I am getting to grips with grandad's tractor, my first introduction to mechanical power on the family farm.

ABOVE AND BELOW *I had no idea what an impact my sixth birthday present would have on the rest of my life. Soon I was perfecting my skills in a field next to our home.*

ABOVE AND BELOW In a report on my progress as a 13-year-old at Belmont, the boarding school I attended in Surrey, one master's intentions were thinly veiled.

BELMONT SCHOOL FELDEMORE

Name..*Flux I*.. Form..*VI A*......

Subject..*Science*.......

Place

Throws himself into the Subject with 'gay abandon' and thoroughly enjoys it.

H.C.B.

ABOVE AND BELOW Racing my Formula 6 Barnard chassis in 1971, at Buckmore Park (above) and at Brands Hatch (below), the latter the occasion of my first race win on a damp October day.

9 IAN FLUX RACING
72- SEASON

DATE	PLACE	ENTERED	PLACINGS	TOTAL
APRIL 2ND	FRADLEY	2 RACES	1ST, 1ST	2 1ST
APRIL 3RD	HEDNESFORD	2 RACES	3RD, 2ND	1 3RD 1 2ND
APRIL 9TH	DETLING	4 RACES	1ST, 2ND, 1ST, 2ND	2 1ST 2 2ND
MAY 7TH	DETLING	3 RACES	2ND, 2ND, BD	2 2ND
JULY 2ND	DETLING	5 RACES	3RD, 1ST, 1ST, 1ST, 1ST	4 1ST 1 3RD
JULY 30TH	HEDNESFORD	2 RACES	1ST 2ND	1 1ST 1 2ND
AUGUST 6TH	DETLING	7 RACES	1ST 1ST 1ST 1ST 1ST 1ST 1ST	7 1ST
AUGUST 13TH	BURTON-WOOD	3 RACES	3RD, 3RD, 3RD	3 3RD
AUGUST 27TH	DOVER	3 RACES	BD 1ST 1ST	2 1ST
SEPTEMBER 3RD	DETLING	5 RACES	1ST 1ST 1ST 1ST 1ST	5 1ST
SEPTEMBER 24TH	DOVER	3 RACES	4TH 1ST 1ST	2 1ST 1 4TH
OCTOBER 1ST	DETLING	7 RACES	1ST 1ST 1ST 1ST 1ST 1ST 1ST	7 1ST
OCTOBER 8TH	BLACKBUSHE	4 RACES	1ST 1ST 1ST BD	3 1ST
OCTOBER 29TH	DOVER	2 RACES.	3RD 1ST	1 1ST 1 3RD

TOTAL : WON 36 RACES
2NDS IN 6 RACES
3RDS IN 6 RACES
4TH IN 1 RACE
BD IN 3 RACES

TOTAL ENTERIES = 52

WON APROX 70% of RACES

ABOVE We rebodied the Scarab for 1974 and it looked much better. Here at Croft in North Yorkshire I finished second — my first podium in Formula Vee.

BELOW Dogsbody: I'm at the back of the Formula 1 Token during a test session at Goodwood. In the background is the £650 Pickfords removal van that I'd managed to source for the team.

ABOVE This was the Brands Hatch race where I won the 1975 Formula Vee Championship. I put the title out of reach from my rivals with a victory.

BELOW Celebrating my Formula Vee title with my dad John, sister Carolyn and mum Eileen.

ABOVE AND BELOW I often used vehicles from Graham Hill's Embassy Hill Formula 1 team and parked them outside our house. I loved thrashing around in the little Fiat 126, which was the team's runabout at the circuits. The Ford Transit, pictured with my mum Eileen, became the transporter for my Formula 3 exploits with Ockley Racing.

ABOVE This is my first try-out of a Formula 3 car, Patrick Neve's Safir, at Goodwood in October 1975. I'm clearly visualising a lap with my eyes tight shut.

ABOVE *By January 1976, I still hadn't decided where my future lay and got to test the Formula 3 Modus at Silverstone, but in the end I raced a Ralt RT1 with Ockley Racing that year.*

BELOW *The highlight of 1976 was the prestigious Formula 3 support race at the Monaco Grand Prix where I finished eighth in the Ralt RT1. I had Bette Hill and Jackie Stewart offering me encouragement from the pits.*

ABOVE I'm looking very proud of myself here as a fully fledged Formula 3 driver.

ABOVE *This is the remains of my Ralt RT1 after my qualifying roll at Thruxton in April 1977. I was already on pole position at the time.*

BELOW *I would have won at Donington Park in June 1977 if I could have stopped daydreaming. Here am in the lead from Geoff Brabham and Derek Warwick but Geoff got past and left me to finish second.*

ABOVE Motorcycle racing legend Giacomo Agostini was one of the finest gentlemen I ever met. I helped Dave Price and Ian Dyer run him in a Formula 1 Williams FW06 in the 1979 Aurora AFX Championship.

BELOW For the last three British Formula 3 Championship rounds of 1979, Dave Price offered me the chance to deputise for Nigel Mansell in the Unipart March 793. Here I am leading Mike Blanchet's Lola at Silverstone.

ABOVE *The man in the three-piece suit is Dr Josef Ehrlich, who ran me in cars of his own design in Formula Atlantic for three years, starting in 1980.*

ABOVE This is the final round of the 1980 Formula Atlantic Championship at Brands Hatch, with me leading away in the Ehrlich RP5. Tucked in behind is David Leslie, who won this race and the title.

BELOW Before the 1981 Le Mans 24 Hours, we prepared Ian Bracey's Ibec in Dr Ehrlich's premises. Here's the car in the scrutineering area before the race, with me one of the pushers, nearest the front of the car.

ABOVE *Powering my Ehrlich out of the Mallory Park hairpin in 1981. This was a period where my technical understanding improved no end with lots of engineering input.*

BELOW *At Ehrlich in 1982 I had a Japanese team-mate, Masanori Sekiya, who went on to become the first Japanese winner at Le Mans in 1995.*

been running Tony Dron in a Unipart-sponsored Formula 3 March in 1976, but then lost the Unipart deal. Unipart went instead to Dave Price, who continued to run Ian Taylor and Tiff Needell in 1977. That left Alan just looking after Phil Silverstone in Formula 3 and Adrian Hall in Sports 2000 and also servicing road-going motorcycles. I took my March 773 to him to run it. I had a spare engine left from my Ralt days — well, there was an engine knocking around that nobody seemed to 'own' — and so we popped that into the back of the March. We were set for the season ahead, but I had no money and it was a bit piecemeal.

Alan was really good to me. He let me work at Cloud Engineering and we basically ran my car on overspill from Adrian Hall's and Phil Silverstone's racing budgets and the money we were getting from looking after the motorbikes, although we had a travel sponsor for the race at the British Grand Prix. I think we did the whole year on no more than £10,000 — just a third of the previous year's budget with Ockley.

I was up against people like Nelson Piquet and Derek Warwick that season. Unfortunately, it was the beginning of a massive hike in budgets because Piquet and Chico Serra came over from Brazil and spent whatever it took to win. Spare cars started to appear for the wealthy drivers and they had several engines. They had T-cars when I was lucky if I could afford T-Cut. If a bloke goes to a team owner with £60,000, the guy isn't going to say, "Well, we only need £35,000." The team is going to take it all and spend it on more testing, spares, things like that.

My March 773 wasn't ready for the opening race, at Silverstone, but Phil Silverstone's March 753 from the previous year was lying around so he let me use that and I finished sixth. But over the rest of the season the best results I could achieve in my own car were just a few fifths and sixths.

One of the races at Donington Park was wet. Qualifying had been dry and I lined up on the third row of the grid but I wasn't at all hopeful for the race because my wet tyres were absolutely shagged and I didn't have any money for new ones. I told Alan I was going to jump the start because that was my only chance. I jumped the start good and proper. I must have reached the first corner, Redgate, before the others had a chance to get going. Sid Offord, the clerk of the course, came running down to our pits and Alan said, "Hands up, I guess that's a 10-second penalty." Sid said, "No way". Because I had done it so blatantly, I was hit with a one-minute penalty. It paid off though. By the end of the race, I was third on the road but the penalty only dropped me to sixth in the final classification because so many people had gone off and the field was strung out.

My personal highlight of the season was qualifying fourth in the Formula 3 race at the British Grand Prix at Brands Hatch. I got away from the grid really well. First time round, Derek Warwick and Nelson Piquet had a massive shunt ahead of me but I managed to avoid that, so I was in second place coming out of Graham Hill Bend. But I hadn't realised how big the accident had been behind me — I'd only seen a couple of cars spinning — and when I set off on the Grand Prix loop, still second and counting my blessings, the race was red-flagged. At the restart 90 minutes later, the clutch went as I tried to leave the line.

Another of my best races was the European Championship round at Donington Park in August. I'd been given a set of free tyres and I had a fantastic dice with Slim Borgudd in his Ralt all the way through. He finished sixth and I was seventh, but I really enjoyed that scrap.

But really that year was an education in how not to do things. We were based in Chiswick and it was 'party city' because Alan knew all sorts of people around London. We were having a great time drinking all over London and I was in a club of party people. I met a load of people who are still friends to this day.

But I also got up to something else, a dark secret that nobody in racing knew about.

I'd got chatting to some lads in Chiswick and they'd explained how they made a bit of extra money to keep themselves going. They went soliciting. One evening I went with them and they showed me what to do. We would hang around the toilets at Piccadilly Circus or Leicester Square at end-of-office hours and just pick up customers. There were all sorts, but mostly city gents on their way home to their wives and families, all in their posh suits. We would offer ourselves for their pleasure, and the money was good.

Nobody at the workshop had a clue about this and of course I didn't want anyone to find out. I wasn't embarrassed about it but I didn't think it was the right thing for people to know about if I wanted to help my prospects of reaching Formula 1. I earned enough to keep topping up the budget, enough for the odd set of tyres here and there.

That year I also went to Le Mans for the first time. We had a guy called Richard Down who was involved with Cloud Engineering. He had a Lola T294 2-litre sports car and we ran it for him with Bob Evans and Martin Birrane as his co-drivers. There had been the hint that I might get a drive and so I tested the car at Goodwood. Considering it was the first sports car I'd driven, I felt I did really well. The car was certainly quite quick. Its BDG engine had about 300bhp, which was twice what I'd been used to in a Formula 3 car. I felt at home in it straight away and it helped that I knew the track very well.

We got to Le Mans and stayed in a farmhouse. We were all down for breakfast on the first morning when a bloke turned up wearing a quilted smoking jacket and leather slippers with a newspaper tucked under his arm. He looked absolutely ridiculous. I thought he might be a sponsor. I said to Alan, "Who the heck's he?" It was Martin Birrane. That was the first time I met the man who would go on to own Lola Cars.

Our equipment at Le Mans was very secondhand and had been used before by Dorset Racing. The wheel rims were certainly questionable. We did practice and testing and all of that, and the car actually ran pretty well. Bob Evans did a time in the top five of the 2-litre class.

But the wheels were still a worry, and Alan said to Richard Down that we really needed to buy some new ones. Down said we could have one new set. We decided that the only person who should have the new ones was Evans, because he was the fastest driver. He started the race and he was running well. We did the first driver change.

My job was to strap the drivers in, that sort of thing. The crew took off the good wheels and put on crap ones. On Down's third lap he didn't come past the pits and we got word back that he'd gone off on the Mulsanne straight. Just past the restaurant, the Lola had turned sharp left and hit the barrier good and hard, and screwed the chassis. The left-rear rim had shattered and turned to powder. The magnesium had given up.

At the end of the year I was quite a long way down the standings in the BRDC Formula 3 Championship, equal 15th, and the guy with the same number of points as me was Nigel Mansell. I really thought that was it for my racing career. I'd been so lucky with the Ockley funding but now there was just no money left and no prospects of getting any.

Then, out of the blue, I got a phone call from Dave Price, who was still running the Unipart cars in British Formula 3. I'd first met Dave in 1976 when we were testing at Goodwood and he turned up with a Formula Atlantic car that he was running for Jeremy Rossiter. Pricey wanted me to come in for an interview about a race drive. I went to his team's HQ in Twickenham. There was a deal on the table for the Unipart-backed drive for the 1979 season and the candidates were Mansell and me.

It was an amazing offer. Pay was £50 per week and a Triumph TR7 to smoke around in. But Mansell got the drive. I never even got to test the car.

I think quite a big part of this was because my reputation — even though people only knew the half of it — had gone before me. I can see that my off-circuit activities probably stopped me getting drives that should have been mine.

Here's an example. In 1978 I'd raced at Cadwell Park and we were staying in this posh hotel. It had a snooker table and we were all playing and drinking. I just don't know why, but I let the fire extinguisher off all over the snooker table. I was pissed, of course, but you wonder why you do those things. People hear about them.

Pricey was very square with me in the end, though, and said that they had taken everything into consideration before deciding upon Mansell. I hated Mansell for years after that.

I was on my uppers. There was no racing for me in 1979. Alan Howell and I went to run Michael Roe's Formula 3 Chevron B47 for John MacDonald at RAM Racing. RAM also had two Fittipaldi cars for the Aurora AFX British Formula 1 series for Bernard de Dryver and Guy Edwards, and we were in the same workshop running Roe's car.

We did Silverstone in March and Michael finished second, which was great. We went to Thruxton for the next race and went out on the piss with Phil MacDonald, John's brother. He looked like shit the next day at the race meeting because he wasn't used to drinking like us. Anyhow, Alan and I got the sack the next day because of that. Apparently, we were leading the team astray.

I was lucky. I got another phone call from Dave Price, this time to ask if I would come and mechanic for Giacomo

Agostini. The motorcycle racing legend — he was a 15-times world champion mostly with MV Agusta — was doing Aurora AFX British Formula 1 in a Williams FW06. I did the whole season with the team, starting at Zolder in Belgium.

Ago was a wonderful man and I still love catching up with him at places like the Goodwood Festival of Speed. At the time I wasn't sure how good he was as a racing driver, but now I know he was very good. He was so lovely to work with too, and such a generous man.

At a meeting he always liked to have a little caravan in the paddock, something that I think was a hangover from his motorcycle racing days. We had a Morris Marina TC to take this bloody caravan everywhere. He used to sit in there and make lunch for us all. He was always cooking up pasta for the mechanics.

When we went to Donington Park, we arrived early and tested on the Thursday. We were having dinner in the hotel that evening. Ago would always bring his girlfriend and sit with the mechanics as we were eating and it was really like a family atmosphere. He asked us what we wanted for lunch the next day, and I jokingly said, "Oh, Ago, I'm a bit sick of this pasta: how about avocado and prawns? That would be nice."

When we got up for breakfast the next day, Ago's car wasn't there. We went to the track to prep the Williams and he didn't turn up until about 1pm. He'd been to Harrods and purchased some king prawns and avocado to keep me happy. He had driven from Donington to London and back just for that.

Working in Dave Price's workshop was frustrating because

Ago's Williams sat in a corner next to the two Unipart Formula 3 cars. One of them had Mansell written on the side but the name should have been mine.

Brett Riley was working in the workshop along with me and also driving as Mansell's team-mate. Mansell's mechanic was Ian Sharp, who hated Nigel because he moaned so much. We only ever saw Mansell in the workshop once, but I guess that isn't unusual. It just all felt very personal to me. There were about 11 of us in that workshop and we are all still good friends.

Towards the end of the season, Mansell had a crash with Andrea de Cesaris at Oulton Park and broke his back. There were three championship rounds left and Dave kindly put me in the car, a March 793 with a Triumph Dolomite Sprint engine. I was getting paid to drive as well as being a mechanic!

I hadn't driven a Formula 3 car for almost a year and the first race, at Thruxton, was tough because I wasn't able to test there beforehand. I finished 14th.

Next came Silverstone. This meeting also had an Aurora AFX Formula 1 race on the bill so it was a bit frantic swapping from my mechanic's overalls to my race suit and back again. Halfway through the Formula 3 race there was a downpour and eight of us — all on slicks — were in the catch-fencing by the time they put out the red flag. I'd been running fifth but I went off first time around in the wet. They let the race run another lap and a load more went off. One was Roberto Guerrero's Argo and it smashed my car up. That meant I couldn't do the final round back at Thruxton. So that was the end of my 1979 season.

CHAPTER 6
SLOW BOAT TO NEW ZEALAND

One of my biggest breaks came while working at David Price Racing in 1979. New Zealander Brett Riley was the number-two driver and also worked alongside me in the team during the week. One day he told me to contact Dr Josef Ehrlich, who'd been running his own Ehrlich cars in Formula 3 for the best part of ten years, and Brett had driven for him in 1978. I knew a little bit about him from the Formula 3 paddocks.

Dr Ehrlich was a clever man. An Austrian Jew, his family had been persecuted before the war and escaped to England. He arrived here in 1938 with nothing. His expertise was in two-stroke engines and in 1947 he set up EMC (Ehrlich Motor Company) to build motorcycles with an engine of his own design. After EMC was forced to close in 1952, he joined Austin to develop a two-stroke engine but that never came to anything, and then he worked in the small-engine department of De Havilland. There he designed a 125cc two-stroke twin that was raced with some success by Mike Hailwood in the early sixties. After De Havilland was taken over by Rolls-Royce, he set up Ehrlich Engineering and got into four-wheel racing, starting in Formula 3 in 1969.

Brett told me that Dr Ehrlich was looking for a driver to race his new Formula Atlantic car in New Zealand in the International Formula Pacific Championship, which took place in the January and February of 1980. I phoned and told him my story, that I hadn't been racing much lately but that I'd done those two Formula 3 races as Nigel Mansell's replacement. Dr Ehrlich asked if I would come and see him at his base in Bletchley. He showed me his new Formula Atlantic car, the Ehrlich RP5, and it was about three-quarters finished. He said he would like me to go to Mallory Park and do a test in it. I went up the night before and did the seat fitting. When I drove it, it went really well.

Almost as soon as the test was finished, Dr Ehrlich invited me to join the team and race for him in New Zealand. He told me the deal: I would have to pay for my airfare and accommodation for the six weeks we were going to be there, but he would cover everything else for the whole ten-race schedule. The series would be run as two races at each track, on five mostly consecutive weekends. He wanted £3,000 from me and I said "yes" immediately. I had £1,500 in savings and I borrowed £1,500 from my parents. This really was my last roll of the dice.

We had to send the car over there on a boat and somehow it got delayed and wasn't going to dock in time for the first race weekend at Baypark Raceway, but that got cancelled anyway. So we were able to roll up early at Pukekohe, venue for the next round, the New Zealand Grand Prix, and do some testing. We arrived on the Wednesday afternoon ten days before the race.

The best thing about Doc's set-up was that I had a Kiwi called Dave Saunders looking after my car. Dave had done some racing in New Zealand, then come over to the UK in the early seventies and spent time with Nicholson McLaren engines and McLaren themselves, and also worked for Dr Ehrlich on Brett Riley's Formula 3 cars. I didn't know Dave from Formula 3 other than to say "hello" but the moment we started unloading our car and equipment from the containers, we got on really well.

Dave was a fantastic mechanic. He put in the right gear ratios at Pukekohe because he knew the place and off I went. Anyway, going down the back straight, instead of pulling 9,000rpm, I was only getting 8,500rpm. He said, "We've got to have that engine apart." Back in his workshop, he opened up the engine and found that one of the camshafts was wrong. The BDA had a standard cam on the exhaust side but it should have been an SCA6 — I can remember that spec even now.

We returned to Pukekohe on the Monday before the following weekend's racing and I was back in the game straight away. My lap times were right on it. If Dave hadn't known about the cams, we would have been up shit creek. This level of expertise was so helpful for a newcomer like me.

I qualified ninth at Pukekohe. It pissed with rain on race day and I drove carefully, keeping in mind that there were another three weekends to go. I finished tenth in the first race, which Kenny Smith won in the March 782 that Teo Fabi had used to win the previous year's title. In the second race of the day I dropped out early.

The following weekend at Manfeild, I qualified eighth. I made a good start in the second race and all of a sudden I was third. I had a brilliant dice for the whole race with Larry Perkins and Brett Riley. It was actually on the national TV channel over there: about 10 laps of us changing places and I ended up finishing fourth.

Then we went to the Wigram circuit just outside Christchurch and the car was really quick round there. I finished third in the first race behind a couple of Ralts driven by the guys who ended up at the top of the points table, Dave McMillan the champion and Steve Millen the runner-up. This is also where I got arrested for flooding our hotel.

We were all staying in the Vacation Hotel in Christchurch and the Vacation chain was Dave Oxton's sponsor. Oxton was one of the leading lights out there and he was being run by Dick Bennetts, who went on to find fame with his West Surrey Racing team. We had a great night having a drink and it all got a bit boisterous. When we finally went up to our rooms at 2am, Bennetts and Oxton decided to hold me down in the lift, then covered me in ice from an ice machine in the corridor.

I thought, "Sod 'em", and lit a fag and stuck it in a smoke alarm, knowing that it would set off the sprinkler system. It's a trick I'd played before. Down came the spray and I removed the fag, expecting the sprinklers to stop after 10 seconds or so, like they had before. However, on this occasion they never turned off, and they weren't operating just on our floor. Water flooded the entire hotel.

Everybody had to be evacuated and assembled in the car park. Dire Straits and their entourage were staying on the top two floors that night because they were playing in Christchurch, so they were all out there too. I can never hear 'Sultans of Swing' without being taken back to that night.

I was arrested and bunged in a cell at Christchurch police station overnight. There were four Hell's Angels in there, tattoos and all sorts, and I thought it was going to be scary. But they seemed to take a liking to me and became friendly.

I had to go to court twice with about two hours in between. It seemed to be a seriously big story and there was a lot of media coverage. I was on the national television news and newspaper front pages. The racing at Wigram was insignificant and my third place didn't even get a mention. It was just all about flooding the hotel.

The consequences could have been a lot worse. I was released and fined NZ$2,000. Doc bailed me out by settling it and never asked me to pay him back — which was just as well because I couldn't have done. He looked after me like a son. His own son, Geoffrey, was with us as well. Geoffrey was ten years older than me and we got on really well.

The last Formula Pacific race was back at Pukekohe and I qualified fourth behind Dave Oxton and ahead of Andrea de Cesaris in a works March. At the start, I decided to go down the outside into the first corner and then there was this massive accident right in front of me. Steve Millen's Ralt, which had been on pole, was suddenly up in the air and barrel-rolled when it came down. I had to take avoiding action and hit a fire truck because it was parked that close to the circuit. They stopped the race. I was able to take the restart but got a puncture and had to pit.

I ended up joint ninth in the points. That wasn't the outcome I'd wanted, of course, but it reignited a spark in me. The mojo was back even though I hadn't won any of the races. In fact I hadn't won a race since Formula Vee in October 1975. I'd had second places and thirds and all that, but no wins.

I think the thing that changed it all was that Dr Ehrlich had complete faith in my driving and my feedback. And in New Zealand it had all worked so well with Dave Saunders. We got the car going really well because Dave had raced, knew all about racing, understood what I was trying to tell him, and we changed the car accordingly. It was great — and about to get even better.

On the way home from New Zealand, Doc said he wanted me to carry on driving for him in that year's British Formula Atlantic Championship. He offered me £40 a week, a Renault 16 road car and use of a flat in a tower block in Bletchley. On top of that I would get half the prize money. As the cash for winning an Atlantic race was £300, that was quite an added carrot for my back pocket.

Besides the race drive, I had a job with Dr Ehrlich. I worked on the cars and learned how to operate a mill, a lathe and an engine dyno. It was a real education in all aspects of the business. As well as car racing, he was running a 250cc team in grand prix motorcycle racing, using Rotax engines. One afternoon I had a Rotax on the dyno and I thought it sounded like it was about to blow, so I switched it off early. Dr Ehrlich could hear any engine on the dyno from his office and he came in to ask why I'd stopped running this Rotax. I said, "There's something wrong with it, Doc, you know, it's going to break." He said, "Oh, start it up again." He pushed me aside and started working the levers controlling the engine. I said again, "Doc, it's going to break." He said, "I don't care, it'll break my way." He pulled a lever — and bang!

That year David Leslie was the dominant force in the Formula Atlantic Championship in his Ralt RT4 and won 11 of the 15 rounds, but I had a really good run at it. In June I took my first win for five years, in the Leinster Trophy at Mondello Park near Dublin. I will admit that I had a stroke of luck to win it, but I won't let that spoil the memory. It was a bit damp and slippery, but we were on slick tyres and that was fine. I was running second to Leslie and when we went into the left-hander out the back behind the pits he put a wheel on the kerb and spun. So I won.

I won again at Snetterton in September and had a host of seconds and thirds as well. One of those second places came at the last round at Brands Hatch. It was the last time my dad saw me race and it went particularly well. It was a 25-lapper on the club circuit and I led 19 and a half of those laps with Leslie right on my arse. Then I came across Roger Orgee coming out of Bottom Bend in his old March and went to lap him. I chose to go left just as Orgee also chose to go left, so I got a bit stuck and had to brake. Leslie went past. I hung on behind and finished a very close second. It was annoying because I was certain I would otherwise have won that race. All the same, it was a good year and I finished third in the points.

My dad died just a couple of months after that race, on 28th December. He was only 49 and had colon cancer. Of course, it was a blow and I so regret that he couldn't stay around to see what was to come in my life and some of the achievements I went on to have, and get to know my kids Coral and William. Losing your dad like that is always going to knock you sideways but I must admit I had a thicker skin by that point, taking into account the tragedy of Graham Hill's accident and going to six funerals in six days.

There was one other thing about that Brands race. The Ehrlich had an aluminium air deflector fixed just in front of the cockpit opening to prevent head buffeting. Doc had put 'FLUX' on this deflector in black capital letters. Tiff Needell was at Brands that day and wrote 'FOR' and 'SAKE' either side with a black marker pen.

As Dr Ehrlich still had the Formula 3 Ehrlich RP4 he'd run the previous year, he decided that we would also do the Grand Prix support races at Monaco and Brands Hatch. For Monaco, we had to take our own fuel and we got that from the Esso filling station that Doc owned in Sywell near Northampton. Use of five-star petrol in road cars had been phased out but Doc still had some left over and we put it in jerry cans. Getting ready to go to Monaco, we ran the engine on the dyno and everything was fine, so we installed it in the car. We didn't test before the race because we knew the car was set-up well.

We arrived and got ourselves prepared. I had two mechanics that weekend. One was Peter Morgan, who had won a Formula Ford Championship in 1978, and the other was Hugh Freeman, who years later helped design Audi's gearbox for Le Mans. I had two good blokes with me. Most of the other teams were roughing it in the campsite but we were in suites in the Loews Hotel. Doc and his family had a suite and we three blokes had a suite.

From the word go I had a top-end misfire, in every session, and we couldn't get to the bottom of it. We changed plugs, changed the coil — we changed a lot of things. We didn't qualify, missing the cut by about half a second.

It transpired that we'd outdone ourselves by trying to be too clever. The five-star fuel had sat in the tank in the Esso garage for so long that it was full of water. That's why we had a bloody misfire.

Back at the Loews Hotel, we had a party for the non-qualifiers. It was a good one and there were quite a few of us because the event had over 60 entries and only 20 made the race. I was good mates with journalist Jeremy Shaw and he had brought his sister Lulu with him. They were staying about 20 miles away in some hovel that they said they'd got for about a fiver. I told Jeremy and Lulu that they could come and crash in our suite. So we all passed out there after the party.

Our suite had a balcony overlooking the hairpin. Next

morning, Doc came in to watch the morning warm-up for Formula 1 from the balcony and brought John Surtees of all people with him. Here was a multiple world champion — on bikes and cars — tiptoeing around and stepping over us, trying not to wake any of us up.

One other big memory that year came in early August. I was testing the Atlantic car at Mallory Park on the Thursday before that weekend's race when the right-hand top-front wishbone cracked. There was no damage to the car as such, but the wishbone was definitely broken and we didn't have a spare with us or at the workshop in Bletchley. Luckily, the Arrows factory was also in Bletchley and Frank Childs, the chief fabricator there, used to work for Ehrlich.

I went to see Frank first thing on Friday and explained that I was racing the next day and would be very grateful for his help. I showed him the broken wishbone and also the unbroken left-hand one for reference. Frank said a jig would be needed to make a new wishbone so we went to the design office. There he introduced me to Ross Brawn — whose dad Ernie I had upset all those years ago in the Firestone place at Colnbrook. Ross said he would take care of the wishbone for me and to leave it with him until the end of the day. I apologised for the short notice.

I phoned at about 5.45pm and asked how they were getting on. Ross said he had done the design and the jig was made, but the machine shop was still working on the part, machining the three bushes it needed. He said they would be done by about 8pm. When I went to collect the new wishbone, I found they had made two, so I had a spare.

After I told Doc what they had done, he said I should take some cash over there to thank them and gave me £50. When I got there, I asked Frank what I owed him, making sure Ross got a bit, and he said, "Is £30 OK?" So I even made a little profit on that. But there aren't many racing drivers who can say that they've had a component on their race car specifically designed for them by Ross Brawn.

We were all set to go again in 1981. Doc was suckered into running a second car for Mark Thatcher, son of the then Prime Minister, Margaret Thatcher, so we converted the Formula 3 Ehrlich into an Atlantic version. Thatcher led Doc to believe that he was bringing a wad of sponsorship from a forklift company for both cars. It wasn't that Doc desperately needed the money but he didn't want to put Thatcher in a car without paying for it because he realised he wasn't that good a driver. Thatcher did a couple of races but at the third one, at Brands, he went off at Paddock Hill Bend and wrote off the car. He just walked away. He didn't say "thank you" or "sorry" or anything to Doc. It left a bitter taste all round.

Doc's motivation for racing then just seemed to disappear. Mind you, he was getting on a bit, in his 70s. He thought that Thatcher had been so disrespectful and I think felt that he'd been misled and betrayed. I believe it was the first time that Doc had ever put somebody in one of his cars because they were bringing money. Nobody ever paid Doc to drive. You drove for Doc.

From that point on, we were scrabbling around a bit. Previously I would have been given a new engine if I wanted one, but now we had to patch up a spare. I wasn't getting the kit I needed to remain competitive and things weren't quite at the same level, so we struggled somewhat for the rest of the season. Nonetheless, I finished fourth in the points behind Ray Mallock, the champion, and Alo Lawler and Phil Dowsett.

My absolute highlight of 1981 was winning at Brands Hatch in May on the Grand Prix circuit in the soaking wet. It was my first win since dad had passed away but mum and my gran were there to see it. It was a special moment and I remember waving to them from the top of the podium.

There was another Le Mans diversion in the middle of that season. It came after I took a phone call from Gordon Horn, whom I had known from Token days. Not long before, Gordon's wife Rosie, who worked as a secretary at Radbourne Racing, had followed up on Tiff Needell's little Brands Hatch prank and very kindly had some 'FOR FLUX SAKE' helmet stickers made — something I've stuck with ever since.

Anyway, Gordon told me that he was going to be running a sports car at Le Mans for a guy called Ian Bracey but had no premises. Bracey's car, called the Ibec, had been built around a converted Hesketh Formula 1 chassis and had already appeared at Le Mans twice but then been stored for the best part of a year. So we brought the car to Ehrlich's place and prepared it for action.

Bracey, who was paying for it all, was an interesting character. His nickname was 'Baked Bean' because he was quite short and extremely round. His father had made his money through an insurance company called Ibec and now Baked Bean was spending his inheritance on racing.

Like quite a few teams, we did the six-hour race at Silverstone as a try-out with our two drivers for Le Mans, Tony Trimmer and Tiff Needell, plus Vivian Candy. Tiff retired the car after 25 laps with a melted piston in its Cosworth engine.

When we went to Le Mans, I asked Peter Morgan to join us again after he'd helped us out with the Formula 3 Ehrlich in Monaco. The Ibec's gearbox was a total nightmare and it haunted us all weekend: I think I must have had the thing apart more than 10 times over the course of our week in France.

In the race the car kept going into the night. At about 2am Trimmer came past the pits without the rear bodywork. It had come off somehow. This bodywork included an integral rear wing so there must have been quite a loss of rear downforce without it. We rushed around to get the spare one out because we were certain that Tony would be coming into the pits on the next lap. But we needn't have panicked. He drove past again, and again, and again. He just kept going. When he finally came in for his regular refuelling stop, he said the car felt better "without the bloody bodywork". The car lasted until the engine cried enough after 15 hours.

We stopped in Paris on the way back and went to a club. A chick caught Tiff's eye. We were all trying to tell him that 'she' was a bloke. Tiff kept saying, "No, no, she's not, she's well fit." He clearly hadn't spotted her massive Adam's Apple.

I had a lucky escape in the pitlane at Le Mans. We had

the garage in front of Steve O'Rourke's EMKA Racing BMW M1 and Eddie Jordan was one of the co-drivers. I was under the Ibec fiddling with something — probably that bloody gearbox again — when Eddie came in far too fast, all locked up. I couldn't move because I was stuck under our car. I was convinced he was going to run me over and he must have finally come to a halt about a centimetre from me.

There was another incident that season that could have seriously derailed my racing ambitions. Thankfully I got away with it but I knew I'd been lucky.

I was still going to Piccadilly Circus and earning money by soliciting. Nobody in racing knew I was doing it. No one had a clue — until one night I got caught in a police sting.

I was in the underground toilets, standing next to this bloke in his 40s, I guess, winking at him and trying to encourage him to do business. He seemed well up for it but the moment he stepped back he and another bloke steamed in and arrested me. Of course, they were coppers. They took me to a nearby police station and then I had to appear at Marylebone Magistrates Court the next day. No one knew about my arrest so at this point I was still thinking I was going to get away with it and not have to reveal my embarrassing secret.

I rocked up to court the next day and didn't have a clue where to go. I'd never been anywhere like that before. I went to a noticeboard and looked for my name on the list. Just as I finally found it, there was a tap on my shoulder.

It was Tim Lee-Davey, well-known racing driver and also a barrister. He asked what I was doing there and I said that I'd been caught for speeding. He said, "Well, your name is listed in the wrong court for that, you should be in court three."

Then, of course, he looked at the noticeboard and written next to my name was the reason for my arrest.

Tim very generously said he would be prepared to come into the hearing and represent me. He said I was likely to get away with a hefty fine but with his help I could maybe get it reduced, perhaps to about £50. And that's what happened. I only got done for £50 but of course I now had a criminal record. Tim never charged me.

Although Tim never told anyone, I knew at that point that the secret was blown to a degree. I stopped doing it after that because I knew I couldn't run the risk. To get caught again would have ruined any hopes I had of racing properly. I'd had four years of no one knowing and I knew my time was up.

None of this came out until many years later and that was only because I mentioned it once on the spur of the moment. I was on a corporate day in Scotland as one of the instructors and afterwards this group went out and got pissed. Everyone was telling stories and I just joined in and blurted it out. It came about because Anthony Reid was asking questions about where my funding had come from. So I told them all that I used to sell my arse. That certainly caused a stir.

Dr Ehrlich's motivation for motorsport thankfully returned at the end of 1981. A motorcycle racing team that was running a new Rotax engine came knocking on his door because they simply couldn't get a handle on it. As Doc really was one of the world's top experts on two-strokes, this fired up his interest again and he was all guns blazing. However, his racing operation was mainly about the motorcycles from now on.

But in the background, Doc had got in league with a fabricator called Len Homer, and we built up a brand-new RP5B monocoque for the 1982 Formula Atlantic season. Obviously I was pleased about that. We missed the opening round at Castle Combe because we were too busy with motorcycle work at the time, including winning at Daytona. But I went to the second race of the season, at Silverstone, and won it.

Initially, it was just me in the Formula Atlantic team, but we expanded again halfway through the year. A Japanese driver, Masanori Sekiya, had come over and bought a new Chevron B56 that he couldn't get to run competitively. He knocked on our door because he and his friend Mutsuaki Sanada, who had come over with him to run the car, knew that Doc still had my old chassis from the previous season.

They did a deal with Doc. The agreement involved them supplying me for the rest of the year with an all-singing, all-dancing Swindon-tuned engine. Doc didn't charge them any money to use his RP5 and we got this superb powerplant in exchange. Sanada even lived with me for a while in Bletchley. We got on well and he would become very important to me later in life.

As in 1980, I finished third in the points, and Alo Lawler took the title. I only had that one win at Silverstone, but my driving — and particularly my feedback — was getting better. I could understand what we needed to do to the chassis to get the car right, and Doc's absolute faith in me really helped. He thought I was the best and, you know, I'd never been told that.

There was a race at Aintree midway through the season, just when Sekiya was becoming my team-mate. Because we were now a two-car team, we had so much kit that we'd had to borrow a mate's £200 Transit. On the Friday evening, I was driving round the track with Sekiya in the passenger seat of this van showing him the lines when we came across Duncan Bain, who was racing against us, and his girlfriend, Jane White.

That moment changed my life, meeting Jane. I found any excuse to go round to Duncan's house near Dunstable on weekends when we weren't racing. We could talk about racing but it also gave me the chance to be in Jane's company.

My last race in the Ehrlich was the Leinster Trophy meeting at Mondello Park in September. It was the first year that the Leinster Trophy itself was awarded to the winner of the Formula Ford 2000 race. This was Ayrton Senna's big year in FF2000 in his Van Diemen and he won. So Senna's name joined mine on the silverware. In the Atlantic race, I finished second to Trevor Templeton's Ralt RT4.

At the end of the 1982 season, Duncan Bain asked me to go with him to the Macau Grand Prix and help with his Formula Atlantic March 78B, so I went as a mechanic with Peter Morgan. It was the last year that Atlantic cars would be the headline act over there before they switched to running the main race for Formula 3.

We were staying in the Hotel Sintra. Near the end of our stay, all the racing folk — about 50 or 60 of us — were having breakfast and I was with Peter and Duncan. All of a sudden, two girls wandered over in our direction, one with a huge bouquet of flowers and the other with a massive bowl of fruit. It seemed a strange thing to happen at breakfast, but I thought that maybe it was a local tradition or something. Then I vaguely realised that I recognised these girls. Anyway, they came over to me and made this presentation for being the best customer in their brothel that weekend. Everyone stood up and applauded: "Well done, Fluxie." Although I remember this clearly enough, I can't recall how Duncan got on in the race.

CHAPTER 7
SOUTH AFRICA AND BACK

Just after I came back from Macau, I was offered an opportunity in South Africa and took it. My role with Dr Ehrlich had changed a lot. Now he was really only interested in motorcycles, so I had been drifting away from the team and was looking for a fresh challenge.

A good mechanic mate, Colin Holmes, had gone to South Africa at the start of 1982 to work for Graham Duxbury, who was going to be competing in the South African National Drivers' Championship. Graham had a Formula 2 March 822 and won the title. Now, Ian Scheckter, Jody's older brother and occasional grand prix driver, had decided to come out of retirement and race as part of the same team, so they needed more personnel. I left for South Africa in early December 1982.

I already knew Graham Duxbury. He had come over to race in England in Formula Ford 2000 in 1980 and had bought a brand-new Reynard SF80 that hadn't worked very well. Halfway through the year, Graham was looking like a tosser but one of his rivals, Frank Bradley, took pity on him and let him have a go in his Van Diemen RF78. Graham went really well in the Van Diemen so Frank suggested a deal. Frank was sponsored by Tredaire, the carpet people, and had an old show car without an engine that he used to take round Tredaire showrooms. He got Graham to do all that, including standing around for three or four hours at the various Tredaire places, and in return Frank loaned the Van Diemen and a van. The deal was that if Graham crashed the car, he had to fix it — but otherwise he had a competitive ride on the cheap. The only thing Graham didn't have was a place to prepare the car. Graham was big friends with Tiff Needell, so one day Tiff rang me to ask if there was any space in Ehrlich's workshop. Doc said "yes" and so I got to know Graham before I went to South Africa. There are so many wheels within wheels in motorsport.

I did the first five South African races with the team, at Port Elizabeth, Kyalami, Killarney, Welkom and Killarney again. Our guys did well as Scheckter won two of those five and Duxbury one. There were another seven races after that because the championship ran over quite a long season, from January to October, but I had to come back to get on with my own racing. In fact Scheckter was such a class act that he won all seven of those remaining races and took away Duxbury's title by a country mile.

I knocked around with Graham's sister Jill for most of the trip. I met her when the Duxbury parents kindly invited me to join the family for lunch on Christmas Day. Jill is the same age as me to within a few days and we really hit it off. In fact we're still friends to this day. She had a nice job training Lipizzaner horses, the white ones you see doing routines that look like dancing. We had a lovely time, including going to see Rod Stewart in the resort of Sun City. I didn't realise at the time that his gig was controversial: he was breaking a cultural boycott of Apartheid by playing in South Africa.

I didn't really know much about Apartheid before I went — but I soon did. We had a black guy, Saul, in the team. The prejudice ran deep and the team manager was forever telling me off for saying "please" and "thank you" when I was dealing with Saul. We stayed in the smartest hotels but Saul was never with us. When we went to a particularly luxurious five-star place for the Welkom race, I asked him where he was staying. He said, "The same place as you." I said, "Where's your room then?" He said, "Round the back." I asked him to show me. He said we'd have to be pretty careful but I did see his accommodation. It was one big room with straw bales laid out to make about 15 very basic beds with sleeping bags. Everyone had to share just one lavatory and one washbasin.

Soon after my return, Duncan Bain called with an offer. He had bought the Ralt RT4/81 that Ray Mallock had used to win the 1981 British Formula Atlantic Championship and asked if I would like to race it for him in 1983. It didn't take me too long to agree.

Duncan also had a Formula 1 Fittipaldi F8 that my Japanese friend Mutsuaki Sanada had run for Tony Trimmer in the previous season's British Formula 1 Championship, which had been revived after a year's break in 1981 but then folded again. Something had gone awry in negotiations with Sanada and Duncan ended up owning this Fittipaldi with a pretty fresh Cosworth DFV engine and a transporter too. He offered me a run in it at Oulton Park in the first round of the short-lived new British Open Trophy series for Formula 1 machinery but I turned that down because I wanted to get used to my Ralt: Formula Atlantic was my sole focus. Tiff Needell raced the Fittipaldi at Oulton and was unlucky as it broke a driveshaft with about 20 laps to go. Duncan then parked it for a few months until Ray Bellm bought it, complete with broken driveshaft, which gave Duncan enough money to carry on running my Atlantic car for the rest of the year.

It was a great year for me in that Ralt. There were seven races that season and I won three of them, at Silverstone, Donington and Brands Hatch. All year long I was fighting for the title with Alo Lawler in his Ralt and I should have won it. We went into the last race, at Silverstone, pretty much neck and neck on points, with me just ahead. Whoever won this last race would be the champion — simple as that. I lost out with two laps to go. I was leading Alo by two or three car lengths. He'd been behind me all race and I was in charge. Then almost within sight of the chequered flag my engine started playing up. It was a stupid thing: a £5 fuel regulator that adjusted the pressure into the carbs had gone tits up. So I finished second in the race and second in the championship.

Most of that year I lived at Duncan's place in Caddington, a village near Dunstable. He had a three-car garage at home that we used as the workshop for the racing team. Jane was still with him, as girlfriend and in effect housekeeper too. Duncan had a company in Bedford called Abdex that made hydraulic hoses and every day he would head off there, leaving me looking after the racing cars and Jane doing the housework. Except it didn't quite go like that.

There was a farm next to Duncan's house. Jane and I spent quite a bit of time with the farmer's son, Tim, who was between us in age. Jane was 19, Tim was probably 23 and I was 27. There was a pub on the A5 called The Horse and Jockey and we often used to go there at lunchtimes and have a few beers. One lovely summer afternoon we came back and Jane got a cheesecake out of the freezer. It had cherries on it. She came up with the idea that we should all get naked on the veranda. She made our dicks hard and got a couple of cherries to put on them. Then she pulled our dicks back at the same time, one in each hand, to see who could flip a cherry the furthest. We did that a few times.

Just for a bit of a chuckle, a few months later I told this story to Stuart Dent, who worked in the advertising department at *Autosport*. Not long after that, Duncan decided he wanted to sell a load of old March 782 parts that he had knocking around and asked me to get an advert placed in *Autosport*. So I phoned Stuart and gave him the list of the items we wanted to sell. Thursday came round and Duncan was eager to see the advert.

He read it out: "For sale: tyres, bodywork, cheesecake 50p a slice." He said, "What the fuck's that about?" I said: "Well, uhm, you know, that publisher has some catering magazines in its stable and they must have left a line on an advert from one of those..."

By this time Duncan had decided we were going to go to New Zealand because he wanted to run me in the Ralt in the International Formula Pacific Championship in the first couple of months of 1984. Between the end of the British season and our departure for New Zealand, I had to go missing for a few weeks because Duncan didn't want to pay me for doing nothing. We got a container from Lep International, a big transport group that Duncan had landed as a sponsor, and I packed the car and equipment. That was me then finished until we travelled.

When we left for our trip down-under, I was feeling less bad about my intentions with Jane because Duncan took a girl called Jackie and left Jane behind. I really was in love with her so I behaved myself over there. Thankfully, the authorities had got over the hotel incident and let me into the country without too many problems.

Peter Morgan came along as my mechanic and my old friend Dave Saunders, who had been so vital the first time I went to New Zealand, got involved as an overseer. While Peter basically took care of the car, Dave would go over it to make sure that everything was OK and do things like compression checks. So we were well set.

We went to Baypark Raceway for the opening race on Monday 2nd January. I was quickest in the testing session on the Friday and the car was absolutely flying. But then the next day we had scrutineering for the event proper and that was when it all started to fall apart. This was the tail end of the 'ground-effect' era and since we'd last run the Ralt there had been a rule change. Flexible skirts were no longer allowed, with effect from 1st January 1984, but this had passed us by. So we had to take off the skirts and raise the car to a minimum ride height of 20mm. Getting into the car was like climbing a mountain.

I went out for qualifying and couldn't get within a second and a half of the times the best guys were doing and I was nowhere near my benchmark from the testing. We had picked up a bit of speed on the straight but lost a load in the corners, such that I had to take some of them in a lower gear. This really knocked my confidence because I'd mastered how to go through those bends when the car had been handling so well on the Friday.

The races this year were run in two parts with race times added together to give the overall results. I finished ninth in the first heat at Baypark, then spun in the second heat, stalled and couldn't restart the engine. And yet three days earlier I'd been expecting to win.

Things didn't get much better at the other three rounds, at Pukekohe (for the New Zealand Grand Prix), Manfeild and Wigram. I ended up only eighth in the points. I'd actually done better four years earlier in the Ehrlich than I did in the Ralt.

Apart from Jane, I came back to nothing — no job, no racing, no home. Duncan Bain no longer wanted to spend his money on my racing. He had enjoyed his time as a team manager but wanted to get back behind the wheel himself. Anyway, the British Formula Atlantic Championship had finished because support had ebbed away.

But at least I had Jane. While we worked out what to do next, we ended up living in Guildford at my mum's house.

CHAPTER 8
GUN FOR HIRE

Desperately searching for new opportunities, I phoned around to see what I could find. I was at the point where I would take pretty much anything to stay around motorsport, even if it was just being a weekend helper for someone. Eventually I got a positive response: "You've called at just the right time, we could do with a hand." This was Paul Vincent, who ran Macdonald Race Engineering and had been involved with Masanori Sekiya's brief campaign with the Ehrlich Formula Atlantic car. Paul said he wouldn't need me all the time but would pay £35 a day for whatever days I did.

Based at Hornsey in North London, Paul was running cars in historic racing. There were two fairly recent Formula 1 cars, a March 781 for John Brindley and that same Fittipaldi F8 for Tony Trimmer, and a rather older Can-Am McLaren M6 for Richard Knight. At first I would just go along on a Friday before a race to help load up, work through the weekend, then unload on Monday. But gradually the team seemed to need me more and more, so it got busier. Travelling from Guildford was a pain until Paul's wife Sue suggested that Jane and I went to live with them in East Finchley as lodgers.

As for my own racing, there was nothing on the horizon for several months. It was pretty frustrating. But then I got a call out of the blue from Alan Eisner, who owned Apollo Race & Rally Wear and supplied the race suits I used. Alan said he fancied a go at "this Thundersports stuff" and asked if I wanted to share his Chevron B8 at one of the rounds, at Donington Park in June.

Thundersports was a new series, started the previous year, and the thinking behind it — John Webb of Brands Hatch came up with the idea — was to bring back some of the noise and spectacle that had been missing from British racing for a while. The concept was very simple: two-seater sports cars of any age, shape or size could take part, from Can-Am down to Sports 2000. The races were a decent distance, with a pitstop and a driver change, and the prize money was amazing. It quickly became very successful.

Of course, I didn't need to be asked twice. The Chevron B8 was quite an old car, dating back to 1968, and up against all sorts of far more modern machinery in the under 2-litre division. Despite that, I set the fastest 2-litre lap and we finished third in our class, even though Alan was quite slow. Recently I was chuffed to see a comment saloon racer Dave Brodie put on twitter: "Ian Flux would've been quick in a shopping trolley. I was at Donington in 1984 when he drove a Chevron B8 in Thundersports against a lot of newer, quicker cars and was right in amongst everything!"

Another Chevron B8 owner, Don Prater, saw what I did in Eisner's car at Donington. He wanted me to join him for the Thundersports race supporting the British Grand Prix at Brands Hatch. I was becoming a gun for hire. We didn't qualify due to a technical problem but I shared with Don again at Brands the following month. That time we ran out of fuel on virtually the last lap when third in our class.

At about this time two March engineers, Rob Gustavsson and Nick Wasyliw, turned up to see Paul Vincent with their new Formula 3 design called the Cygnus. They needed space to build it and so they were squeezed into a corner of the workshop in Hornsey. When they weren't doing their jobs at March, they came down and worked late nights and over the weekends putting their Cygnus together.

They also needed a driver so I was pressed into service for two of the last rounds of the British Formula 3 Championship, at Brands Hatch and Silverstone. We had a very tired Toyota engine at that point but the car felt really good, even though I had lots of people passing me down the straights.

In due course Rob and Nick left March, took out loans and moved themselves and their new company into premises in Milton Keynes. They wanted me to be their salesman as well as their driver. They changed the name of the car to Roni — 'Ro' for Rob, 'Ni' for Nick — and called the company Roni Motorsport.

Meanwhile, Don Prater was keen to carry on in Thundersports with me but wanted a top-notch car, so for the

1985 season he bought the Mazda-powered Lola T594 that Peter Lovett and Ian Taylor had used to such good effect in 1984, winning three races. I took Don to meet the guys at Roni and they ended up running the car for him. That left me pretty squared up for the coming year: my role with Roni had turned into a full-time job, I had a competitive Thundersports seat and there was the chance of some Formula 3 races too.

Only one thing remained to be sorted out and that was where Jane and I were going to live. Obviously it needed to be within reasonable reach of Roni in Milton Keynes. First choice was Buckingham. We went to four estate agents in the town but there was nothing available to rent. Then we thought Stony Stratford would be quite nice and tried three estate agents there. Still nothing. Next stop was Newport Pagnell. We walked into the first estate agent there and I said: "We're having a lot of trouble this morning. We want to rent a house and we've been to Buckingham and Stony Stratford and found nothing there. Any chance you've got something?" The woman in the agent's office replied brightly: "Yes, a place has just come on the market this morning." I said: "Well, we'll have it." She said: "Don't you want to look at it?" I said: "I suppose we do but we're having it no matter what."

So Jane and I finally set up home together properly in November 1984. The house was right opposite a pub called The Dove. Needless to say, we frequented The Dove quite a lot and I quickly became fond of the place and the crowd there. It has been my local ever since.

A nother racing opportunity had come along a little earlier that autumn. Frank Bradley, who had come to the rescue of Graham Duxbury in Formula Ford 2000, told me about a non-championship three-hour relay race at Oulton Park for sports cars, like a Libre race featuring any sort of sports car. Frank was entered to drive a Sports 2000 Aquila RO83S for an outfit called Computer Consortium Racing but for whatever reason didn't want to do it. He asked me if I would take his place. He said they would pay me £200 and put me up in a hotel. I jumped at that.

It was tipping it down at Oulton. You have probably realised by now that I like the rain and I took to the Aquila like a duck to water. Because I was going so fast and this was a relay race, the other drivers in our team would only go out and do the minimum three laps at a time before handing back to me. I just about had time for a cup of tea and a fag before darting out of the pitlane again. In the end, I think I lapped the entire field.

The Aquila was designed by Richard Owen, a one-time BRM apprentice who had worked in Formula 1 with Williams and Shadow before branching out to build his own cars. The first Aquila appeared in 1982 and the follow-up model achieved great success in 1983 when Mike O'Brien cleaned up to become British Sports 2000 champion. Richard clearly liked what I'd done at Oulton and asked if I wanted to drive his Aquila in the last three rounds of the Sports 2000 Championship. It was a popular series and I was up against Sean Walker and James Thomson in their Royales. They dominated that 1984 season and Thomson won the title.

I already knew Sean Walker. The previous year he'd done Formula Ford 2000 in a Pilbeam run by Peter Morgan, the mechanic who'd helped me so much over the years. At the end of that season, Sean had been racing at the same Silverstone meeting where I was hoping to win the Formula Atlantic title. I'd done a deal that weekend to hire the Marlboro Suite at Woodcote corner to celebrate the victory — or not. Anyway, that was the race where that bloody fuel regulator played up and my title got snatched away. But we still had our party afterwards and I invited Sean up to the suite with his girlfriend Nikki. The beers were going round and people were smoking, so I asked Nikki if she would like a cigarette. She very politely said, "Oh no, no thanks." So I followed up, "And I don't suppose you take it up the arse either?" That rather cemented the friendship between Sean and me.

Anyway, those three end-of-season Sports 2000 outings went pretty well. One was a supporting race for the Formula Ford Festival at Brands Hatch and was shown on BBC *Grandstand*. Tiff Needell did the TV commentary with Murray Walker and really enthused about my performance, which certainly pleased mum watching at home. I finished second to Mike O'Brien and set the fastest lap.

After that, Computer Consortium Racing asked me to do the full 1985 B&Q Sports 2000 Championship in their Aquila. The team was run by Len Foster, who was the financial director of Amstrad, Alan Sugar's company, which by that time was flogging cheap PCs for home use in the hundreds of thousands. The concept behind the team's name was that each computer dealer got an extra discount if they put a certain contribution into the racing budget and in return they all had their names on the car. We ended up with something like £25,000 for the season. That was a crazy budget for Sports 2000.

It went brilliantly until Friday 5th July. We were at Castle Combe testing before the following day's race. I'd had a great run of four wins in five races — at Thruxton, Brands Hatch, Snetterton and Silverstone — and was leading the championship. But it went badly wrong that day at Castle Combe. When I turned into Tower corner, a 90-degree right-hander, the left-front upright broke and the Aquila hurtled into the bank on the outside of the corner. It was a big shunt and it completely destroyed the car but mercifully I was unhurt.

I still managed to compete that weekend thanks to Frank Bradley. He let me drive his Royale and I finished second, so that kept my title hopes alive. That was quite a gesture from Frank — what a great bloke.

Then we went to Brands Hatch the following weekend. Another generous guy, Anthony Llewellyn-Davies, lent me his old Lola for that race. It was the day of Live Aid and that evening lots of us watched it on TV in the Kentagon, the bar and restaurant at Brands, and of course knocked back a few beers. I remember the evening very clearly but not what happened in the race.

After that Royale's Alan Cornock stepped in and loaned the team a new RP38 for the rest of the season. However, my title prospects effectively vanished when I got a very dispiriting phone call. I'd also won another race with the Aquila at

Silverstone in June but afterwards the scrutineers disqualified me because reverse gear didn't work. Now the man on the phone was telling me that the points for two of my other wins were also going to be taken away as further punishment. Suddenly I was 90 points down.

That left me with no hope of clawing my way back into contention for the title. I did get one more win, at Thruxton, but Sean Walker duly became champion. He was driving a Shrike P15, which was Richard Owen's latest design and looked almost identical to an Aquila, with the same kind of swoopy body. Between us, Sean and I won 13 of the 16 Sports 2000 races that year.

What about the Formula 3 Roni, you may be wondering? In the end I only raced it once, at Snetterton in August. By this time, a Volkswagen engine was the thing to have in Formula 3 and it took a while to get one, probably because money was tight. Eventually Gil Baird, boss of Tech-Speed, helped us out by lending a spare Formula 3 motor. I knew Gil and his team because they raced in Sports 2000.

I drove the truck to Snetterton on the Friday to do some pre-race testing. Jane and I got there before the Roni guys and unloaded the car and gear on our own. I checked all the wheels and tweaked the set-up. By the time the others turned up, I was ready to go out and try the car for the first time with the VW engine. Immediately my times were very respectable.

Next day in official practice, I just couldn't get near those times. The car didn't feel quite right, not as positive in its handling, but I couldn't put my finger on what was wrong. I qualified 22nd out of 28. I overtook quite a few people in the race and finished 13th.

Unbeknown to me, the Roni guys had agreed to stay over after the race and do some more testing on the Monday. Dave Scott had been on pole for the race and they put him in the car, so I was just a mechanic for the day. Dave went around and around and they changed this and they changed that. He never got within two tenths of me. That was a relief.

It's a truth in motorsport that there are only two reasons why things ever go wrong: either the driver's shit or the car's shit. The easier thing to change is the driver. So, if two drivers do exactly the same time as each other, it's the car that's shit. But if one driver goes a second quicker, it's the other driver that's shit. It's very simple, really.

Meanwhile, I was quite enjoying Thundersports with Don Prater, even if our results were nothing special. Trouble was, the two main classes in the series were split at the 2-litre mark and the Mazda rotary engine in Prater's Lola T594 was a 2.3-litre unit, so we were up against some big-banger Can-Am cars. These included John Foulston's Chevy-powered Lola T530. Foulston usually planted this monster on pole and then he and his co-driver John Brindley would romp away into the distance. It proved hard to make much of an impact and our best result was only third overall at Brands Hatch in July.

The highlight of that Thundersports season was the last round, at Brands in October in front of a huge crowd. This was the European Grand Prix meeting where Nigel Mansell scored his first Formula 1 victory driving for Williams. I pulled out all the stops in practice and managed to stick our car on the front row next to the Foulston/Brindley Lola — 2.3 litres versus 5.0. I was pretty chuffed about that and went to celebrate in the Kentagon. I was at the bar chatting to Gil Baird and his engineer Marvin Humphries when Gil suddenly offered me a drive in the European Formula 3000 Championship for 1986. Wow!

Gil said he would supply everything. All I had to do was just turn up and drive. I was in heaven. Maybe the grand prix dream wasn't over after all? I bit Gil's hand off and said "yes".

That deal only lasted an hour. I chatted away with various other people and ended up having a beer or two too many. Staggering off to the outside area of the Kentagon, I tripped over a step, fell on the ground and struggled to get back on my feet. This happened right where Gil and Marvin were standing. That was the end of that brief Formula 3000 dream. I'd managed to screw myself yet again — but on this occasion in record time.

Still hoping to do Formula 3000, I stupidly started running, just locally for about three miles along the pavements. I thought the cars would be a bit more demanding to drive and the races would also be longer than I was used to, at 45 minutes or so. But after running every morning for about ten days, my legs were hurting so badly that I had to go to the doctor. He was a great supporter and used to give me a free medical for my race licence every year.

He couldn't tell me the cause of the problem and suggested I visited a physio. I went along to the guy the doctor recommended and he used a video machine to film me running on a treadmill in his gym. I'd only been on it for about five minutes when he said I'd done enough. He told me my trainers were rubbish, which hadn't helped, but also said I wasn't cut out for running and could ruin my legs if I carried on and might end up not even being able to race. He said I needed to find another way of getting fit because running wasn't for me. I took that to mean that I should spend more time in the pub.

So that was my only dalliance with getting fit in the way that a lot of people understand it. But actually I was adequately fit anyway because people who drive racing cars regularly always are. That's a fitness course in itself.

Meanwhile, no other opportunities came along, Formula 3000 or otherwise. Because there was no real Formula 3 programme happening with Roni, I'd found it hard to shift any cars in my role as salesman. Rob Gustavsson said they couldn't really afford to keep me on, rather overlooking the fact that I'd brought them all of Don Prater's budget, which kept them afloat to start with. So I was out of work again.

CHAPTER 9
A SPOT OF
BEAUJOLAIS

The first person I phoned after the Roni job came to an end was Gerry Corbett, who ran the Silverstone Racing School. Just a few weeks earlier I'd been chatting with him at the Brands Hatch Formula Ford Festival. He knew I was now living in Newport Pagnell and said he'd be very happy to give me a job as an instructor at the school if I was interested. At that point, of course, I didn't know that the writing was on the wall with Roni. I started with Gerry in January 1986, pretty much full-time.

The school ran Van Diemen single-seaters and MG Maestro hatchbacks. The people there were a great crowd to work with and the other instructors included the likes of Anthony Reid, John Pratt and Eugene O'Brien. Sometimes our demonstration drives for the would-be racing drivers turned into full-on races. The instructors would be sent out of the pits in five Maestros at 15-second intervals with three customers in each car. We would wait down at Becketts for the others to arrive and then

126

have a full-on five-car race with the punters on board. We never actually hit each other, but my word, it was close!

As for my racing in 1986, it was another pivotal year. Computer Consortium Racing weren't intending to continue in Sports 2000 so I needed something new. This time there was no scratching around because I'd had so much success in 1985 and was in demand. Just before the end of that season, Mick Mobberley, who ran Hi-Tech Motorsport, told me that he had a Sports 2000 deal for me and I might like it. Initially, I just thought, that's great, I have something. And then I heard the details.

Mick had obtained backing from a computer company called Syscom and they were putting up £20,000 just for running costs. Mick had been to see Richard Owen and got the loan of a Shrike P15, which was certainly the car to have. As for the engine, he'd sorted that with Neil Brown, who'd built the championship-winning engines for the previous two years. Mick said I would be paid £250 per weekend and could have half the prize money. He asked, "Does that sound good enough?"

Too bloody right it was. It was perfect. And I was going to carry on doing Thundersports with Don Prater.

To top things off, I got a phone call from Ian Taylor. We'd been friends for yonks, going back to our Formula 3 days. In fact I'd first met him in 1973 when he was doing Formula 3, battling with Tony Brise, while I was still a Formula Vee driver. Ian and Tony were very aloof and I got the impression that they didn't feel they needed to be mixing with the likes of me. But when I was doing Formula 3 in 1977, Ian came back to the category driving with Tiff Needell in the Unipart team. I got to know Ian and his wife Moya really, really well that year. Ian and I had a great relationship. Mind you, part of that is probably because we never ended up going wheel-to-wheel with each other — we were just never on the same piece of tarmac.

Anyway, Ian said he was putting together a team of professional drivers for BMW customer track days. Previously BMW had used salespeople for track demonstrations but too many cars had got smashed up when punters were let loose and track insurance had become a problem. So Ian had come up with the idea that if there was a professional racing driver sitting in when a guest was driving, it would do away with the worry about insurance because the racing driver in effect would be the insurance. BMW liked that plan.

Ian offered me £100 a day, massively more than the measly £40 a day I was getting at Silverstone. I think there were about 14 BMW days in that first year. We would drive the whole range of BMWs but if you were pally with Ian, which I was, you would get the pick of the bunch, the M3. And then you wouldn't have to sit in while the Billies drove around, you would be the one doing the driving, so that was the job everyone wanted. I seemed to get it more than most.

Working with Ian was wonderful. Everything was done properly. There was no expense spared and it seemed to be a world away from the racing school at Silverstone.

One of Ian's BMW events that I recall particularly well was at Ingliston in Scotland. There were about 20 of us instructors and we all flew business class from Heathrow to Edinburgh. There really were some proper people involved: racers like Gerry Marshall, James Weaver, Tiff Needell, Mike Wilds — and even Marcus Pye from *Autosport* because Ian was still racing and doubtless wanted favourable coverage.

It wasn't long before word got around about what Ian was doing for BMW. Soon Rover wanted him to run customer days for them as well. And so, in that first year, there were 10 Rover days as well as the 14 for BMW. It was all very good for my bank account.

I was very happy with my racing as well, especially in Sports 2000 with the Shrike. I had some sensational dices with Mike 'Fulmar' Taylor, who was in a Royale RP42. I took eight wins across the 16 rounds and Mike claimed six, but it was nip-and-tuck between us all season long. And I became champion.

One of the two races neither of us won was at Snetterton. It was towards the business end of the year and the championship was getting to a perilous state. We were both on the front row and I squeezed Mike towards the pitwall away from the start line and caused him to shunt. I came by at the end of the opening lap with a huge lead. He was furious, naturally, but there was a title on the line. I got three points on my race licence for that but you were allowed up to 12 before you got a ban. I figured it would be good value. Mike had a brand-new crash helmet for that race and my team boss Mick Mobberley told me that when he got back to the pits he threw it so hard into his pit garage that it's probably still rolling around there to this day.

Other than that, we really enjoyed our battles and became very good friends.

People never seem to realise just how competitive Sports 2000 was. There were so many entries that not everyone could qualify for the races. They were proper little racing cars and the driver could make a real difference with his engineering inputs. The only thing that spoiled it a bit with the Aquila and the Shrike was that Richard Owen had designed the bodywork to conceal the rear wheels because he thought this gave an aerodynamic advantage. To my mind, it made the car look a bit like hover mower.

In Thundersports, I did five of the nine rounds alongside Don Prater in his Lola T594. It was a season to forget because our Mazda engine was unreliable and we struggled. A solitary third place at Donington was our best finish. For the race at the Birmingham Superprix, Don agreed that I would have Ian Taylor as my co-driver but that all came to nothing when the race had to be cancelled because the heavens opened.

Of course, Sports 2000 and Thundersports were both championships that had been the brainchild of Brands Hatch boss John Webb. What with those categories and also Formula Atlantic, I had done rather well out of Webbie. And then there was Thundersaloons, which Webbie started in 1985.

When I got involved with Thundersaloons, it came about through contacts I'd made many years earlier. The connection went right back to Ian Ashley and the Token Formula 1 team. Ian's best mate was a chap called Mike

Smith. They'd gone to school together and were very close. I'd got to know Mike and stayed in touch. Now Mike had a Thundersaloons project, a Vauxhall Chevette powered by a Formula 2 Hart engine. It had been built by a very reputable specialist, Dave Cook Racing Services, so I knew it would be a proper piece of kit. I went to Oulton Park to test the thing and it immediately put a big smile on my face. Dave Cook was there to run it and I thought it was all going to be great.

Next thing I knew, I got a phone call from a chap called Tony Adams at the Vauxhall dealer in High Wycombe. This dealer was Davenport Vernon and he was the boss there. He told me that Davenport Vernon would be sponsoring the team, which was very kind of him, but then he dropped the bombshell: Davenport Vernon would also be running the car. I asked what had happened to Dave Cook. Tony Adams told me that he was too expensive, so the boys in the Davenport Vernon service department were going to look after the car instead. Sure, the car looked like a Chevette, but it was a bit different from the Chevettes they were used to.

The whole thing turned very sour. Mike and I did six races and didn't finish any of them. The car was so quick that we qualified on pole every time but it always broke, because these Vauxhall guys simply didn't know how to bolt the thing together properly — but, to be fair, why should they have done? They had no experience of racing.

The failures were mostly driveshafts and CV joints. Dave Cook had told the Davenport Vernon people that everything about the car was on the limit — that's why it was so quick

— and things needed to be replaced before they broke. He had advised them to fit new CV joints for every race but they never did.

Still, I did get one good break out of that association. Davenport Vernon entered the Beaujolais Run in November with three new Vauxhall Astra GTEs and Tony Adams asked if Jane and I would like to drive one of them. The Beaujolais Run had become quite a big charity event and the objective was to drive down to the Beaujolais wine-producing region in France and bring back the first bottles from that year's harvest. The Astra GTE had just been launched and Adams thought it would be great PR for his business to have three of them take part painted up in the firm's colours. I thought, "Why not?"

Adams himself drove one of the cars and he invited footballer Terry Neill to have the third. Terry was the celebrity among us. A Northern Irishman, he was a huge figure at Arsenal because he'd not only played for the team but gone on to great success as the manager, winning three FA Cups in a row. We got on like a house on fire and had a real laugh.

The event was competitive up to a point. The idea was to reach Beaujolais in the shortest possible distance and involved regularity sections where you had to travel between checkpoints quite sedately and hit a particular target time. It took us about three days to get there with all these stipulations. Our three Vauxhalls more or less followed each other in line astern for the whole run. I never really gave the competition side much thought and just did the route. But when they announced the winner, it was Jane and me. We'd won by about three miles.

I couldn't work out how that had happened but found out later. Vauxhall sourced tyres from various tyre companies and our Astra GTE had a different brand from the other two. Our Continental tyres had fractionally taller sidewalls and that accounted for the difference. Still, a win is a win, isn't it? I will take them any way they come.

When we got back, we found out that our team had raised £11,000 for charity. TV personality Leslie Crowther came along on the charity's behalf and we handed him one of those giant cardboard cheques.

The other thing I won in 1986 was the BRDC Silver Star. That capped the year brilliantly. The British Racing Drivers' Club gives this honour annually to the most successful driver in national racing. Of course, Jane and I went to the awards evening to collect it. We were looking at a list on the wall to find out where our seats were and she saw Stirling Moss's name. She turned around to me and said: "Stirling Moss? I thought he was dead!" All of a sudden, she felt two hands on her shoulders and a voice said: "No, my dear, I can assure you that I am still very much here." It was indeed the man himself.

I was riding the crest of a wave and at the end of the year I took Jane out for dinner and proposed to her. A few months later, on 7th February 1987, we were wed. We had our honeymoon in Madeira but had to cut it short because I needed to get back for a Sports 2000 test at Thruxton. When we got home, the test had to be called off because of snow. Jane wasn't best pleased.

Sports 2000 was again good to me in 1987 but not quite

as good as in 1986 because this time I didn't win the title. We had the same Shrike P15 but the team now had a new sponsor, John Bond-Smith's West Oxfordshire Motor Auctions, and the car was turned out in turquoise rather than white. Again, Mike 'Fulmar' Taylor and I were at each other all season, and this time we pulled off even more of a rout. We won all 15 races, seven to me and eight to Mike, and he claimed the crown. The deciding factor came at Oulton Park in August when I made a stupid error. Trying to keep up with Mike, I hit the tyre barrier at the Foulston chicane and pushed a wheel back into the tub. In a season that was see-sawing so much between us, I just couldn't afford a non-finish and that scuppered my chances.

Looking back on those two years of racing against Mike in Sports 2000, I think he was consistently the fiercest rival I ever encountered in my entire career. He had the speed, he knew how to run a proper team, he was competitive. You knew you had to be the best of the best to beat him. There were no short cuts to beating Mike, it had to be spot on in every way. It was always so close and often we were just a few centimetres apart. I feel sorry for the blokes who finished third in the years we were up against each other.

Over the years, I have been involved with quite a lot of businessmen who've gone racing as amateurs and none of them took it as seriously as Mike did. He ran a highly successful printing business, Fulmar, but the moment he came through the circuit gates all the business side of him was set aside and he was as professional as Ayrton Senna. He was totally dedicated to how he'd chosen to spend his leisure time and enjoy the rewards of his business success.

I also had another season of Thundersports in 1987, sharing a Can-Am Lola T530 with former Formula 1 driver Mike Wilds. This turned out to be the best car I ever raced — my absolute favourite.

The T530 had been a real star car in Can-Am, winning two titles, for Patrick Tambay in 1980 and Geoff Brabham in 1981. John Foulston had been running one since the beginning of Thundersports in 1983 and then Burke Ratcliffe Racing — a team owned by Nigel Burke and Andrew Ratcliffe — bought two of these beasts from movie star Paul Newman's team and started running one of them in 1986 for Mike Wilds, usually with Ratcliffe co-driving. Now the team manager, Roy Kennedy, whom I'd known for ages, stuck me in it for the new season. The 5.7-litre Chevrolet V8 pushed out something like 650bhp. Without any traction control or other driver aids, the physical effort you needed to hustle this thing around tracks like Oulton Park and Brands Hatch was immense, and it required all your skill too, especially in the wet.

If nothing broke, the car finished first or second, but Foulston and his usual co-driver, John Brindley, beat us to the title. We won twice — both times at Brands Hatch — but they had three victories.

Mike Wilds and I had a really good relationship all season but there was a big dispute right at the end of the year. After the Thundersports season had finished in early September at Oulton Park, there was one more task for us: a Peterborough

Motor Club meeting at Silverstone. The BRDC put up a big trophy for the fastest lap of the season at Silverstone on the National circuit. It was a lovely thing called the Chris Bristow Trophy, which went on to become the trophy given to the McLaren *Autosport* BRDC Young Driver of the Year. Thundersports never went to Silverstone so this meeting was our chance to claim this silverware. Burke Ratcliffe Racing decided to enter both T530s into an allcomers race, so I drove one and Mike had the other.

Because of the varied nature of the entry and our speed around the short National circuit, we knew we would only really have two laps to gun for the quickest lap before we would start getting into traffic, and that would spoil things. As expected, Mike and I locked out the front row in qualifying, and we came up with an agreement: whoever made the best start would be free to go for the fastest lap with no attack from the sister car. Luckily, that was me.

I was in the lead on the opening lap coming down to Woodcote corner and I wasn't defending. I didn't even look in the mirrors because there was no need to. As I dropped it down to second gear, I felt a bit of a bump at the back of my car but just kept my focus on getting through Woodcote as quickly as possible because the second lap would be the key one. Sure enough, I got the fastest lap and that was it — the Chris Bristow Trophy was mine. When I got into the traffic, I started looking behind me to see where Mike had got to, but I couldn't see him anywhere. So I took an easy win.

It turned out that it was Mike who had nudged me at

Woodcote. He'd lost control, speared into the barrier and done a whole load of damage to the car.

After the race, Mike was moaning that he was much quicker than me and just wanted to get ahead to give himself a chance of the fastest lap, but I reminded him of our agreement. Nigel Burke was very unhappy about it all and Mike got the sack.

One other opportunity came along that year: I had my first tin-top race. Dave Cook, who'd built the ill-fated Vauxhall Chevette Thundersaloon 'that I'd raced the previous year, prepared a Honda Prelude for a guy called Des Winks to race in production saloons. I'd stayed in good touch with Dave because he liked me doing testing for him and valued the quality of my feedback. Anyway, there was a 500-kilometre production saloon race on the Brands Hatch Grand Prix circuit in September and Winks needed a co-driver, so Cookie suggested me. We finished third overall in the Prelude and won our class.

CHAPTER 10
THE FLUX EMPIRE EXPANDS

That November Jane told me she was pregnant. Previously she'd had complications and had been told that the chances of her having any kids were limited. She used to like a drink and we'd gone out one night to a club in Milton Keynes with some friends. We were in the taxi home when Jane asked the driver to pull over because she was about to be sick.

The next day she was still feeling ill and I just put it down to over-indulgence the night before. But when she was still rough the day after that, I told her I thought she should see a doctor. She went along reluctantly and the doctor said he thought she should do a pregnancy test. Six months later, on 14th May 1988, our daughter Coral arrived.

At the end of 1987, I was offered a chance to expand my international repertoire into America, a market the Fluxie brand had yet to conquer. Sports 2000 was growing in the USA and Andrew Broadley, son of Lola founder Eric, asked me to do some development work on a new Sports 2000 car that Lola was planning to sell in America. I asked Richard Owen, who had loaned me those Aquila and Shrike cars that had brought so much success in the category, if he minded me doing this work with Lola on the T89/90. He said it would be fine, because Lola's programme was just an American one with the aim of selling cars out there. In any case, Richard's priority was also to sell cars and he felt he had nothing more to gain from lending me a free chassis for yet another season.

I did a lot of testing and then Lola asked me to go to Florida to debut the car in two events in January 1988. Even better, I could take Jane with me too. Carl Haas, the company's US importer, ran the car for me. Straight out of the box at Sebring, I won. Then we went to Moroso (now called Palm Beach International Raceway) and there I had a typical race-long battle with a guy called Steve Knapp in a Tiga, swapping the lead continually, but I ended up second.

While I was in Florida, Chris Crawford of ADA Engineering found out I was there and got in touch. ADA had built its own Cosworth-powered Group C2 car, the ADA 03, to run in the World Sports-Prototype Championship, including at Le Mans, and the team was debuting it in the Daytona 24 Hours. I already knew the car because I'd done a day's testing with it at Silverstone. The Daytona race was only a few days away and they'd decided they wanted another driver. They already had Ian Harrower, who was part of the ADA set-up, Wayne Taylor, whom I'd met when racing in South Africa in 1983, and Stanley Dickens, who I also knew from Formula 3 in 1977, so I was going to be the fourth driver.

Soon after I arrived, I bumped into David Hobbs, who'd raced at Daytona a lot. I knew him well and he was so helpful. He walked the circuit with me, a combination of most of the banked speedway and a twisty infield section. Jane came along and when we tried to walk up to the top of the banking she couldn't make it because she was so heavily pregnant. David told me all the things I needed to know, such as the turn-in points. He explained that because I wasn't in the quickest car, there was no need to go to the very top of the banking. The idea was that you always gave the faster cars room at the top, and it was up to them to make the pass on you.

The first time I sat in the car was for night-time qualifying. I'd never driven a racing car in the dark, it was pissing with rain, and the lighting on the banking was dreadful. I was nervous almost to the point of shitting myself.

The mirror set-up on the ADA really wasn't suitable for the banking because the view didn't show the higher part of the track, although it was fine for the infield bit. Anyway, I was looking in the mirrors and I hadn't realised that I'd wandered up the banking to the top strip that Hobbo had told me not to use. Suddenly there was a roar alongside and Eddie Cheever in a Silk Cut Jaguar XJR-9 came blasting past about 40mph quicker. He just about squeezed between my car and the wall but took off one of my mirrors. He was on a qualifying lap and thought I knew he was coming through, but of course I hadn't seen him at all.

I came into the pits and made up a story about there being an electrical fault. I really needed to get my breath back.

Throughout practice there was loads of trouble with the electrics anyway and we had a perpetual misfire. The car spent a lot of time in the pits and none of us did many practice laps. The car still wasn't working properly in the race and by the time I had my first stint we were already three laps down on the leaders. I wondered what the point was. The car only lasted a few hours.

After we came back home, I did thousands more miles for Lola around Snetterton trying to develop the car through the course of the season. Towards the end of the year, it was a bit embarrassing when Lola supplied a chassis to Sean Walker to race in the penultimate round of the British Sports 2000 championship. It meant that in effect my promise to Richard Owen about not helping a rival manufacturer hadn't been honoured after all. Still, I was able to set the embarrassment to one side when Lola built another chassis and asked me if I wanted to do the last Sports 2000 round, the race at the Formula Ford Festival. I won it. That meant I won the Formula Ford Festival support race for Sports 2000 three years in a row. I've always been very proud of that.

I did another Thundersports season in 1988 with Burke Ratcliffe Racing — by now simply known as BRR — in the Lola T530 but the wind had rather gone out of the sails of the championship. John Foulston had had a whale of a time in Thundersports ever since the start of it all and won loads of races but a few weeks after the last round in 1987 he had been killed testing at Silverstone. As Foulston had also bought Brands Hatch a couple of years earlier and taken over from

John Webb, he had become the real driving force behind Thundersports. Without him, the impetus went out of it, with fewer races, less prize money and smaller grids.

As Mike Wilds had shot himself in the foot with the Burke Ratcliffe guys, I got my mate Ian Taylor to drive with me for the opening two Thundersports races either side of the Easter weekend and we won the first of them, at Oulton Park on Good Friday. Then there was a four-month hole in the season and after that I teamed up for two more races with John Brindley, who'd partnered Foulston for four years. We won both of them, at Snetterton and Brands Hatch, and I became champion after four of the five rounds.

Through Thundersports, I'd become very friendly with Colin Pool, who'd raced a variety of cars in the series and was now running a Tiga TS86 in the 2-litre class. The BRDC had just introduced its own sports car championship for Group C2 cars but was short of entries and allowed some Thundersports cars to join in too. Colin normally shared with David Leslie but he had some other commitments and so I filled in when needed. Colin and I did two of the BRDC races together and we won both, at Silverstone in June and Brands Hatch in September. I also did the last Thundersports race of the season, at Oulton Park, with Colin in the Tiga, and we finished second.

All that left me with a pretty good record in sports cars in 1988 even if I didn't get that many outings. It's worth a quick recap: Sports 2000, three races — two firsts and a second; Thundersports, five races — three firsts and a second;

BRDC Group C2 sports cars, two races — two firsts.

As I had quite a lot of spare weekends, I was open to other offers and managed to secure my first ever run in the British Touring Car Championship. It was at Donington Park on 14th May, the day Coral was born. I was there at the hospital when she popped out at 6.42am and then I rushed back to Donington.

The car was a Ford Sierra RS500 Cosworth that Karl Jones was racing for Asquith Autosport. This Donington round was a one-hour race with a pitstop, and the team needed a second driver. Vic Lee, whom I'd got to know through working with Ian Taylor, was trying to support Karl's efforts and got me the drive.

It seemed like a good opportunity because RS500s were doing all the winning, but we weren't very competitive, and the car went out with a blown turbocharger before my stint. I didn't have much of a frame of reference because the whole thing was new to me, so I wasn't aware at the time that Asquith Autosport was very underfunded. It was only when I got in Sean Walker's Andy Rouse-prepared RS500 a year later in the equivalent race that I realised just what Jonesy had been up against. It was like comparing a Mini to a Ferrari.

The BTCC wasn't the biggest show in British racing back then, like it is now, but it was getting television coverage and the drivers were beginning to become known by the public. It looked like a category where there was money to be made and it was certainly on my radar. I would love to claim that I was a mystic and could predict the six-figure salaries that manufacturer teams would be paying when they arrived in the mid-nineties, but I could certainly see that the series was on the up.

Vic Lee was operating Toyota Supra Turbos in the BTCC that year but was struggling with them. Whoever had done the homologation for the car at the governing body, the RAC MSA, had made it carry an extra 150 kilograms to counteract the fact that it had a twin-turbo engine, but it had no more horsepower than a single-turbo RS500 so it was always going to struggle. Anyway, Vic offered me two late-season drives in one of the cars, at Brands Hatch and Silverstone, and I accepted. To prove the point, the best I managed in it was 14th place at Brands.

In between those Toyota races, I also reconnected with Karl Jones and his RS500 for the Tourist Trophy at Silverstone, a three-hour race that counted towards the European Touring Car Championship. It was quite a warm September day and the heat within the car was intense. The clutch pedal was near the exhaust and got incredibly hot. I was wearing my usual thin-soled Westover racing boots and my left foot became so painful that I struggled to change gear. Still, I had a good ten-lap battle with Tom Walkinshaw in his works Holden Commodore and really enjoyed that.

By a somewhat roundabout route I also ended up doing two late-season races in Lionel Abbott's Group N production version of the Sierra RS500 Cosworth. This all started on a BMW driving day at Donington Park when I was chatting to the bosses at a Derby-based firm called Minitec. They were

ABOVE *After a strong British Formula Atlantic season in 1983 with a Ralt RT4/81 run by Duncan Bain, we took the car to New Zealand but had a frustrating time there.*

BELOW *With Davy Jones at Wigram in New Zealand in 1984. The Lep firm sponsored the pair of us in the Formula Pacific Championship.*

ABOVE My first Thundersports race came in the summer of 1984 when I shared Alan Eisner's Chevron B8 at Donington Park.

BELOW In Thundersports in 1985 I raced Don Prater's Mazda-powered Lola T594 against the big-banger cars but still had some success. This is the Lola on the way to a podium finish at Snetterton.

ABOVE *My last Formula 3 race, at Snetterton in August 1985, was the one and only outing for the Roni chassis. I climbed from 21st on the grid to 12th place.*

BELOW *I had my first full season in Sports 2000 in 1985, driving an Aquila. Here I am subtly pushing rival Mike O'Brien's Shrike over the 'penalty line' to win at Silverstone in June.*

ABOVE Now in a
Shrike, this is me
leading Mike 'Fulmar'
Taylor during a 1986
Sports 2000 duel.
Mike was one of the
fiercest and best rivals
I ever had.

LEFT Getting ready
to tie the knot to
Jane, with best
man Tiff Needell.

ABOVE *Celebrating with 1987 Thundersports team-mate Mike Wilds after winning at Brands Hatch in August in our Burke Ratcliffe Racing Lola T530.*

BELOW *Burke Ratcliffe Racing had two Lola T530s and put Mike Wilds and me in them for the Peterborough Motor Club meeting at Silverstone at the end of 1987. The idea was for one of us to win the Chris Bristow Trophy for the year's fastest lap of the National circuit — and I achieved it.*

ABOVE *In 1988 there was more Thundersports with the Lola T530, my favourite race car, now sharing with Ian Taylor. This is Brands Hatch at Easter.*

BELOW *Here I am, on the left, teaching team boss Vic Lee how to drive one of his own Toyota Supra Turbos. I can't remember who paid the bill for this little tap...*

ABOVE Racing a Sports 2000 Lola in 1988, I managed to take a third victory in the Formula Ford Festival support event at Brands Hatch.

ABOVE For the European Touring Car Championship Tourist Trophy at Silverstone in 1988, I shared this Sierra RS500 Cosworth with Karl Jones until the car broke.

BELOW After we had persuaded sponsors Minitec to give up backing Rob Murphy, I jumped in and shared this Group N Sierra RS500 Cosworth with Lionel Abbott.

ABOVE Ricky Fagan (left), Ian Taylor and I brought this Mercedes 190E home third overall and first in class in the 25-hour version of the Willhire endurance race at Snetterton in 1989.

BELOW Prize-giving for the Willhire 25 in 1989 with Ian Taylor (centre) and Ricky Fagan.

ABOVE AND LEFT
On my way to a BTCC podium at Brands Hatch in 1990 with Sean Walker in his Ford Sierra RS500 Cosworth. You can tell I had to work hard in this hour-long two-driver race and afterwards I was even spotted drinking some water.

ABOVE My first race in a TVR Tuscan was at the Birmingham Superprix in 1990 and I finished second despite wearing unsuitable shoes.

RIGHT One of the best experiences of my career came with a Jaguar XJR-15 in the three-race series that supported the Grands Prix at Monaco, Silverstone and Spa in 1991. And I got paid very well.

One of my favourite photos: battling with Tiff Needell on the way to third place at the British Grand Prix support race at Silverstone in the Jaguar XJR-15.

ABOVE *After Nigel Mansell won the British Grand Prix, the XJR-15 race came next and when I stepped onto the rostrum it was surrounded by thousands of people shouting my name.*

BELOW *The first appearance of Halfords in the British Touring Car Championship was in 1992 on my Roy Kennedy Racing BMW M3, seen at Thruxton.*

ABOVE *With team boss Roy Kennedy when the waters were smooth at the start of the 1993 British Touring Car Championship.*

BELOW *This was the second visit of the British Touring Car Championship to Donington Park in 1993 and here I am in the Peugeot 405 Mi 16 ahead of both factory Renault 19s.*

ABOVE *After my friend Ian Taylor sadly lost his life at Spa in June 1992, I was asked to take over his Rover 216 GTi for the last four races of the season.*

BELOW *One of my stranger assignments was co-driving with Mike Lindup of the band Level 42 in his Citroën 2CV at Pembrey.*

supporting a young driver called Rob Murphy in a two-car Formula Vauxhall Lotus team but weren't very pleased with his progress. They asked if I would go along to a test day at Snetterton and observe. They wanted me just to hang around in the background and watch how the squad was operating.

Murphy was a lot slower than his team-mate, Peter Hardman, so midway through the day I phoned the guys at Minitec to tell them that this youngster wasn't their man. But I suggested that Hardman should at least try Murphy's car to make sure there was nothing fundamentally wrong with it. We came up with some excuse to make this happen and after only three laps Hardman was faster by one second a lap. Still, I wanted to give this kid a chance. Now that I knew Lionel Abbott, who raced in both the BTCC and production saloons, and told him he could charge Minitec a hefty sum if he let Murphy have a few races in his Sierra RS500 Cosworth. So that was agreed.

We decided to prepare Murphy properly and give him two or three test days before his race debut. That was great for me too as I earned £500 a day to go along and mentor him. During this testing, Lionel kept getting in the car — it was his, after all — to check that the set-up was right and everything was OK for the driver. Whenever Lionel got in it, he was much, much faster than Rob. The guys at Minitec were aware of all of this and eventually turned around and asked me to do a couple of the races, at Pembrey and Thruxton.

Pembrey was a two-driver race and I shared with Lionel but went off and got stuck in the gravel. It got better at Thruxton where I finished third behind Mark Hales and Kieth O'dor. I had made the right impression and it looked like I was all set to do more in 1989.

There was one other race in 1988 that warrants passing mention. My mate and old Sports 2000 rival Sean Walker had a Tiga GC287 that he shared with Paul Stott in the BRDC's Group C2 championship and they also took in Britain's two 1,000Km races in the FIA World Sports-Prototype Championship. For the second one, at Brands Hatch in July, he asked me to be the third driver. It was a terrible car — Sean rates it the worst he ever raced — and I was quite glad when a CV joint broke five laps into my stint. My main memory is Jochen Mass blasting past in his Sauber-Mercedes when lapping me.

CHAPTER 11
TURNING TO
TIN-TOPS

A longside my racing, I was building up a good reputation by this time as a test driver, something that I enjoyed. It really started in Sports 2000. I never advertised myself but word got round that I did a good job, giving plenty of technical feedback, and people just rang up.

Even though I hadn't been trained as a mechanic, I'd built race cars for other people and had run them for myself. I'd accumulated a great bank of knowledge from all the different roles I'd had with various teams, in particular with Ron Tauranac at Ralt and then Dr Ehrlich. I'd learned what needed doing to make a car work and how a car should feel when operating at its best.

The more cars I drove, the easier it became to judge. I guess I'm fortunate to have a very high level of sensitivity and can detect even minute adjustments. For example, I can feel two clicks on a damper. People who wanted my advice knew that I could get the most out of a car as given to me and then suggest the right way forward to get even more out of it.

Ultimately, I think I became even more skilled as a test driver than a racer. Winning races needs a totally different mindset from testing, but that's in me too. Knowing how to win was something that also came to me as I progressed through the early stages of my career.

When I started racing in karting and in Formula Vee, it was all easy. I didn't need to be aggressive or competitive because I seemed to win so comfortably. It became a bit of culture shock when I moved to Formula 3 in 1976 because that was the first time I'd come up against really talented drivers wanting to get to Formula 1. I realised pretty quickly that I had to be much more forceful in my driving to either maintain a place or gain a place.

I've always loved the feeling of winning. Goodness knows where it comes from. Genes-wise, my parents wanted to do well in business, but I wouldn't say they were hell-bent on winning.

My testing ability was certainly helping my career at this time. Lola were so pleased with my efforts with their Sports 2000 car in 1988 that they sent me to America again at the start of 1989. I did the same two races — Sebring and Moroso — and this time reversed my results, finishing second at Sebring and then winning at Moroso. After those events, Lola asked me to go back for the first proper round of the Sports Car Club of America championship at Road Atlanta — and what a circuit that was. I remember travelling over there with James Weaver, who was doing race-by-race trans-Atlantic commuting driving the Dyson Racing Porsche 962, and thinking, "Look at me, professional racing driver flying to the States…"

I finished third at Road Atlanta, beaten by two Swifts. I was close enough to these American-made cars to get a really good look at them. Like my Lola, they had a flap on the rear edge of the bodywork but theirs was much more flexible. Down the straights, I could see it move such that it sat almost flat, giving them a real advantage. We all thought Formula 1 broke new ground when DRS (Drag Reduction System) came in 20 years later but I certainly saw a primitive version of it on those Swifts.

Back in the UK, I was due to take part in the BRDC C2 Championship again. BRR had bought an Argo JM19 fitted with a 5.7-litre Chevrolet V8. All seemed set and we went to Snetterton for some pre-season testing. On my fourth lap, I was coming down to the Russell chicane — the old super-quick one, not like now — and going quite carefully because I was running the car in. I gave it a bit of gas coming out of Coram but when I came off the throttle to go through Russell the pedal collapsed and jammed against the side of the monocoque. I went flat out into the tyre wall and earth bank. Luckily, I was only winded, but the chassis was wrecked.

It was one of the biggest shunts I'd ever had. In motor racing you're bound to have a few accidents, hopefully ones that won't hurt you too much, but I never worried about it much. If you think too much about crashing, it can screw you up, so really you have to put it to the back of your mind. Anyway, there's nobody holding a gun to your head when you slide into a cockpit and press the throttle. It's your choice, after all.

Crashing that Argo screwed my racing prospects for 1989 because the new season was about to start in anger and only limited choices remained. Most of the intermittent opportunities that then cropped up involved being someone's co-driver in tin-top races.

The best of those chances was in the British Touring Car Championship. As in 1988, I took part in the two-driver race at Donington in May, this time with John Cleland in his works Vauxhall Astra GTE. We won the 2-litre class — which turned out to be the only win I ever had in BTCC.

Initially I'd agreed to do this race with Sean Walker, who was now tackling the BTCC with a Graham Goode-run Ford Sierra RS500 Cosworth. Just a couple of days after agreeing to join Sean, I got a call from Dave Cook, who was running the factory Vauxhall programme and asked if I could partner Cleland. Greed took over as usual: Sean was going to pay me £500 for the weekend but Cookie offered £1,000. So I declined Sean's offer but he was all right about that. He hired Damon Hill instead and they finished fourth overall.

Of course, I knew Cookie from the Thundersaloons Chevette that he'd built, and I'd also raced against Cleland in that series. I've always liked John because he tells it like it is. On my barometer of good blokes, he's someone I would always go out for a beer with.

John did the opening stint and then I took over. They put on two new front tyres for me at the pitstop and away I went. On my third lap, John and the rest of the Vauxhall team — including his dad Bill, Cookie and engine man John Dunn —

were all on the pitwall waving their arms like crazy and urging me to slow down. They needed the point for fastest lap in class to go to Cleland and I was looking like I might go quicker. So I had to back off. All the same, we won the class and finished ninth overall. Job done.

Cookie was really keen to get me to be John's full-time team-mate the following year, when they switched to a Cavalier, but Bill Cleland, who was an important guy in Vauxhall circles and had the purse strings, didn't want anyone who was going to cause John problems. In the end they took Jeff Allam and he was the perfect choice.

A month after Donington, I took another tin-top class win but it was much, much harder. This was at Snetterton in the traditional Willhire 24 Hours, which this time became a 25-hour race to mark the sponsor's 25th anniversary. I'd done this production saloon race the previous year in a Mercedes 190E with Ian Taylor and Ricky Fagan. We had a great team but the clutch went very early in that earlier race. Somehow we fixed it with a can of Coca-Cola and it lasted the duration, but we were never in contention. Anyway, we put the band back together for 1989 — same car, same drivers. This time we finished third overall and won our class.

I knew we had to be well prepared. Through Tom Walkinshaw, I'd got to know the Silk Cut Jaguar team's keep-fit guy, Tom Ryan. I went to see him because I'd heard that the team used a special energy drink to help keep drivers going during the longer stints. It was powdery and you had to mix it in your drink bottle. I hadn't got a clue what it was. For all I knew it could have been some kind of drugs cocktail. Anyway, he gave me some of this stuff.

Ian, Ricky and I all drank some. You had to drink half-a-litre of this mixture half an hour before your stint and then pee as much as you could — two or three times — before you got in the cockpit. Everything was going fine and in the middle of the night we were leading our class and running second overall. Then I got into the car at 2am. Within two laps, fog came down and the pace car came out. We were behind this bloody thing for two hours. Of course, I'd had all this drink and now I needed a pee.

I got on the radio to Steve Beeches, our team manager, and told him I was busting to go. He was adamant that I couldn't stop anywhere or come into the pits, because then I would have to drop to the back of the crocodile of cars behind the safety car. He told me I would just have to relieve myself in the car. I'd never done anything like that before.

I had to build myself up to do it. I started, but every bump I hit seemed to shut off the peeing valve. It must have taken me three laps to finish. I came in at the end of my two hours and Ian Taylor got in. On his out-lap, he got on the radio to Steve and said, "Blimey, Fluxie must have been working hard during his stint, the seat is soaked with his sweat." Steve had to tell him what had really happened.

The following Thursday, Ian and I did a corporate day for Rover. At the end of the day, Ian did the usual finale, standing on stage and presenting trophies to the best punters — driver of the day, that sort of thing — while we instructors cheered.

When it finished, Ian told everyone that he had one more prize. He brandished a big disposable nappy and told all the clients what had happened to him the previous weekend. Thanks Ian.

Going into 1990, things seemed to be looking up in terms of a full-time ride. With Minitec on board, Lionel Abbott was drawing up a fantastic plan for a Production Saloon programme with the assistance of Dennis Nursey of Middlebridge Racing. Nursey was going to get two Nissan Skyline GT-Rs from NISMO, Nissan's motorsport arm, and Minitec had £60,000 available to run them for Lionel and me. It was all very exciting.

But the Skylines didn't show up. This dragged on and on, for three months, and still we had no cars with the season nearly upon us. Through my own Nissan connections, I tried to find out what was going on and nobody seemed to know anything about Nursey or any deal. It was all a bit of a mystery. Kieth O'dor of Janspeed did get his hands on one and ended up winning a lot of the races.

Lionel and I tried to convince Minitec that turning to a Sierra RS500 would be just as strong but we had done such a good job telling them about the Skyline that they didn't want to go for it. I didn't know what I was going to do. Lionel soon got himself a deal to drive a Saab but I had nothing.

Minitec's boss, Mel Morris, was great. About a week after the company decided to pull out, he phoned to apologise that I'd been left in the lurch and offered to pay me the £20,000 that I'd been due to receive anyway. All I had to do in return was turn up for the occasional sponsor day with them. He just wanted to make sure that I had some money to live on. It came monthly, so I couldn't spend it all down the pub.

In July that year, Jane and I went to Bournemouth for our first family holiday with Coral, who was a toddler. When we were having dinner one night, Jane told me she was pregnant again — so that meant William was on the way. We had the Minitec money coming in, we had equity in our house, and I had some prize money tucked away too. We increased our mortgage and moved into a bigger house on 1st December 1990.

While the Minitec money provided me with financial stability, that year I was just a jobbing racing driver with nothing much on the horizon. Twice I shared Sean Walker's Andy Rouse Engineering-built Ford Sierra RS500 Cosworth in the British Touring Car Championship and we got pretty good placings, fourth at Donington in April and third at Brands Hatch in July. The BTCC was an incredibly strong scene at that time: there were at least a dozen RS500s and eight of them were capable of winning races. I also had a race in Lionel Abbott's Saab at Thruxton and finished second.

So, I spent 1990 just picking up the occasional drive wherever I could, but there was one that was really special.

I did my first ever TVR Tuscan Challenge race when I took Gerry Marshall's place for the Birmingham Superprix in August. The opportunity came out of the blue and I can only think that Gerry put in a good word for me. However, the weekend stands out in my memory above all because I got the biggest bollocking I've ever had in racing *and* I was disqualified from the race.

Beforehand, I went to Snetterton for a test and fell in love with the Tuscan right away. You had to get it sorted out to your liking and you really had to drive it properly. You had to treat the car with respect as it could bite you back if you whacked the throttle pedal too hard, but I liked the idea of this category of racing because the nut behind the wheel could make such a difference. This was only a few weeks after the second of my two BTCC races with Sean Walker and suddenly the RS500 seemed pale by comparison. The Tuscan was way better — and much more fun to drive.

The feature event at the Birmingham Superprix was a round of the International Formula 3000 Championship. When we arrived, Eddie Jordan, who was running one of the top Formula 3000 teams, invited Jane and I to join him and Ian Phillips for dinner at their hotel the evening before qualifying. All of Eddie's sponsors were there and I had a good chat with one of them. He agreed to give me £250 to put his company's sticker on my crash helmet for the Tuscan race. The next morning, I headed over to the Eddie Jordan Racing awning in the Formula 3000 paddock to meet this guy and he handed over the two stickers and the £250 in cash. Happy days.

When I went to go back to the TVR paddock, the pedestrian walkway was blocked because they were closing off the roads for the action to take place. I founded myself stranded — and my session was about to start.

I did find a route, a long way round, but by the time I got to the TVR paddock all the cars had gone to the assembly area. There was no one around and there I was on my own in my normal clothes. I knew my helmet, balaclava and gloves would be in the car but my race suit was in the team's truck — which was now locked. Fortunately, the wife of another driver, Chris Maries, was still there in his team's coach next door, so I darted in and asked if I could borrow Chris's spare overalls — but I still had no boots. I sprinted down to the assembly area in my posh shoes but at least now wearing overalls. It was all so last minute that I didn't even have time to put the stickers on my crash helmet.

Chris Schirle, TVR's competition manager, had driven my car to the assembly area and parked it at the very front of the queue. He gave me this most enormous telling-off in front of everyone. "Who do you think you are, Ayrton Senna?" he yelled. I got in the car feeling deeply embarrassed.

Even though I wasn't wearing the right footwear, I managed to heel-and-toe in my smart shoes and got to grips with the car as best I could. The plan for qualifying was to do a couple of laps on old tyres and then come in and put new ones on and go for a time. When I came in after those preliminary laps, Chris lent into the cockpit and said, "I've bollocked you once, I don't want to have to do it again." I suppose he wasn't too impressed with my initial efforts. So, I was really fired up when I went back out on the new tyres. I thought I probably had only two laps to do a time because the session was quite short. Bang: row two on the grid!

Because I'd never competed in a Tuscan before, I was a bit

unused to it all, but the race went brilliantly. On the green-flag lap, I weaved around to get heat into the tyres, like we did before BTCC starts. Chris Hodgetts made a good getaway from pole and I was left having a bit of a dice with rally driver Jimmy McRae, who was in the guest car used for the series, and John Kent. I got the better of them and finished second. I was up on the rostrum, pretty pleased with myself, but just as I stepped off, I heard the public address crackle into life: "Ian Flux to the clerk of the course's office immediately, please."

John Nicol, the clerk of the course, chucked me out of the results for excessive weaving on the warm-up lap. I couldn't believe it. That was a new one to me. That was it, I was out. And I got another flea in my ear from Chris Schirle. It wasn't the noise of the engines that was ringing in my ears after that meeting, it was the sound of his voice at high volume.

All the same, I'd enjoyed driving the TVR Tuscan and it was an experience that ultimately transformed my racing life.

CHAPTER 12

MOVING ON UP IN A BIG CAT

Early in 1991, Ian Taylor came to visit us in our new home and took me to Millbrook for a company car show. On the way back, he said he had a proposal for me concerning his BMW and Rover customer days: he said he thought I was sufficiently trustworthy to run some of the days myself! I nearly jumped out of the passenger door: "What me?" But he had observed me with the clients and other professional drivers and thought I could handle the responsibility — and bear in mind that he and I knew each other well.

Ian's operation was going well and he had a lot of clashing dates coming up in the year ahead. He knew that he and his right-hand man, Bill Coombs, couldn't cover it all so his plan was that I would take charge when needed. A management role! Ian put me straight on £250 a day.

I guess the other instructors involved must have respected me because it all worked out very well. People did what I told them. I enjoyed that.

I had to allocate the cars to our instructors. These events, which sometimes lasted two or three days, involved the manufacturer's entire range. Obviously, that meant there were some dull cars, particularly at a Rover event. No one really wanted to be in an automatic Metro all day but a top-of-the-range SD1 was nice enough. I tried to share the cars out fairly.

You can never stop racing drivers being competitive though. All the boys on these events were great fun, particularly guys like Karl Jones and Pat Blakeney. The final thing we used to do on one of these days was some fast demonstration laps with customers. We would stick them in three at a time, and give them an out-lap, a fast lap, and in again. These laps weren't supposed to be timed, of course, but they were. The marshals were our people, not circuit staff, and they would time you from the pit exit back around to the pit entrance. This was really important to all of us: we all wanted to be in the top three!

One of the instructors was John Stevens, who was a bit older than the rest of us and always wore a cravat. He'd held the Formula Ford lap record at Thruxton when he raced and then turned to coaching. He'd done a bit of work with Nigel Mansell in 1985 just before Mansell won his first Grand Prix for Williams. Mansell always said that Stevens had found him 0.7sec per lap. There was massive coverage in national newspapers about 'the man who taught Mansell how to race' — great for him, honestly, but it was journalism at its best.

Anyway, we were doing a two-day session at Oulton Park and I was in charge. On the first day, it got to that time in the afternoon where we were all going out to do the quick laps. Stevens turned up, ready to do his timed run in a Maestro Turbo, but he had just one young lad with him who weighed next to nothing. I asked him where his other two passengers were. I knew exactly what he was doing and he was taking the mickey. But a queue was forming and I really didn't have time to argue, so I told him to set off. About a minute later I got a call on the radio: "Fluxie, Fluxie — John Stevens has crashed at Knickerbrook."

I spoke to Ian Taylor and he told me to put Stevens on marshalling duty the next day as a punishment. In the morning, I ran through the cars and finished the list, and then told John he would have to go and marshal at Knickerbrook. He kicked up a right stink. I had to put him in his place but everyone else was on my side.

One big memory came at Donington Park on a BMW day. It was a lunchtime and we were doing demonstrations up and down the start/finish straight using two 320is, one with new anti-lock braking (ABS), the other without. The idea was for the drivers to set off together, zoom up to 70mph, weave through some cones and then slam on the brakes. We had a bowser there to make the circuit wet in this braking zone.

We wanted the driver of the non-ABS car, a lovely old boy called Steve Roberts, to exaggerate his braking so that it looked really dramatic and unwieldy, while Tiff Needell in the car with the new-fangled system would come to a nice tidy-looking halt. But Steve just chugged down the track and wasn't making the point at all. Ian Taylor was shaking his head. He turned to me and said, "I'm going to have to sort this out." He marched down to Steve's car and told him to get out. Ian was going to drive it himself.

I guess Ian had a lot on his mind because he completely forgot he was in the non-ABS car. Off they went, side by side, Ian on the left-hand side of the track, close to the pit wall. A few seconds later there was a huge bang. Ian had put his 320i square into the pit wall, good and hard. I remember the feeling of relief that swept over all the instructors that day. Everyone knew from that point forward that we all had credit in the bank… If the boss could slip up, then so could we!

When you're paid to coach someone, you have to know what you're signing up for. I always considered that I was in control of the car, even in the passenger seat. I would make guests feel at ease, take the pressure off them and use the wheel if I needed to. I had one or two minor scares, but nothing major. I've heard some awful horror stories from other instructors, but they're the ones who I think don't always pay proper attention to what they should be doing. I've never had a terrible experience.

Mind you, there was a bit of a moment on a Mercedes day at Knockhill. I was instructing an attractive female customer and giving her some extra laps. We went through the chicane and headed to Clark's and I asked her what she was up to that evening. We got to the corner and because my mind was on her, and not her driving, I hadn't said "brake" or given her any instructions. She was still flat on it… so we ended up bowling through the gravel. She was going quickly enough for us to get through all the gravel and come out the other side, with some assistance from me on the steering wheel.

Work life was going well, particularly now I was the trusted one with Ian, but there was still the racing to sort out. The plan was to try to make a full-time impact on the British Touring Car Championship.

Right at the end of the previous year, I'd done the last BTCC round, at Silverstone, in BRR Motorsport's BMW M3 run by Roy Kennedy because the regular driver, John Llewellin, hadn't been available. It was the last race in which those 2.3-litre M3s could take part before the series went all 2-litre. I finished fifth in class, behind class winner John Cleland's Vauxhall Cavalier and three other M3s, two of them crack entries for Frank Sytner (Prodrive) and Jeff Allam (Vic Lee).

For 1991, Kennedy swapped the 2.3-litre engine for a Prodrive-prepared 2-litre unit to suit the new regulations. We knew we had a reasonable car but money was always tight. I scratched around trying to get funding but it was hand to mouth, so I was only able to do four of the first five races and then the very last one at Silverstone when we had some backing from Absar Batteries. The results were no good and at Donington the gear lever came off in my hand.

But there was very good news on another racing front. It came in March, the month my son William was born, on the 22nd. Not long before his arrival, I received a fax from Japan. It was from Mutsuaki Sanada, who had lived with me in Bletchley all those years ago when we were racing for Dr

Ehrlich. He said he had good news: a drive for me in a new one-make series for a new model of Jaguar supercar built by Tom Walkinshaw Racing. I would get £10,000 in cash per race.

I had no idea what this series was about so I phoned Andy Morrison at TWR to find out more and he filled me in. It was called the Jaguar Intercontinental Challenge and there were going to be races for XJR-15s at three Grands Prix — Monaco, Silverstone and Spa — with the champion driver getting $1 million. I nearly fell off my chair.

Amidst all the scrabbling about for the BTCC deal, all of a sudden 1991 was up and running. It was all go and I really had something to get my teeth into.

The XJR-15s were mostly owned by various customers but run centrally on Jaguar's behalf by TWR. The cars Sanada-san and I were going to drive were owned by a Japanese outfit called The Room, which had something to do with racehorse breeding, and besides the two race versions the guy behind all this had also bought eight road-spec XJR-15s.

The first time I drove the XJR-15 was at Silverstone in the circuit's revised form after all the modifications that had been made over that winter, with the new Vale section and the Bridge/Priory/Brooklands stretch. I loved the car from the word go, especially its big V12 engine. Everyone who was going to Monaco for the first race was there and I wound up third fastest on the day. Derek Warwick was quickest and David Leslie was next, but David had plenty of experience because he'd done all the testing for Walkinshaw before anyone else got their hands on the cars. I don't know why, but the new-look Silverstone seemed to suit me well.

With the first race looming, Sanada-san phoned to say he was getting a mate of his to deliver my fee for the three races. I was expecting £30,000 in cash but what arrived was more like 8,000,000 Japanese yen in a dustbin bag. Once we'd tipped out this mass of banknotes, it took Jane and I about three hours to count it all.

We had half-completed an extension on our house and the builders wanted £6,000 to finish it, so I gave them about £7,000-worth of yen and left it to them to exchange it. Whenever I could, I used the yen to pay for other things and took the same approach, overpaying and leaving the legwork of changing the money into pounds to others. It took about three years before I'd finally spent it all. Of course, everything cost me quite a lot more that way — I often overpaid by as much as 25 per cent — but it was just the easiest way to deal with all this bloody yen.

At Monaco I qualified on the fourth row of the grid and was going along quite nicely until John Nielsen had a massive crash in front of me at Tabac with two laps to go. I avoided him but spun round and was going backwards towards the swimming pool. I sat there waiting for the bang but thankfully it never came. I was so relieved at not having a shunt or even putting a mark on the car that I did something like a 27-point turn to get it headed in the right direction again without touching anything. After all, it was a £500,000 motor.

Not only did I get well paid — the most I ever earned

in racing — but we also lived the high life. In Monaco we stayed at the Loews Hotel and I had a suite. I was on my own, though, as William had been born only six weeks earlier and Jane didn't want to come because she was worried it would have been too difficult with a baby. That was such a shame — it would have been lovely for her to have been there.

The next race was at Silverstone. I qualified fourth and made a good start. I got into the lead when Derek Warwick and David Brabham hit each other and Cor Euser spun. I stayed in front until lap 17 out of 20, holding off Juan Manuel Fangio III, but at Club, a second-gear corner in an XJR-15, I missed a gear and Fangio went straight past. I stayed with him initially but then my rear tyres gave up the ghost and Bob Wollek got ahead of me too. But I was still on the podium.

Our race was immediately after the British Grand Prix and Nigel Mansell had sent the crowd crazy by winning in his Williams. Although the start of our race had been delayed because of the circuit invasion by the fans, it was fabulous on the podium because there were hundreds and hundreds of people below when I stood up there. It was a really special moment, one that I will remember forever. No one really cared about Fangio, because he wasn't the proper Fangio, and Wollek was French. I was the homegrown hero and they were all shouting my name.

At the last race, at Spa for the Belgian Grand Prix, I qualified on the third row. Tiff Needell had a big crash at Eau Rouge during practice and did a lot of damage but the TWR people got it repaired for the race. Matt Aitken of Stock Aitken

Waterman record-producing fame was there because he owned David Leslie's XJR-15 and he spent a bit of time observing the rebuild of Tiff's car. When the TWR guys fitted new rear light lenses, he watched them take the parts out of their boxes and saw that they were supplied by Porsche, the same as on a 924. That set him thinking. He did some research and found that TWR's price for the part was ten times Porsche's price. He spread that news around pretty quickly.

JaguarSport had built up a massive display area where they were going to hand over the $1 million to whoever won it at the end of the race. Before the race had even started, this had all been taken down because Walkinshaw was so pissed off about what Aitken had been telling all and sundry in the paddock.

We only got the truth about that championship many years later. Win Percy, one of Walkinshaw's own drivers, was supposed to win it and to that end his engine received a proper going over beforehand. If Win won, JaguarSport, which was run by TWR, wouldn't have to pay out. Strange as it sounds, the deal for this final race was that the chequered flag would come out some time between lap 10 and lap 15. Nobody knew when, other than Walkinshaw himself, but the idea behind this was to reduce the possibility of any 'arrangements' between drivers — and doubtless to improve the chances of Percy being in front when the flag was shown.

At the end of lap 10, Cor Euser was leading in Charles Zwolsman's car from Armin Hahne in some German bloke's car. By now it was obvious that Win wasn't going to prevail, so the flag came out at the end of lap 11 and this time Hahne was in front. Only recently I found out that the two of them, Hahne and Euser, had indeed come to 'arrangement' and agreed to share the prize money 50/50. That seemed like a good outcome to me because they're both good guys and deserved to relieve Walkinshaw of the money. Of course, you'll be wondering how I got on in the race. Not that well: I finished eighth.

That wasn't my only visit to Spa in 1991. I'd never raced there before, so I thought that there couldn't be a better way to learn the circuit than to do the 24-hour touring car race, which took place three weeks earlier. With the Japanese funding and Sanada-san driving as well, we had a strong budget to bring to the right team.

I got in touch with Roger Nevitt from R&D Motorsport and we put together a deal to do the race in a Sierra RS500, with John Sheldon as the other driver. Malcolm Swetnam was going to be the team manager and that was a good thing because I'd known Malcolm for ages and knew the team weren't going to be cutting corners and would be able to prepare a good car. The team was also connected with Mountune Engines, which was important. The deal was that the sponsors from the Jag would put up a massive chunk along with Dunlop, because Sanada was tied in with Dunlop from his Japanese racing.

There was a second car, a 'rent-a-car' Sapphire RS Cosworth 4x4 driven by a British guy, Ken Grundy, plus a Belgian and a Frenchman. Their deal was that the three drivers paid their contributions in instalments: one-third before the car left England, one-third after the qualifying session and the rest after the opening hour of the race.

Qualifying ended at midnight. At a quarter to midnight, I was finished, job done, overalls off, relaxing, when Malcolm came rushing over. He explained that the team was in the shit. The drivers of the other car had been too slow and none of them had qualified — so the last third of the budget wouldn't be forthcoming.

He told me to go to the caravan behind the garage and put on Grundy's spare overalls and his crash helmet. The overalls were far too small and the helmet was so big it was spinning around on my head. Malcolm said when he gave me the signal I was to come out of the caravan, march straight through the garage to the car, not speak to anyone, climb in — it was already warmed up — and set off. When I came back in, I was to do the same thing in reverse and go straight to the caravan.

After an out-lap, I had just one lap to set a time. That wasn't a problem because I'd done plenty of laps in my own car and now knew the circuit quite well. Back in the pits when I got out to stride back to the caravan, I could see all three drivers of this second car were cheering because the car had got into the race — and then they looked around and realised that all three of them were standing there! They had been completely in the dark about our little plan.

When I eventually saw Malcolm afterwards, he said, "Congratulations, you've just outqualified yourself!" I'd gone faster than in my own car.

Our car retired from the race but, as irony would have it, the other car finished.

CHAPTER 13
MURRAY KNOWS MY NAME

On the strength of my Jaguar XJR-15 performance at Silverstone in 1991, I got some funding together for a better go at the British Touring Car Championship in 1992. Tiff Needell had a sponsor called Bankhall, an investment company run by GT racers David Warnock and Paul Hogarth. I got on really well with them and they agreed to give me some backing for the start of 1992, in the same BMW M3 that Roy Kennedy was now running in his own right. Besides Bankhall, I also had Halfords on the car. I'd met their marketing manager, Gil Duffy, on a Rover day at Donington Park and locked him in the car for ten high-speed laps until he agreed.

My car wasn't able to run at the front because it was an older-spec M3 and now the top teams, Prodrive and Vic Lee Motorsport, were running new-shape BMW 3-series cars. Despite my best efforts, and having the honour of fabled team manager Keith Greene looking after me at races free of charge, our results in the first three races were disappointing, so no more money was immediately forthcoming, although Halfords chipped in halfway through the season so that we could do the British Grand Prix support race at Silverstone.

I knew I had to get some decent TV coverage for Halfords on BBC *Grandstand* and thought that could lead to something afterwards. I hatched a plan and told Roy Kennedy about it. During the race, I was going to come into the pits and he would lift the bonnet and fiddle around for a bit, then I would give him the thumbs-up when to shut it so that I could come flying out of the pits just in front of the leaders. I could time this to perfection because there was a big TV screen for the crowd in full view of our pit so I could watch that and see the leaders approaching.

I came out in front of John Cleland's Vauxhall and Tim Harvey's BMW and held them up for three laps, then let them go ahead and stayed as close to them as I could to make sure we got maximum TV exposure — and to show everyone that I could keep up with the pacesetters in my out-of-date Beemer. Halfords were over the moon. But we still had no money to continue so that halted my BTCC ambitions yet again.

A few weeks before the British Grand Prix, there had been a dreadful period following Ian Taylor's death in a Rover 216 GTi during a British Rover Cup round at Spa. Ian wasn't just a boss to me in his driving venture but a wonderful friend. When he'd started that driving business, he'd got me in on the ground floor and had been so good to me. A few days after his death, his wife Moya spoke to the team and to Rover about the possibility of me driving for them and the upshot was that I did the next four races.

Not long after agreeing to that, I got a call from Ian Harrison of Prodrive's BTCC team asking me to step in and drive one of their BMWs for the rest of the season after Alain Menu injured himself in a paddock quadbike accident. That was a fabulous offer. Unfortunately, though, one of the four remaining BTCC rounds clashed with a Rover race and of course my loyalties were with my mates at Ian Taylor's team. Obviously, I hoped we could sort something out for the other three BTCC races but Ian told me it was all or nothing with the Prodrive car, so that was that. Kris Nissen got the BTCC gig.

Still, I did get one more BTCC race at the end of that year, courtesy of Peugeot. Robb Gravett had been racing a factory 405 Mi16 all season but for the last round he had a new car and so the team wanted to run the old one with a second driver. The team boss, Mick Linford, phoned and asked me to do a test on the Silverstone club circuit. I thought it was just going to be me at the test, but when I arrived I found that Bobby Verdon-Roe and Ray Armes were also taking part.

We all did lap times, and it came down to a shoot-out between Bobby and me. He reckons to this day that he didn't get the drive because he wasn't smart enough. Having been a mechanic, I've always realised that the first people you need to get onside are the mechanics and engineers. Bobby thought he was beyond all that back then — but I know he soon realised that this wasn't a good idea.

We had the test and I think after the initial runs I was 0.2sec up on Bobby — it was very close. Then I said to the mechanics that I thought it was time I tried the car on new tyres and they duly obliged. Obviously, I had the best of the new rubber and then they stuck Bobby in the car. He couldn't get near my time, so I got the drive.

That final BTCC round at Silverstone in 1992 was the famous race where Steve Soper and John Cleland, the championship leader, had their huge set-to and crashed out, leaving Tim Harvey to take the title. I finished ninth and that gave me two points, one point more than Gravett had managed all season.

Mick and the boys at the Peugeot team were pleased with that and liked me, so they also put me in for the TOCA Shootout at Donington Park four weeks later. That was great and I thought it would be the impetus to get me a regular drive with the team for 1993. My BTCC career had been a bit patchwork up to that point but I thought I was in with a shot of some full-time work.

This was the first TOCA Shootout. None of the factory-supported BMWs were entered so the new champion, Tim Harvey, couldn't take part, but he was there driving the safety car. Otherwise most of the top guys were there, including John Cleland, Andy Rouse, David Leslie and Jeff Allam. The concept was that the race started with the grid in reverse order and after 10 laps, halfway through, the last car on the track at the end of every lap would be black-flagged, until just four cars were left. Then Harvey would be sent out in the safety car to bunch everyone up at the end — the Shootout.

I managed to get into that final four — and finished fourth. I also got fastest lap, which turned out to be the one and only fastest lap ever achieved by a Peugeot in the BTCC. I featured a lot in the TV coverage and at one point Murray Walker, bless him, said, "There's Ian Flux — he hasn't had much driving this year, but he's doing really well here." That was what finally convinced my gran, who was 90 by then, that I'd made the big time!

My hopes for a full-time Peugeot seat in the 1993 British Touring Car Championship sadly came to nothing. As I expected, Peugeot did indeed run two factory cars that year but unfortunately for me Robb Gravett had a say in who his team-mate would be. It had been a one-car team when he went there and he'd obviously been pretty smart in getting this stipulation written into the contract. Although Mick Linford wanted me, Robb didn't, so the drive went to Eugene O'Brien.

Mick was a good man and said he still wanted me to be out there in a Peugeot, so he gave me the previous year's car free of charge. Roy Kennedy could run it for me and all we had to guarantee was that it went back to them at the end of the season in some kind of running order. It didn't have to be pristine but they didn't want to get it back as a ball of scrap.

Halfords were impressed with what I'd done at the British Grand Prix support race in 1991 and sponsored me again. Halfords had just done a deal to stock Silkolene oils and brought them aboard too. Dunlop also kindly provided me with free tyres for the whole year. So we went into that season with two good sponsors, a free car and free tyres. I was nicely set after all.

I was generally quicker than the factory Peugeots of Gravett and O'Brien for the first half of the season and scored points in five of the first seven races. But then they got some new cylinder heads and I didn't, so I struggled after that. And it wasn't just on track that things started going wrong. A company called Lauramite Developments was another backer to the tune of £25,000 and this money was basically going to be my wages for the season. But only £5,000 of that ever materialised despite me chasing the Lauramite bloke all season long. I must have turned up on his doorstep about 15 times but I never got to see him. He had me over.

There were glimmers of light though. At one of the Donington rounds, a chap called David Enderby came up to me during the pitlane walkabout. He said he liked the way I raced, gave me his business card and told me to call him in the coming week. His card had a Grolsch beer logo and said he was the marketing director. Of course, I followed it up. David had no budget for sponsorship but he did agree to give me some beer. I had visions of a couple of cases appearing on my doorstep at some point but a truck turned up with two pallets of the stuff and these were forklifted off into my driveway. I had to clear space in the garage to make room and get some neighbours round to help me drag the pallets into the garage. We had a good summer with all that beer on hand.

As well as BTCC in the Peugeot, I did a Prosport 3000 race in 1993. Prosport was a single-model sports car category that Chris Taylor had set up the previous year and I'd done the testing of the prototype car for him. He used this as a 'celebrity' car and offered me a race in it at Donington. By this time it was a bit of a hack and had done hundreds and hundreds of miles.

I think Chris expected me to do this race for nothing but I said he'd have to pay me £250. That was pretty cheap but I needed to make the point that as a professional driver I had to be paid when I raced. I knew what Chris was like and before qualifying I decided I had to have the money up front. He said he didn't actually have £250 but offered me three brand-new gear ratios instead. He told me I could sell them for £100 each and end up with an extra £50. I thought "oh well" and took them. Luckily my old mates at Roni rebuilt loads of gearboxes and I knew they would buy them off me. What with my touring car money troubles, I was £20,000 down but at least I now had some gear ratios.

Peter Hardman was the dominant driver in Prosport. He'd won the 1992 title and went on to win the 1993 series too. At Donington on the long circuit, I fought with him for the lead but it all went wrong on the last lap. Coming out of the Melbourne hairpin, the lock nut on the gear lever came loose as I went for second gear. By the time I'd rammed it into a gear, Thorkild Thyrring had come past me. Then I had the same trouble at Goddards and dropped to fifth by the end.

The gear ratios weren't my only 'payment in kind' that year. I co-drove a Roger Dowson-prepared Group N Ford Escort RS Cosworth with Peter Clarke at Silverstone and we finished third. When we came down from the podium, I asked Peter about the £500 fee we'd agreed. He said he would give me an option. He said I could have the money or I could go to the

Leeds premises of his family business, Silentnight beds, and choose a bed. He said I could look round the showroom and have whatever bed I wanted. So Jane and I drove up there and on the way I said we were going to get the most expensive bed in the entire place, even if she didn't like it. The price tag was £1,230 — and that was in a sale — so that's the bed we had. I still sleep on that same bed today.

There was another occasion. Dave Beecroft had built a sort-of Clubmans car for Mike Smith, whom I'd raced alongside in Thundersaloons. They'd tested it for a few days with Smith driving but hadn't really got anywhere. Beecroft is quite a forthright bloke and he'd told Smith that his feedback was crap. There was a bust-up and Mike told Dave to put someone else in the car to sort it, but Dave would have to pay for it.

So Beecroft asked me do a day with the car at Oulton Park and we agreed on £250. When I arrived, I asked him if he had my money. He said he would have it by lunchtime but I wasn't sure I trusted him. Anyway, at lunchtime, a bloke turned up in a van with a brand-new fridge, still in its plastic wrapping, and loaded it into the back of Beecroft's race truck. By the end of the day, Beecroft still didn't have the cash — but offered me the fridge. I really didn't want the fridge. But I was beginning to think I might never see the money so I put the seats down in my road-going Daewoo and managed to fit the thing in. Jane and I didn't need another fridge but at least we could put it in the garage and keep Grolsch in it. So, that year I'd been paid in gear ratios, a bed and a fridge, and also got two pallets of beer. It was an interesting career.

CHAPTER 14
TAMING THE BEAST OF BLACKPOOL

After my first TVR Tuscan experience in 1990 at the Birmingham Superprix, another opportunity came along at the end of 1993, courtesy of — in a roundabout way — Nigel Mansell. This was the year that Mansell, after winning the 1992 Formula 1 World Championship, went off to try his hand at Indycar racing and won that title too. So when it was announced that he was going to do the end-of-season TOCA Shootout in a Ford Mondeo, it was a big deal and a massive crowd poured into Donington that weekend.

There was also a TVR Tuscan race on the bill. Mansell was entered for that as well — and so was I. My Tuscan was owned by Clive Greenhalgh, who ran one of TVR's biggest dealerships, Team Central in Perry Bar, Birmingham, and normally raced the car himself. On this occasion, though, Clive asked me to drive instead because he really wanted to see his car beat Mansell's.

There was a test day and that went really well. I was

quickest, ahead of the top guys Colin Blower and Mark Hales, champions in 1992 and 1993 respectively. My car was run by Chris Smith of Streber Motorsport and we hit it off instantly because we had the same outlook on things, always trying to find an advantage when we could.

Mansell wasn't at the test day so the first we saw of him was in qualifying. He had a special engine built by John Reid at the TVR factory. I lined up behind Blower and Hales, then Mansell was just in front of me. Unfortunately, Mansell had a big shunt in the touring car race and had to go to hospital so there was a hole on the Tuscan grid where he should have been.

Before the race, I asked my crew to change the tyres from left to right and turn them around. You weren't allowed a new set of tyres so I thought that would give us a small advantage because of the wear. In the closing laps, I was fighting with Blower for the win and barged past him into McLeans to take the lead. But when I came down to the chicane at the end of that lap, my car snapped away from me and spun round and round and round. The tyre had suddenly deflated. When the car was checked, it was found that the valve on the wheel was the wrong kind, a long one that stuck out, and it had been torn away. It must have happened when I passed Blower. It was a story of what might have been: if only I hadn't tried to be too clever about the tyre wear and if only the offending wheel had been fitted with the correct stubby valve. Still, I got fastest lap and was awarded 'Driver of the Day'.

I went off to celebrate at the end of the day and was in

the bar with some racing mates. There was a nice guy there who kept wanting to buy everyone drinks but no one seemed to know who he was. He turned out to be Mike Lindup, keyboard player for the band Level 42, and we got on well. I didn't hear from him again until the following year when he invited me to co-drive with him. I hadn't even realised he raced so I asked him what his car was. Well, it was a Citroën 2CV, and he wanted to pay me to join him for a two-driver race at Pembrey. We finished third and I earned £1,000. I don't think many people can ever have been paid a grand to race a 2CV.

Anyway, back with TVRs, Clive Greenhalgh had been impressed with my efforts at Donington and asked if I would race for him for the whole of 1994. The deal was that he would pay my expenses and I would get to keep all prize money. We missed the first two rounds because we weren't ready, so my first outing was on Bank Holiday Monday at Castle Combe on 2nd May, the day after the dreadful weekend at Imola where Roland Ratzenberger and Ayrton Senna had been killed.

I was in a massive battle for the lead with Colin Blower and John Lyon, an older guy who was having a one-off drive in Gerry Marshall's factory-run car. I got ahead of Blower into Tower on the last lap and stuck to the inside to stop Lyon getting ahead. So that was my first Tuscan win and it was a really great race. I won again at Thruxton, the fifth round, and that put me only one point behind Mark Hales, the championship leader.

The next race was a one-off overseas round at Zandvoort in the Netherlands. I got a misfire on the warm-up lap when one of the spark plugs fouled on the Rover V8 engine so I had to go into the pits and start the race from there. From dead last, I got up to fourth place by the end. Chris Hodgetts was a convincing winner that weekend and I don't think I could have beaten him but I would certainly have finished second but for the plug problem.

That was the first weekend I really experienced the social side of the championship. It was immense fun with lovely lunches at the tracks and parties after the races. Thanks to dear old Peter Wheeler, TVR's owner who also raced in the series, it was all done in the best possible way. It was competitive, fun and often outrageous. Even if there was some aggro on the track, it was forgotten about half an hour later. I've never experienced anything quite like it in racing before or since.

Still, I behaved pretty well — unusual for me — on that Dutch weekend. The evening before the race we all went into Amsterdam, just down the road, but I returned to our hotel reasonably early and went to bed. All the mechanics stayed there the whole night and came straight from a strip club to the circuit the next morning.

After that, Mark Hales did a lot of the winning and became champion, but I did get one more win, at Silverstone near the end of the season.

Another memory of that 1994 season is going up against the great Gerry Marshall in four of the rounds. It was the first time I'd raced against him but of course I'd loved watching his heroics behind the wheel for donkey's years. Later, Gerry used to tell people that he beat me in Tuscans, but he never did, and nor did he outqualify me or set a better faster lap. I was very proud of that.

I carried on in the TVR Tuscan Challenge in 1995, still with Clive Greenhalgh's Team Central and still run by Streber Motorsport. It was a season of transition, with the old Rover V8 engine being phased out and the new Al Melling-designed AJP V8 coming in. At first only John Kent, Steve Cole and Peter Wheeler had the new engine, and I didn't get one until May. At the end of the season, though, I went on a run of seven straight wins in the last eight races, counting heats and finals, and also led the eighth until the diff broke. This streak was too late for the title, which went to John Kent, but it showed what I could do.

I had a third full TVR Tuscan season with Team Central and Streber Motorsport in 1996, by which time I had also landed a fabulous ride in the British GT Championship, as you will find out in the next chapter. When there was a clashing date, the British GT gig took priority, but that only happened twice. By this time, though, the Tuscan Challenge often had more than one round at a circuit on the same day, and unfortunately on the first clashing weekend the Tuscans actually had three races, so while I was at Donington winning in British GT I was missing three chances to score Tuscan Challenge points at Knockhill in Scotland. So although I won two of the first three Tuscan races, at Silverstone and Oulton Park, after seven rounds I had a sizeable deficit in the standings.

Martin Short was the championship leader at that point but

then he lost the plot. At Oulton Park in the eighth round, for example, he was in the lead but picked up a gearbox problem. That slowed him down but he was desperate to keep me and John Kent behind him. I thought he was driving like an idiot and in the end I couldn't avoid spinning him out of the way at Cascades because he was so slow through there. If he'd been realistic, he could have let John and I go by and hung on for third place, but he chose not to, and didn't get any points. One aspect of the art of racing is knowing when to let someone through. If you're beaten, let your rival go.

I finished second to Kent in that race. That put me on the front foot and I won four of the next five rounds to get my momentum going. Then Shortie took a win before I scored four more wins in five rounds. I won the title with a round to go and Shortie lost it because he didn't use his head — and I've told him that.

Another thing about that Oulton Park race was that the team entered two cars for the first time. I got a new car, a green one, and Bobby Verdon-Roe came aboard to drive my old yellow one. Bobby, remember, was the guy I'd had over in that British Touring Car Championship test for Peugeot at the end of 1992. For the final round, the big Donington event where the touring cars were running in the RAC Tourist Trophy race, there was this idea of wanting to prove that I could win in either of our Tuscans, so I swapped cars with Bobby.

To get people talking, we pretended that Bobby and I had a £10,000 bet about whether I could win with his car. This story spread everywhere and even the track commentator, Alan Hyde, picked it up and started announcing it. It was great PR for TVR and Ben Samuelson, the company's press guy, didn't deny it — there was no need to quash this great rumour spreading all over the place. Anyway, I led until three laps from the end when the diff packed up. The diffs were marginal on those cars.

One of my proudest moments in a Tuscan came at Cadwell Park that year. It was a hot day. In the Tuscan, if the water temperature went over 100°C, the timing would be automatically retarded and you'd lose 15 horsepower. If you then went over 105°C, you'd lose another 15 horsepower. I was in the lead but the engine was beginning to overheat and I had Bobby Verdon-Roe and Jason Yeomans right behind me. As I was getting concerned about the temperature, I let them both through. I dropped back a bit and watched them. With a lap or two to go, they both made a move on each other at the end of the Park Straight. Jason went off to the outside and Bobby to the inside. By then I had my engine temperature back under control and I drove past them both and on to the win. I congratulated myself on being such a professional.

I remained with Streber Motorsport for 1997 but now with backing from a different TVR dealer, Brooklands Exeter, because Clive Greenhalgh had sold up and gone to live in Spain. As the champion, I had a lot to live up to but I got a strong start to the season and won the first three races. Then we went to Brands Hatch, using the long circuit, and I always went well there. I was leading from Jamie Campbell-Walter but let him through so we could put on a bit of a show, with me staging a few attempts to pass before I was ready to do it for real. Trouble was, someone dropped a load of oil and the race was suddenly red-flagged — with me still second. So I lost that one through my own stupidity.

After that, the season developed into a fight between Bobby Verdon-Roe, who was now driving for the TVR factory, and me. It all went down to the final race at Silverstone. I had to win it, but I needed Bobby to finish lower than third for me to claim the title.

My friend Dave Loudon, who has won lots of one-make championships himself, came over as I was strapped in the car on the grid. He leaned into the cockpit and said: "Fluxie, you have to win this as slowly as you possibly can." I had to be ahead but also had to keep the pack behind me as tightly bunched as possible because that could spell all kinds of bother for any of them — hopefully including Bobby. There would be no point scorching out in front of everyone and having no control on what was going on in my mirrors.

I had had a word with fellow racer Ian McKellar and he was on-side. I got away in the lead but I could see Bobby right behind me so I knew I needed to slow down. Then Jamie Campbell-Walter overtook Bobby, which was good, and I willed McKellar to do the same.

We were on the International circuit at Silverstone, with the old chicane out the back. When Bobby was behind me, I'd been driving off the track on the exit of the chicane to try and throw crap into his radiator, but that never worked. All I did was manage to put a hole in Campbell-Walter's radiator and he dropped out.

I was still trying to go slowly and I wince when I recall the lap times. A normal time was about 1m 10s but I remember seeing 1m 19s on my pit board. I was that desperate to hold everyone up.

There was a yellow flag at Copse on one lap. I hit the anchors as soon as I saw it, put my hand in the air and trickled through at about 20mph. Bobby was right behind and nearly shot past — which would have earned him a penalty — but managed to check up. It caused pandemonium in the queue behind.

I was using all 30 years of my accumulated motor racing knowledge and experience. All the things I'd ever had done to me or heard about — I was throwing it all at that race. Eventually, Bobby did finish second and won the title, but it certainly wasn't for lack of trying on my part.

In truth, I lost that championship at the previous event, at Mondello Park in Ireland, where Bobby had won. I went out drinking the evening before the qualifying sessions and got very drunk. The circuit was damp for qualifying and I went out on wets and set a provisional pole time. Then the track started to dry and we put slicks on but the tyre change was very slow. By the time we were ready for me to do my quick lap, the session was just about to end. I was only on the fifth row of the grid for my heat.

Making my way up the order in the race, I came up against Steve Cole at the exit from the Esses. He braked for no apparent reason — you didn't need to brake there — and I ran up the back of his car and ended up on top of it. Although both our cars could be repaired in time for the final, in the end there was only space on the grid for one of us because of the way the results of the two heats turned out. As I was unfairly deemed to have caused the accident, Cole got into the final and I was out.

But there was one way to get into the race. If I went to every driver and got them to sign a piece of paper agreeing to let me take part, I would be allowed in. Eventually they all signed. I climbed from the back, 27th, to fifth place at the chequered flag, which was quite an achievement around Mondello. But it was that qualifying session that had put me in that position and cost me a better result.

Bobby Verdon-Roe was a great rival. We had some great races in Tuscans and never once made contact — well, not deliberately. He was, without question, the best person I ever drove against in those TVRs. He had the speed and the racecraft — and he was just such a good competitor.

CHAPTER 15
THE TEXAN CONNECTION

The guy who ran my TVR Tuscan, Chris Smith from Streber Motorsport, asked me to do some demonstration drives for passengers in a Porsche 956 at Goodwood in October 1994. Little did I know it on the day, but this led to a wonderful opportunity.

There were lots of guests and I wheeled them around one after another in the passenger seat. I wasn't hanging around, lapping in about 1m 12s, which was a pretty sensible time around Goodwood. It was the one and only time I drove a 956 and I enjoyed it. The turbo boost was chattering and I earned £500 for my day's work. I drove home happy.

About two weeks later, one of the passengers phoned me. It was James Stevenson, who ran Nigel Mansell's Ferrari and TVR dealerships. James said he'd been so impressed by his run with me that he'd put my name forward as a driver coach for an American who was going to come over and race a Tuscan the coming season.

This was Jake Ulrich. I coached him all the way through 1995 but he was always at the back of the Tuscan grids. We worked together a lot but he just drove at a certain pace and that was it. Even though I used to jump in his car and back-to-back it with mine to make sure all was well, it was hard to make him any faster. We got on really well and he liked having me around.

Jake phoned early in 1996 and said out of the blue that he wanted us to race together in the British GT Championship. He asked me what car I thought he should get. Because he wasn't really on the pace, it needed to be the best car out there. Going on the previous year's Le Mans form, when a McLaren F1 GTR had won outright, I told Jake that I felt we needed one of those. He said he'd been thinking exactly the same thing.

Paul Lanzante had looked after the winning McLaren at Le Mans. I knew Paul because he'd run Colin Pool's Thundersports Tiga back in 1988 when I did a couple of races in that car. When I called him to talk about Jake's plan, Paul couldn't quite believe it was for real to begin with, but I assured him it was, and we fixed a meeting. Paul was still sceptical and said I'd be in for the high jump if I was wasting his time.

Jake and I went down to Lanzante's place. Paul saw that Jake was genuine and that he really did want a McLaren. They also hit it off and liked each other. However, there weren't many McLarens available. But there was one possibility because Ray Bellm, who owned two Gulf-liveried cars that had been incredibly successful in the BPR Global GT Endurance Series in 1995, was planning to buy new McLarens for 1996 and sell these older ones. We went to Bellm's place and viewed both cars in their iconic blue and orange Gulf colours. They looked identical to me but we picked one, the one that had done more of the winning in 1995 and had also finished fourth overall at Le Mans. Ray and Jake shook hands on a deal for £400,000 and Jake organised the funds there and then in front of us all. Next morning, Jake sent his guys to pick up the car.

So we were all set and Jake agreed to pay me £1,000 per race. Before the season, there was a media day at Silverstone and everybody was gobsmacked when this McLaren turned up. It had been a well-kept secret. It was still in Gulf blue but Jake had changed the orange bits to yellow.

The British GT races lasted about 45 minutes and included a mandatory minute-long pitstop where there could be a driver change if wanted. Our plan was that I would always do the start and build up as big a lead as possible before handing over to Jake, who would then do his steady best but inevitably slip back.

The first round, at Silverstone, went to plan until Jake dropped the clutch at the pitstop and the car didn't move. But next time out, at Donington, everything went perfectly and we won quite comfortably. In the remaining six races, however, Jake was never quite able to hold on to our initial advantage and we ended up with two seconds, two thirds and a fourth. Nevertheless, that gave us the class title but a two-and-sixpenny Darrian took the overall honours.

So, with my TVR Tuscan Challenge crown as well, I was a double champion in 1996! I was 40 years old and it was a golden period of my life... except for one thing.

That year I stupidly fell out with my sister Carolyn in a big way. It happened soon after she'd brought mum along to Brands Hatch to watch me winning in the TVR Tuscan. It was great to have them there, especially as Carolyn was so pleased to see how well I was doing. Up to that point she'd taken no interest in my racing because she'd been turned against it back in my very early days, in Formula 6, when she'd been dragged along to race meetings at the age of 12 or 13. I remember her saying to me, "It was always all about you — all I ever got was a piano and I hated it."

Not long afterwards, I guess it was all about me again. It was mum's 65th birthday party and we all went over to Carolyn's and my brother-in-law Rob's house for a party. It was a little bit tense. Anyway, we were in the middle of lunch when Wills, who was five, wandered off and started letting off the party poppers that were planned for later, with the birthday cake. Carolyn thought Jane and I should have kept a better eye on him and stopped him doing that — and she said so. Regrettably, I snapped and said, "Right, we're off."

We didn't speak for five years after that. What broke the ice was when Jane and I went to Spain with the kids for a holiday. Via a racing connection, we stayed in a holiday villa that was supposed to have a swimming pool but when we arrived... no pool. Coral and Wills were massively disappointed. Now, Carolyn and Rob had their own place in Spain, about 45 minutes away, and it not only had a pool but a granny annexe as well. I phoned to tell Carolyn what had happened and she invited us over. We ended up staying for the rest of the week — and that put everything back together again.

If I could live my life all over again, the only thing I'd change would be to make sure I didn't fall out with my sister.

At the end of the 1996 season, Jake did a track day on the Grand Prix circuit at Silverstone with his mates so we could give them all a ride in the McLaren. That was the last time the car ever went on a track. Although Jake decided he wanted to do British GT again in 1997, he preferred to run a different car. Wisely, though, he decided to keep the McLaren.

Paul Lanzante turned it back into a road car. All that needed to be done was fit a proper handbrake and a silencer system and away you go. Other F1 GTR owners did this too so it was quite a familiar practice. Lanzante maintained the car and MoT'd it every year until 2013, when Jake sold it. I reckon he's the only person ever to make a proper profit from doing British GT: he'd paid £400,000 for the McLaren and sold it for £8.5 million!

Not long before that, I'd been chatting to a fellow driver who'd made a bit of cash when a supercar he'd raced had been sold. He told me that he'd collected up all the trophies he'd won in the car and his overalls from that time and got good money for it all from the car's mega-rich buyer. That got me thinking and I phoned Lanzante to suggest a similar deal for all my stuff from that title-winning year with the McLaren. Paul said, "I'm very sorry to tell you this, Fluxie, but as far as the new owner is concerned the worst thing about that car is that it did British GT races. He was only interested in it because it did well at Le Mans: you'd better forget that idea!"

Anyway, back to 1997 and Jake's new car. He and I had noticed that the Lister Storm GTS had been quick in the hands of Tiff Needell and Geoff Lees in its 1996 BPR GT outings. Lister boss Laurence Pearce liked the idea of one of his cars in British GT and showed me the design for the new version he was building. It looked great and Jake decided to go for it. Laurence did him a good deal for £350,000. Lister only built two of these new Storm GTL versions and the other one was used as a factory car for Le Mans and the new FIA GT Championship.

The two Listers were finished about three weeks before the opening British GT race of the season. Geoff Lees and I spent 10 days going round and round Pembrey in South Wales getting them sorted and ironing everything out. They were on different makes of tyres: Jake's car was on Dunlops, as his McLaren had been, because I could get free deals with Dunlop and they'd been over the moon about our title in the McLaren; the factory car was on Michelins. At Pembrey, which is very bumpy, the Michelins gave a much better ride, and in fact they proved to be superior in every way — but they weren't free.

It was all looking good when we turned up at Silverstone for the first race on the first weekend of April. I put the Lister on pole before Jake got in to do his five laps to qualify himself to start. He overtook John Greasley, who had just come out of the pits in his Porsche 993 GT1, and somehow ended up on the kerb going into Becketts. The Lister just took off and flew over the catch-fencing into the barrier. It was a massive shunt and the car was totalled.

Jake was taken straight to the medical centre and I hurried there with Laurence Pearce to see how he was. We found him on a hospital bed and the first thing he uttered was, "Laurence, don't worry about the £350,000." He hadn't paid a penny for the car up to that point. Looking back, it would have been sensible for him to have come testing with us for at least one day and got some experience of the car.

We missed a race while the Lister was being repaired and came back for the third round, at Donington, which we managed to win. But that shunt basically screwed our season. Jake didn't have much confidence anyway and the crash just sucked more out of him. He was never the same after it.

One happy distraction that year was winning a race at Brands Hatch to celebrate the 30th anniversary of Formula Vee. It was shown on the BBC's *Top Gear*. Tiff Needell and I had a great battle for the lead, Tiff in a brand-new GAC, me in a much older Scarab. On the last lap I was right with him and thought I would chance it coming out of Clearways and sprint to the finish line in third gear all the way, hoping the engine would take being buzzed. Tiff slightly fluffed his gearchange into fourth and I won by a nose. Ten years later there was a 40th anniversary and I finished second, this time driving a lovely modern GAC.

Back in the British GT Championship, Jake and I stayed with the same Lister for 1998. I always qualified well, third or fourth every time, but we didn't win a race. We had two podium finishes, but we were now up against Tiff Needell and Julian Bailey in the other Lister, and this now had a full carbon-fibre monocoque. I could pretty much match them but they were too quick for Jake, so it was always an uphill struggle. Otherwise, the main opposition was Tim Sugden and Steve O'Rourke in Steve's EMKA Racing McLaren F1 GTR and John Greasley and Magnus Wallinder in their Porsche 993 GT1.

The biggest problem for Jake was the Lister's carbon brakes. He never seemed to get the hang of them and I think it was because he just didn't press the pedal hard enough. They needed to be really hot to work properly. As in our McLaren year, I always did the first stint and then Jake would take over. He would do all right for the first couple of laps, while the brakes were still quite hot, but then slip further back as they cooled off.

The championship's penultimate round was at Spa in Belgium. This race, the first overseas event in the history of the series, looked very tasty money-wise because of a prize indemnity insurance policy that Jake had taken out. It was a form of gambling and suddenly seemed to be all the rage in motor racing at that time. Jake knew that I was short of money and had put £5,000 into this policy on my behalf. Don't ask me exactly how it worked, but if either Lister were to win the championship, which now looked like quite a long shot, I would receive £65,000. So it was like a 13/1 bet if you think of it in normal betting terms. Any other championship outcome meant I would get nothing. Instead of sharing with

Jake, I teamed up with Ian McKellar, while Anthony Reid joined Julian Bailey in the lead car.

Everything went all right in qualifying with our cars second and third behind the O'Rourke/Sugden McLaren comfortably on pole. In the wet first half of the race, O'Rourke fell back through the field, as he usually did being an amateur driver, and our Listers ran 1–2, Bailey in the lead, McKellar second.

Because radio communication is so hard at Spa with all the elevation changes, Laurence Pearce had bought an enormous broadcast mast to make sure that we could hear the pits-to-car radio all the way around the circuit. This was working perfectly until the crucial time when the track was drying out. Our generator ran out of fuel and the radios went down just as the call went out to get Bailey into the pits to swap to slicks. O'Rourke brought the McLaren in, put Sugden in the car with slicks, and away he went. Bailey didn't come in until the following lap — and that lost lap made all the difference. Reid lost the race by just over a minute, which is pretty much what Bailey was forced to give away with that extra lap on the wets. Those four and a half miles cost Lister the championship and lost me £65,000.

CHAPTER 16

AFTER THE LADDERS, THE SNAKES APPEAR

I did a fifth season in the TVR Tuscan Challenge in 1998 but after so many good times it turned to shit. This time the money came from Steve Beeches, who often helped out in the pits at my races and had been a personal sponsor for the best part of six years. Steve had a haulage company called Saints Transport and was about to buy some new lorries. Saints split its fleet across three different manufacturers — MAN, Scania and Mercedes — and operated about 20 vehicles from each. Steve was planning to buy six Scanias but asked MAN if they'd consider a deal whereby they'd give extra discount to cover the cost of running the Tuscan for the year and have their branding on the car. So that's what happened.

Initially the car itself was Jake Ulrich's, the one he'd raced in 1995 when he'd first come over from America. Jake had been so good to me in my career that my biggest worry was to make sure I gave his Tuscan back in one piece. I didn't bother with insurance because I didn't have accidents and in any case

I wouldn't have been able to afford it. We only planned to use Jake's car until we'd put together a new one. We wanted to find out what Martin Short had done on his trick car and then build one exactly like his — and we were in the process of doing that.

Still, I wasn't unhappy with Jake's car and managed to win the second round, at Donington. But next time out, at Oulton Park in early May, I had a massive shunt. It happened when the throttle pedal jammed under the roll cage going into Island Bend, one of the fastest corners on the circuit with the least run-off. It was flat in fourth gear with a little dab of the brakes just as you go in, but because the throttle was stuck open I didn't get that dab and that made all the difference. I went off at about 140mph and smashed the right-front into the wall.

I was concussed and properly bruised but I managed to get out relatively unscathed. What worried me most, more than my own state, was how I was going to tell Jake what had happened to his car. I was taken to the medical centre and Jane rushed over there. Apparently, I said to her that we must make sure the kids, who were now ten and seven, didn't get to hear about it. She told me that would be difficult because they were standing at the end of the bed... I was so out of it I hadn't noticed.

Thanks to TVR and some of the other teams rallying round, we put together a replacement car for Jake without breaking the bank, while I got hold of my new one to race for the rest of the season. But I struggled and didn't win again.

One reason why I lost form in Tuscans that year was because there was something wrong in my marriage. I didn't know what it was but deep down I knew things weren't right between Jane and me. Something had happened and I could feel it all the time. I'm sure it took the edge off my game.

It wasn't until many years later, long after Jane left me, that I found out what it was. She had been sleeping with someone else. It was Ian McKellar, my on-track rival and supposed friend, someone I'd coached and looked after. It was a huge betrayal. I haven't spoken to him since I found out.

In British GT with the Lister, I think I was less affected because I knew I wasn't going to win. With Jake as my co-driver, I couldn't beat Tiff Needell and Julian Bailey. But so long as I put in a good performance and got somewhere near their fastest lap, that was OK. In TVRs, however, I was expected to win.

There was a highlight at the end of 1998 that was quite unexpected. I was invited to drive a Ferrari 250 GTO in the RAC Tourist Trophy Celebration race at the very first Goodwood Revival. It came about through Tony Dron. He regularly raced historic cars owned by Harry Leventis, including this GTO, but on this occasion he needed a co-driver because it was a two-driver race.

I had a chance to test the car beforehand at Silverstone. Earlier in the year it had broken its crown wheel and pinion and now had a replacement fitted, but it was far too tall. It would have been ideal for a road trip down to the South of France but the car was just too long-legged for the track. So Tony and I were never competitive at Goodwood and finished only tenth in the race.

The big thing about the Goodwood Revival, of course, is all the period character. For that first one, it was a particularly special novelty to see everyone dressed in keeping with the era. Everyone but me, that is. I just couldn't afford the £600 needed to buy the old-style race overalls we were all supposed to wear so I looked a bit out of place in my brightly coloured modern race suit. That did raise some eyebrows.

All GTOs are special, of course, but this one was extra special. When new in 1962, it was going to be raced by Stirling Moss, but then he had his big accident at Goodwood. With Stirling's career at an end, Innes Ireland mostly drove it that year and the highlight came when he won the Tourist Trophy, the famous event that 'my' race was celebrating. When I drove it, the car was worth about £1.25 million, but today it must be at least £30 million.

Another memory of 1998 was a coaching assignment with an unusual twist. At Donington on the April day I won what turned out to be my last ever Tuscan race, Mike 'Fulmar' Taylor, my old rival from Sports 2000, asked if I would help his son Mark, who was just starting out in Formula Vauxhall Junior. We went to Croft and did two days there with his team, Jonathan Lewis Racing, which was running three other drivers besides Mark.

Although Mike had employed me solely to instruct Mark, Jonathan saw a chance for the entire team to benefit and asked me to play along with a plan. At about 3pm on the first afternoon he told the drivers they were done for the day and explained to them that I was going to do five laps in each of the team's four Van Diemens. Then he pulled me aside and said he wanted to make an 'unbeatable' car. I had to pick the best chassis, the best engine and the best gearbox across the four cars.

James Hanson's car had the best chassis, with more feel than the others, while Mark Taylor's had a really strong engine, and I liked Antonio Pizzonia's gearbox. Pizzonia, a 17-year-old Brazilian who'd come over to make his name, was the team's most promising driver so that evening the mechanics cracked on to assemble this mega-car for him. He went on to win something like the next eight races on the trot and became the champion.

The end of the 1998 British GT season with Lister brought my relationship with Jake Ulrich to a close because he decided to stop racing. He was feeling the pressure of combining his racing with a demanding business life — not long afterwards he became CEO of Centrica, which owns British Gas — and he really should have stopped at the end of 1996 when we won the championship and left on a high. But it all got too much for him and that was understandable.

That meant the TVR Tuscan Challenge was all I had for 1999. I had another change of team and this time I ran with Bert Taylor at Countdown Developments. It was all done on a bit of a shoestring because we ran on the budget of my teammate, Steve Hyde, who had some backing from Barclays Bank. It was really only enough money for one car but we divided it into two. The season got off to the worst possible start.

The first two races were a double-header at Oulton Park on the first weekend of April. On the first lap of the first race, I tried to take the lead at Knickerbrook. There was a massive kerb on the inside and I used all of it. I smacked it hard and remember thinking to myself, "Goodness, that was a big hit." It wasn't until I got to the slight left-hander under the bridge at the top of Clay Hill that I realised I had no steering whatsoever. Having gone off the previous year at the worst place to crash at Oulton, it had taken me only 12 months to find the second worst. I had time to get on the brakes and scrub off some speed but it was still one hell of a shunt.

Peter Wheeler, the TVR boss, was really kind. Luckily the crash hadn't destroyed the chassis but there was a lot of damage and Peter arranged for Bert Taylor to get all the bits he needed to rebuild the car free of charge in time for the next race at Donington. But the engine was a different story. There were good TVR engines and not so good ones. We eventually discovered that the Oulton crash had cracked something and for the rest of the season I had to race with a sub-standard engine.

But there was one highlight that year, at Castle Combe, and it came with a bit of an underhand tactic. It was the only race the Barclays bosses were attending all season and I wanted to put on a good show. I qualified mid-pack on the sixth row but told Bert I was going to jump the start.

As I formed up on the grid waiting for the start, I slotted it into first gear and immediately started rolling forward. You could see it on the onboard camera: as soon as the cog was in,

I was moving, as if the clutch was dragging. Of course, there was no problem with the car whatsoever, but I couldn't have slammed on the brakes and risked stalling in the middle of the pack, could I? The only thing for me to do was to keep the power coming on. I had to go — and I led for quite a long time! Afterwards, the officials weren't happy about it and wanted an explanation. Then they went to Richard Hay, whose Hay Fisher firm provided the film coverage, to see what the camera had captured — and it looked exactly as I'd described. I got a slap on the wrists but at least Barclays got some great coverage.

This was my last proper year in the TVR Tuscan Challenge and it had given me some truly great days. I did the occasional race after that, but nothing serious. My last ever race in Tuscans was at Castle Combe in 2000 driving a car built by Colin Blower. Colin's regular driver, Jamie Campbell-Walter, was away and Colin asked me to stand in. In qualifying, there was something wrong with the fusebox and the car only ran intermittently, and we couldn't sort it out for the race. I struggled along with it and finished third.

There were lots of great people in the TVR Tuscan Challenge and Colin was certainly one of them. I'd raced against him in Production Saloons, when he was driving a Mitsubishi Starion, and I'd got to know him well. He was a clever engineer and saw how to make the most of grey areas in the regulations. One example on his famous 'number five' Tuscan was the windscreen, which was positioned at a much shallower angle than everyone else's. The rules stated that the windscreen had to be the correct one for a Tuscan but there were no stipulations about its position or angle of rake. That must have given him a few mph on top speed.

I raced one other front-engined brute in 1999, a Chrysler Viper, in the British GT Championship round at Silverstone supporting the British Grand Prix. David Clark, the owner, invited me to a Mallory Park test to get used to the car but there was a problem on the day and I never got to try it. So my first acquaintance was in qualifying at Silverstone, where the weather looked a bit threatening.

The team had wet tyres ready in the pits, complete with air bottles for the wheel-guns on a portable trolley. It was all very congested in the pitlane because part of it was cordoned off for the Formula 1 cars. The Viper was left-hand drive, something I wasn't at all used to, and when I pulled in at our pit I managed to knock the trolley. David Clark's wife was standing on it and fell off, breaking her arm.

It was very unfortunate. All the same, I couldn't believe it when Clark tried to sue me. For a start, she shouldn't have been standing on the bloody trolley, and really she shouldn't have been in the pits at all during the biggest meeting of the year where only minimal crew were allowed. So much for being a good team-mate. Ian Titchmarsh, the renowned circuit commentator and a solicitor in his day job, kindly acted for me and knocked that nonsense on the head.

CHAPTER 17
NEWSPAPER ASSIGNMENTS

Before we leave the 20th century, I need to tell you about a media side-line that turned out to be enormous fun and put me in the cockpit of some very special competition cars.

It all started in 1994. Paul Fearnley, the International Editor of *Motoring News* and the newspaper's British Touring Car Championship reporter, had written his end-of-season review of the 1993 BTCC in which he had selected his top 10 drivers of the year. He had put me in at number 10 — for trying hard, I think — and that was very good of him. Soon afterwards, *Motoring News* decided that they wanted to publish track tests because rival magazine *Autosport* did so. *Motoring News* wanted someone with a good name who would be thought worthy enough to drive people's precious cars. Paul phoned one day to offer me the job at £250 per day plus expenses.

Most people think I wrote these articles myself but Paul put the words together from my comments after the tests. We would squirrel away and I would give him my thoughts about the car. Paul did this until he left the newspaper in 1998, after which it was usually Matt James who wrote the words. Sometimes the tests were published in *Motor Sport* rather than in *Motoring News*, which — just to add to the confusion — changed its name to *Motorsport News* in 2000. So, *Motor Sport* was and is the monthly and *Motorsport News* was and is the weekly, but they're no longer sister magazines.

I loved all this. It opened so many doors. I ended up driving cars I would never have dreamt I would ever be allowed near, including most of the world's top rally cars.

My first mission was to go to Snetterton to test the Paul Stewart Racing Dallara F394 that Jan Magnussen drove to win the 1994 British Formula 3 Championship. It was my first run in an up-to-date Formula 3 car for nine years, as that's how long had passed since I raced the Roni, also at Snetterton. It was a good experience except for the embarrassment of running wide on my first out-lap and sliding onto the grass. I came straight into the pits to have the car checked and got a bit of a ticking off from Andy Miller, who was running the car.

Another car I drove during that first year with *Motoring News* was an Audi A4. This took place at Donington the day after the FIA Touring Car World Cup, where Frank Biela and Hans Stuck had raced for Audi. I rocked up early and all the very efficient German mechanics were there ready for me with Stuck's car. They asked me to start by going out for three laps: an out-lap, a flying lap and an in-lap.

When I arrived back in the pits, all the mechanics were smiling and I wondered what on earth I'd done to get this reaction. It turned out they thought I'd gone 0.5sec quicker than Stuck had managed all weekend. What they didn't realise was that the test was on the National circuit, not the full track that had been used for the World Cup. It was only by chance that my lap time as I was easing myself into it had been so similar to a full lap time. I didn't set them straight for a while!

There were a lot of great tests in 1995, my first full year of doing these articles. One that was a real honour was a chance to drive the Harrods-sponsored McLaren F1 GTR that Andy Wallace, Derek Bell and Justin Bell had nearly driven to victory at Le Mans that year but ended up coming home third after last-minute gearbox dramas. This was just about the most important car I'd ever driven at that time and came before my British GT season with Jake Ulrich.

The test was on the Silverstone Grand Prix circuit. At the time I was enjoying a strong winning run in the TVR Tuscan and I wrote in the story that the McLaren was only two seconds a lap quicker than the TVR, even though it cost £625,000 rather than £25,000. That really pissed off Ron Dennis.

One of the test drives I enjoyed most that year was in European Rallycross Champion Will Gollop's Peugeot 306 at Croft. It was a four-wheel-drive machine and had a turbo 2-litre engine. I've never driven anything like it. First of all I did three laps with Will alongside and then he let me go out on my own for a few more laps. I didn't do very well so he got back in as a passenger. He was a lovely bloke and really tried to help me, wanting me to get the most from the car. Eventually I started to feel like I was getting to grips with it.

When I went back out on my own, Will's guys timed me over a three-lap run and at the end of that I was only about 10 seconds off his time. He thought that was pretty good and I was pleased with myself. Various other pros went out in the car and none of them could get within 20 seconds of him. The way I'd been able to achieve some mastery of the car made the experience very special.

In rally cars I was often able to sit alongside star drivers. Without question, the best ride I ever had was with Hannu Mikkola in a left-hand-drive Ford Escort Mk1 in 1995. This came about in connection with the 25th anniversary rerun of the London-to-Mexico Rally. As on the original event in 1970, Hannu and his navigator, Gunnar Palm, won this modern version. Afterwards, Ford took the car to Mark Higgins's rally school in Wales for a media day in the snow.

Actually, this 1995 *Motoring News* test wasn't my first run with Mikkola. Back in 1977, during my Formula 3 days, I'd gone along to a press day for the RAC Rally at an army proving ground at Bagshot with my mechanic Alan Turner, who'd been Mikkola's mechanic on Ford rally cars a few years earlier. Hannu greeted Alan like a long-lost friend and then offered me a ride with him in his Toyota Celica 2000 GT. It was absolutely amazing. Hannu did things with that car that I couldn't possibly have done myself. Then I got into a Vauxhall Chevette with a guy called Will Sparrow and it wasn't impressive at all.

Anyway, back to Wales in 1995. We spent the evening before the test with Hannu and David Sutton, who was running the car, and we all had a lot to drink. That seems to be the way in rallying! There were loads of great stories. The next morning, there was plenty of snow and we went to the rally school. I jumped in the passenger seat and away we went for 10 laps of a forest stage.

This stage had a long, steep, downhill left-hander with a particularly big tree on the right-hand side of the rough track. First time round we missed the tree by about three inches — and, don't forget, it was on my side of the car. I thanked my lucky stars and figured that Hannu would get his eye in on the next run. Every time we missed that tree by three inches! He was an incredible talent.

The best rally car I drove was a Toyota Celica GT-Four, also in 1995. This took place at a general test day at a Michelin place in hilly farmland somewhere in the middle of France and Toyota's regular driver Marc Duez was there. The course was a private lane but occasionally farm traffic needed to use it and proceedings had to be paused. Before each run up and down this lane, marshals at the top and bottom had to confirm that it was clear.

I was allowed plenty of blasts in both directions and I loved it. The car had unbelievable get-up-and-go. For my last session, our photographer, Malcolm Griffiths, got in the car beside me to do some in-car shots so I tootled up to the top of the hill so he could get those in the can. Then I turned the car around for a final quick run down the hill. The marshal said it was clear to go and off I went, determined to beat the best time I'd recorded so far.

RIGHT The start of my journalistic career came in 1994. The beauty of the job with Motoring News was that I got to drive some fantastic cars.

BELOW One of my first tests for Motoring News was a session in Hans Stuck's Audi A4 at Donington Park the day after the FIA Touring Car World Cup in 1994.

MOTOR RA

Flux signs for *MN*

MOTORING NEWS has a new staff member. The editorial office has swallowed its pride and secured the services of a *bona fide* racing driver.

Show me a motoring journalist who doesn't fancy his chances behind the wheel, and I'll show you the next Liberal Prime Minister. To be fair, our office has had its Great Sporting Moments – an 11th place overall and class win on the Circuit of Ireland, a Formula First lap record, a Ford P100

ABOVE My championship-winning year in TVR Tuscans came in 1996. For the first half of the season I drove this yellow version, pictured leading Colin Blower and John Kent.

BELOW One of my most treasured possessions is this original Jim Bamber cartoon that he gave me after winning the 1996 TVR Tuscan Challenge.

AN 'INFLUX' OF TVR's

ABOVE *It was a privilege to share Jake Ulrich's McLaren F1 GTR in the 1996 British GT Championship and we won the GT1 class title.*

RIGHT Autosport *was very kind and came up with this special tribute cover when I won both the British GT Championship and the TVR Tuscan Challenge in the same season in 1996.*

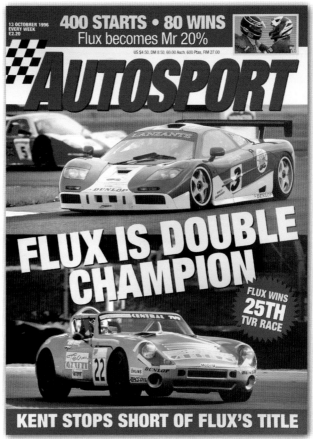

13 OCTOBRER 1996
EVERY WEEK
£2.20

US $4.50, DM 8.50, 60.00 Asch. 600 Ptas. FIM 27.00

400 STARTS • 80 WINS
Flux becomes Mr 20%

AUTOSPORT

FLUX IS DOUBLE CHAMPION

FLUX WINS
25TH
TVR RACE

KENT STOPS SHORT OF FLUX'S TITLE

1996 TVR TUSCAN CHAMPION **1996** BRITISH GT1 CHAMPION
15 RACE WINS • 8 x 2ND PLACES • 3 x 3RD PLACES
18 POLE POSITIONS • 15 FASTEST LAPS • 10 LAP RECORDS

*The above would not have been possible without
the financial support of the following:*

**JAKE ULRICH • F.A.I. AUTOMOTIVE
DAEWOO CARS • DUNLOP MOTORSPORT
CLIVE GREENHALGH • SAINTS TRANSPORT
ACE VEHICLE DELIVERIES**
To all of whom I am eternally grateful, Fluxie

ABOVE *All the pots from 1996: I took out a special advert to thank those who had helped me along the way.*

ABOVE *My first chance to drive a McLaren F1 GTR had come in the summer of 1995 when I tested the Harrods car that came close to winning Le Mans that year.*

BELOW *The 1997 TVR Tuscan Challenge started well for me, but the wheels soon came off the campaign.*

Bobby Verdon-Roe vs Ian Flux

44

There was no real malice in the Flux and Verdon-Roe battles in TVR Tuscans, but the racing was tense and extremely high quality.

Flux had a huge lead in the championship in 1997 after a strong start, but wrong tyre choices and mechanical problems at exactly the wrong time gave Verdon-Roe a whiff of the crown. He caught up with Fluxie's points haul and the title was balanced on a knife edge – the final round at Silverstone was where it would all be decided.

Flux shot off into the lead with Verdon-Roe in his wheeltracks, but Flux needed BV-R to be third or lower to win the crown.

They'd driven past a yellow flag at Copse five times during the race, and Flux hatched a plan. As the pair headed to the right-hander on lap six, Flux slammed on the anchors, put his arm in the air and slowed to walking pace. Verdon-Roe locked up, nudged into the back of his rival and narrowly avoided overtaking him. Flux continued round the corner at 30mph and accelerated away, giving himself breathing space, meaning BV-R had a snake of cars in his rear view mirrors.

Flux's plan didn't work – neither did the one when he drove across the chicane gravel in an effort to kick up the stones and cause BV-R's radiator to puncture (it did manage to break third-placed Jamie Campbell-Walter's windscreen though).

BV-R came home in second place and it was enough to hand him the crown.

HANG ON, I HAVE A CUNNING PLAN: Flux tried everything he could to foil Verdon-Roe in the final round at Silverstone in 1997. His plain failed, though

Ian Flux vs Mike Taylor

Talk about Sports 2000 and most people will recall the 1986 British Championship. Ian Flux and Mike Taylor engaged in some of the most ferocious physical contests in the history of the category. "It was war, but only on the track," recalls Flux, who clinched the title with two races to run.

There were only two drivers in the running that year – Flux in the Shrike and Taylor in the Royale. "We kept hitting each other and we had to tape all our bodywork on before the race," says Royale boss Alan Cornock.

A Snetterton race proved a turning point in the contest. "Mike couldn't afford another non-finish," says Flux. "So as the lights went green, I smashed into him and took him out on the spot."

Having watched Rupert Keegan pull a similar one on Bruno Giacomelli at Thruxton from a few behind in F3 in 1976, Flux knew it would work.

"He protested me for dangerous driving and an endorsement, but he didn't finish the race – that was crucial to winning the championship."

That moment aside, most of the battles went to the flag and in 32 races during '86 and '87, each won 15 and finished second in 12, so that year with Taylor turning the tables to win the '87 title.

"That year stands out. It was brilliant, the track we remained friends," says Flux. "People ask and loads of people remember it. God knows how much bodywork we got through."

YOU TINKER, TAYLOR: Ian Flux (right) had to resort to rather suspect tactics to defeat the tenacious Mike Taylor (left) in Sports 2000 back in 1986

ABOVE *I was the only driver to appear twice when* Motoring News *counted down its list of greatest motorsport rivalries in 1997. One was that year's TVR Tuscan duelling with Bobby Verdon-Roe, the other my Sports 2000 encounters with Mike 'Fulmar' Taylor back in 1986–87.*

ABOVE Unbeknown to me at the time, Donington Park in 1998 proved to be my last ever TVR Tuscan Challenge victory.

TVR Tuscan Challenge
MOST RACE WINS

Wins	Driver(s)
26 wins	Ian Flux
24 wins	Lee Caroline, Steve Guglielmi
19 wins	John Kent
17 wins	Mark Hales
16 wins	Jamie Campbell-Walter
15 wins	Bobby Verdon-Roe
14 wins	Colin Blower
13 wins	Martin Short
12 wins	Chris Hodgetts, Gerry Marshall
9 wins	Ian McKellar
8 wins	Andy Britnell
7 wins	Mike Jordan, David Mason, Jay Shepherd
6 wins	Michael Caine, Steve Cole, Richard Hay
4 wins	Jeff Allam, Troy Dunlop, Phil Hindley
3 wins	Phil Keen, Chris Stockton, Simon Wayne
2 wins	Bob Sands
1 win	Gavin Cooper, Tony Dron, Richard Finney, Mark Goddard, Tim Harvey, Chris Maries, Richard Stanton, Steve Sutcliffe

RIGHT One of my proudest achievements was my success record in TVRs, as immortalised by Motorsport News.

ABOVE AND LEFT As part *of a* Motoring News *track test, I managed to win a Mondeo Eurocar race that was shown on BBC* Top Gear, *by spinning presenter Tiff Needell off at the last corner.*

ABOVE To help mark 30 years of Formula Vee, I took part in two races at Brands Hatch in 1997. One was a British championship round and I had a great battle with Jeremy Clark, beating him to second place.

BELOW The Ferrari 250 GTO I raced at the maiden Goodwood Revival in 1998 was worth £1.25 million at the time. Its value now is at least £30 million.

Motoring News Motorsport HEROES

46

STUART SMITH
BriSCA F1 National Points Champion 1969-'81; World Champion 1969, '72, '80, '83, '84, '85
b 4/8/46

THE man who made a sport. Stuart Smith is a legend in BriSCA Formula One stock car racing. Winner of 13 successive National Points Championships, plus six world titles and 500 final victories in a career that began in 1965 and ended 21 years later, is a record unlikely ever to be beaten.

Such was his persona – charismatic, ruthless, seemingly unbeatable – Smith was a driver fans either loved or hated, but always respected. Undeniably, in a sport that was concentrated in the north-east, his contribution to BriSCA F1 was highly significant.

For one thing, it put bums on seats. Everyone who went to see him in action would either marvel at his driving skill or cheer someone else on to beat him. Famous battles between Smith and Dave Chisholm, Len Wolfenden and Doug Cronshaw during the Seventies and Eighties gave the sport cult status.

Through his skill and showmanship, Smith brought BriSCA F1 to a wider motorsport audience. If ever there was a man a sport owes a huge debt to it is him. *"His charges through the opposition in BriSCA F1 will always remain with me,"* **Michael Straughan, Wakefield**

"The biggest name in stock car racing – ever," **David Hill, Rushton**

ROB SPEAK
b 14/3/72
BriSCA Formula Two World Champion 1991, '92, '94, '95, '96, '97, '98, '99; National Points Champion 1989-'99

THERE can be no argument as to who is the best driver of all-time in BriSCA Formula Two stock car racing. Rob Speak is unquestionably the best there is and probably the best there ever will be. His record in a sport that has more than 600 registered drivers is as remarkable as it is emphatic.

He has won the world title eight times in the past nine seasons, and the National Points title every year since 1989. Speak is now at the stage of his career where he finds winning

40-car races from the back of the grid – sometimes with one arm resting on the side of the cab for the last few laps – less of a challenge.

It was only a question of time before he stepped up to the more powerful Formula One stock car class, and during 1999 he made his move.

He made an immediate impact. No-one uses forceful tactics in a forceful formula of racing as he does and clearly reputations matter little.

The new millennium is geared for him to establish a new order in the most spectacular motorsport in Britain. A huge talent recognised by an ever-growing band of fans.
"Anyone who denigrates oval racing cannot have witnessed Rob Speak on a charge. Breathtaking." **Rob Lees, Southport**

KEKE ROSBERG
F1 world champion 1982
b 6/12/48

ONE of the most laid back and popular characters to win the world F1 title.

Rosberg, born in Sweden of Finnish parentage, meandered into Formula One, initially with tail-end teams such as Theodore, ATS, Wolf and Fittipaldi.

He took over from Alan Jones at Williams in 1982 and, in a front-line team, was thrust into team leadership when Carlos Reutemann quit after two races.

Rosberg won the title despite only one race win, the Swiss GP at Dijon, although he did benefit from the absence of Ferrari stars Gilles Villeneuve, who was killed at Zolder, and Didier Pironi, who suffered terrible leg injuries at Hockenheim.

Earned huge respect by storming to victory at Monaco in '83 on slicks in damp conditions, but is best remembered for his 160.938mph pole lap at Silverstone in '85, despite the fact he had a slow puncture.

Rosberg moved to McLaren a year later but was outpaced by Alain Prost, retiring from F1 in '87. He returned in '91 via the World Sportscar Championship with Peugeot and then the German Touring Car Championship.
"That qualifying lap at Silverstone. Brilliant." **Nigel Routley, Derby**

45

TOP TEN
National racing drivers

1	Barry Lee (17)	6	Ian McKellar Jnr (76)
2	Gerry Marshall (19)	7	Steve Soper (79)
3	John Cleland (33)	8	Marc Hynes (103)
4	Ian Flux (38)	9	Barrie Williams (105)
5	Andy Rouse (41)	10	Rod Birley (113)

ANDY ROUSE
BTCC champion 1975, '83, '84, '85
b 2/2/47

THE most successful driver in British Touring Car Championship history with 60 outright wins to his name.

Rouse started in Formula Ford, winning the Castle Combe championship in 1970. He switched to saloons and won the Ford Escort Mexico series in '72 and, after involvement in the ill fated Broadspeed Jaguar XJ12 programme, won the BTCC in '75 in a Triumph Dolomite.

He started his business, Andy Rouse Engineering, in 1981 to build and prepare cars and then hit a purple patch behind the wheel in the mid-Eighties, winning the BTCC in '83, '84 and '85 in an Alfa GTV6, Rover Vitesse and Ford Sierra XR4 respectively.

Rouse was also instrumental in the formation of TOCA, of which he remains a director. After running the works BTCC Toyotas in the early Nineties, Rouse restored his links with Ford by running and driving its Mondeo.

Retiring from racing in 1993, he continued to run the Fords until '96. He plans to unveil a new saloon formula of his own next month.
"A touring car maestro and a great engineer." **Marcus Fuller, Kings Lynn**

40

MURRAY WALKER
The nation's favourite talker
b 10/10/23

PUT your average motorsport fan in front of a microphone and they would dry up quicker than a frog in an oven.

Murray Walker has faced more than his fair share of criticism of his dramatic commentary style over the years, yet he remains one of the most admired figures on the safer side of the pit wall.

It is often said that Murray could make drying paint sound interesting and, given the processional nature of some grands prix, he has had a lot of practice. His 'pants-on-fire'-style stems from an unquenchable passion for motorsport instilled in him from an early age – his father raced motorcycles. Partnered by the laidback James Hunt over the Eighties, Murray kept an army of dedicated F1 fans on the edge of their seats.

Hundreds of drivers have come and gone, but he has always been there. Sure, there's been some great blunders along the way, such as: "Nigel Mansell is the last person in the race, apart from the five in front of him." But that makes Murray what he is. There will come a time when his words of wisdom will cease, and F1 will be a poorer place.
"He can make the dullest race sound like an edge-of-the-seat extravaganza," **Peter Warner, Wrexham**

41

EDDIE IRVINE
F1 world championship runner-up 1999
b 10/11/65

YOU either love him or hate him. With a huge ego and a bank account to match Irvine says it like it is. If somebody was crap, well, he'll tell them. If he thought the car was crap, well…he'd say it was.

Irvine pulls no punches and is happy to embrace the life of Riley: birds, booze, fast cars, big boats, helicopters and more birds. The James Hunt of the Nineties, the Englishman was, predictably, one of Irv's heroes. During four seasons at Ferrari, however, he may be remembered more for being in Schumacher's shade.

Irvine is never shy of controversy. Who can forget the post-race hoo-haa with Ayrton Senna after his debut GP at Suzuka 1993? A series of crashes, a ban and scorn from the F1 fraternity followed, but Eddie soldiered on and through hard work has earned respect.

Irvine is a star and a welcome breath of fresh air to a rather dull Formula One paddock. We are also thankful because, for one magical season, he almost pinched the title when nobody gave him a prayer at the start.
"Anyone who gets the word 'arse' into a press release is a hero!" **K Quinnell, Sittingbourne, Kent**

39

IAN FLUX
Five national racing championships ranging from Formula Vee (1975) through to TVR Tuscans (1996)
b 11/5/56

IAN Flux is a born entertainer as well as a racing driver. Throughout a career which spans more than two decades, he has proved his speed and guile in a variety of cars, but more than that, he has the ability to relate to race fans as an real character.

He started his career as a single-seater aspirant in the early Seventies after having worked as an F1 mechanic with Graham Hill's fledgling GP team. He worked his way through the ranks to Formula Three in 1977 but chose the wrong chassis at the wrong time. He switched to Formula Atlantic and was championship runner-up three times, before a switch to sports cars.

He fought legendary duels in Sports 2000 in the late Eighties and combined that with a championship-winning performance in the Thundersports category in 1988. He also picked up a win in the Willhire 24 Hours in the process.

More recently Flux has been a leading player in the TVR Tuscan Challenge series. He took the championship in 1996 but has experienced appalling luck since. Despite that, his record of 99 wins to date is one few drivers can dream of matching.
"The last real character in national motorsport," **Steve Beeches, East Meon, Hampshire**

38

STIG BLOMQVIST
World rally champion 1984
b 29/7/46

FOR half of his career, people wondered what Stig Blomqvist might achieve if he drove something other than a Saab and for the other half, his rivals wished they had never found out.

The supreme exponent of front-wheel drive in the 1970s, Blomqvist's turn of speed in the upright, under-powered 96V4 beggared belief and earned him victories on the 1000 Lakes and the RAC as well as countless successes on the Swedish.

He gave a glimpse of his versatility by leading the Swedish in a Stratos, then branched out at Talbot, but it took the Quattro to demonstrate the full scope of his talent. A technique honed on Saabs was perfect in four-wheel drive's infancy and given a free hand, he would surely have won more than one world title.

He never prospered to quite the same degree at Ford and Nissan, but it was a measure of the esteem in which the laconic Swede was held that he remained a sought-after driver long after he ceased to be a winner at world championship level.
"The quiet personality belies a steely determination," **Tim Bulwer, Pulborough, West Sussex**

37

ABOVE Motoring News *polled its readership in 1999 to ask for their all-time motorsport heroes and I was thrilled to make the list in 38th position.*

ABOVE *Radical was the first — and only — company to actually pay me to use my image rights, which they did in this advert. It was part of a long association with the company.*

BELOW *I went globetrotting in the FIA Sportscar Championship in the early 2000s, sharing the Team Sovereign Rapier with Mike Millard, pictured here at Magny-Cours in 2002.*

ABOVE Mike Millard and I were class winners in the Team Sovereign Rapier in the last ever FIA Sportscar Championship race at Nogaro in 2003.

BELOW I took part in an Invitation GT race in Bahrain in 2004 alongside John Griffiths in this Porsche 935. It was all going swimmingly until a wheel fell off.

ABOVE One of my most emotional days behind the wheel was being reunited with Graham Hill's last Formula 1 car, the GH2, from the time I worked for him. The experience, for a 2004 article in Motor Sport, *brought tears to my eyes.*

BELOW I had a long association with Kevin Riley racing a Mosler in the British GT Championship, Spanish GT, Dutch Supercars and the Britcar series between 2006 and 2008.

IAN FLUX

47 ▼ 9

Has a career that would make a great book, although you'd have to censor most of it...

One of the great characters of national motorsport, Ian Flux has raced in almost every area of the sport.

What really made him stand out was his character: he was a true showman. He could liven up any race meeting, whether through his spectacular driving or by making the odd inflammatory comment on a circuit PA system.

But he's not just a joker: when the lights go out he is a real racer. His career began as a mechanic with Graham Hill's F1 team, but led to stints in Formula Three and touring cars. More recently he has turned to sportscars, and is fondly remembered for his TVR Tuscan title in 1996. He still races today, and he's still very quick – and a great laugh. **RL**

ABOVE Ten years after its first reader poll, I was still included in the Motorsport News *Heroes poll in 2009, and I was still inside the top 50.*

BELOW Phil Abbott (left) got me into the Radical firm and then got me back onboard from 2010 until 2014 doing promotional driving.

ABOVE In 2014 I raced my old friend Sean Walker's Osella PA3 and won outright at Donington and Brands Hatch.

BELOW Here I am on my way to a class win at the Silverstone Classic in the Mazda 323F in 2018.

LEFT *My last ever race: I finished third overall, and first in class, in the Mazda 323F at Knockhill in 2018.*

BELOW *I was delighted to have a Formula Atlantic Trophy race named in my honour at Thruxton in 2021, and my grandson George, plus my kids Coral and William, came along to show their support. That's one of my old Ehrlich cars parked behind.*

I slammed up through the gearbox, really pushing, and came to a long left-hander with a sheer drop on the outside and a rock face on the inside. Going at probably 75mph, I was halfway around this bend when, all of a sudden, a Renault 4 appeared. It was coming towards me and there was no way I was going to stop in time. I had to make a split-second decision: rock face or sheer drop? I chose to steer towards the rock and managed to stop without damaging the Toyota. But the little Renault toppled over the edge and disappeared.

I was sure the driver must have been killed. Malcolm and I got out and sprinted back to where it had gone over the edge. We peered over. The Renault was about six metres down, perched on its wheels on a ledge, and thankfully the farmer was clambering out. He looked a bit groggy but he gave us the thumbs-up. That was a massive relief.

A week after my test, the Toyota team was banned from the World Rally Championship for using an illegal mechanism that moved the turbo restrictor plates out of the way when the car picked up speed. That was why the car had felt so incredibly fast when I drove it.

One of my most glamorous tests in those early years was also in France, in 1996 when I drove a British Touring Car Championship Renault Laguna at Issoire. Those Renaults were prepared and run by Williams Grand Prix Engineering and we flew there and back in a day in the team's private aircraft. Several journalists with track experience were invited and there was a bit of competition between us about who was going to be quickest. It was only three years since I'd raced a BTCC

Peugeot 405 Mi 16 but the Laguna was night-and-day different. It was a proper built-for-purpose tin-top and was just so easy to drive.

The same year I finally got to drive my first Formula 1 car, at Donington Park. It was the Lotus 87B that Elio de Angelis raced in 1981 and by this time it was owned by my old rival Sean Walker, who had just won the FIA Historic Formula 1 Championship with it. It was in John Player Special colours and really looked the part, a proper Lotus from Colin Chapman's time. Bob Dance, the long-time Lotus mechanic who had worked with Jim Clark and Graham Hill in the sixties, was looking after it. Bob had helped me when I was in Formula 3 so it was lovely to have him in charge for the day. Another former Lotus guy, Chris Dinnage, who had been Ayrton Senna's chief mechanic, was there too.

After Sean had warmed the car up, it was my turn. Over the years I'd always wanted to put my arm up and twirl my finger to have the engine started but I'd never had the chance to do so. When I gave that signal, it was Bob who started the Cosworth DFV for me. That was a truly special moment.

I have learned over the years that you don't need to dawdle about in cars that are meant to go fast. In fact, that's the just about worst thing you can do. If you drive reasonably quickly straight away, you can warm up the tyres and brakes and get the car into its 'zone'. It helps you to prepare for doing some decent laps.

I knew the lap times around Donington like the back of my

hand and I had it in my mind that a 63s would be a good one for this car. My first lap was something like 64.5s. I thought that was respectable enough. I felt well within myself.

I got 10 laps, so the whole run lasted only about 12 minutes. It was all over too soon but it was a wonderful experience all the same. It wasn't the car's speed as such that blew me away, because I'd driven quicker machinery than a 15-year-old Grand Prix car, but it was just the entire sense of occasion about it all. The article was published in *Motor Sport* and I always enjoy looking at my copy and bringing back the memories.

In 1999 there was a two-car Formula 1 test at Donington for *Motoring News* in a Williams FW08C and a Benetton B194, as raced respectively by Keke Rosberg and Michael Schumacher, and owned by Richard Eyre and Dave Shelton. The idea was to work out the difference in flat-bottomed technology across two cars that were 11 years different in age, from 1983 (when new regulations required flat-bottomed cars) and 1994, so we tried to run the test with as much similarity in both cars as we could. I had 10 laps in each car.

My times were around 64s in the Williams and 57s in the Benetton. The biggest difference was going through the Craner Curves on cold tyres on the out-lap with each car. The first time I went through there in the Williams I was doing probably 90–100mph and could feel that there was very little grip. Doing the same thing with the Benetton, I just wanted to accelerate because I could feel good grip being generated from the floor.

My kids Wills and Coral were there that day. Coral was 11

and she has since said to me that she wishes she'd been a bit older because she didn't realise the significance of me driving those cars. As far as she was concerned, it was just dad driving more noisy cars. But when she now looks at the photos of me doing it, she realises how much that meant.

In 2004 I got into the Formula 1 car that meant the most to me. *Motor Sport* invited me to sample the Hill GH02, which I'd helped build as part of the team 30 years earlier but unfortunately it had never raced. The car was owned by a very pleasant Swiss man called Klaus Fiedler and I tested it at Dijon. It still had the GH1 rear end, the trick the guys had discovered back in 1975 at Paul Ricard in that final test.

When I first went out in the car, the throttle was sticking a little, so I pitted straight away. There's nothing scarier than a sticking throttle and it always puts me in mind of poor David Purley. In this case the cable had just got a little out of line with the pedal and it was fine after we'd adjusted it with a couple of washers. Then I did five more laps: an out-lap, three quick laps and an in-lap.

The emotion of driving the GH2 was really something. So many memories went through my head while I was behind the wheel. I thought back to building it, the all-nighters, the night of Graham Hill's plane crash, all the team members we lost, what a dreadful time that had been for all of us involved, what could have been — all of it. I had tears in my eyes while I was in the car.

At that time I still thought the Benetton B194 was the best car I'd driven but that was blown into the weeds one day at Donington in 2010. I was there working for Radical but Martin Brundle was also present doing a feature for Sky Sports F1 about a F2004 Ferrari. It was Rubens Barrichello's car but had Michael Schumacher's name on it. The car was being run by Paul Osborn through his Cars International dealership.

After Brundle had finished doing his stuff, Paul came along to the Radical garage and asked if I fancied a go in the Ferrari. I thought he was taking the mickey. I asked Radical if I could take a little bit of time off from my work for them and they virtually frog-marched me down there. They knew that I wouldn't get a chance like that every day.

When I got to Paul's garage, he told me there was one proviso. He said they wouldn't muck about altering anything. Either I fitted in Brundle's seat or I didn't. Of course, I said that wasn't an issue — and I fitted like a glove anyway.

They explained how it started up. I was all ready to go and the engine was running when Paul wandered over and told me to switch it off. He leaned into the cockpit and said, "Fluxie, I know you can't afford to fix this, so don't crash it. Off you go…"

He said I could do 10 laps. On my third lap, I beat the time I'd done in the Benetton. On my sixth lap, I got down to 55.1s, which was 0.6s off Brundle's best. As I came past the pit board, I saw the lap time and decided I would leave it there and come into the pits. I thought that if I went any quicker, Paul's words might come back to haunt me. When I arrived in the pits, Paul asked why I'd stopped early. But I knew that I was right to do so and thanked him profusely for the opportunity. It was best to walk away gracefully.

Driving the Ferrari was such an incredible experience. In most proper cars with downforce, you would approach the chicane at Donington and brake at about 100 metres. In the Ferrari, the first time I went past the 100-metre board, I hit the brakes out of instinct, but then found I was having to accelerate again to the apex. I soon got that out of my system. By the end of the run, I was braking at the 50-metre board without any panic, although the pressure on my lungs then made me cough and I couldn't start breathing properly again until halfway down the next straight. This may make you wonder about the state of my physical fitness but it's actually the only occasion I've ever been affected like that, because the Ferrari's acceleration and braking were so powerful.

Besides all the highs I had when track testing, there were some lows too. My most frustrating experience came when I did a race at Donington Park in 1998 in a Formula Palmer Audi single-seater for a story in *Motoring News*. I tested the car beforehand and was fifth quickest on the day, but when I turned up for qualifying that weekend, I was last. I couldn't work it out because the car didn't feel any different. Then in the race it went well enough and I climbed through the field to tenth place.

I only found out the explanation for my hopeless grid position about six years later when I bumped into someone with my trolley in Tesco's. I apologised and when I looked up I saw it was the guy who'd engineered me in the car that weekend. He told me that I wasn't given any turbo boost for qualifying because the championship organisers didn't want an old 40-something racer showing up the youngsters. But in the race I had turbo boost again and was able to overtake people.

There was amazing variety in the *Motoring News* assignments. I was sent to an autograss event and told I was only going to get a go by myself at lunchtime, but I ended up doing three races in three different types of car, one some kind of saloon, the others single-seat specials. It was a weird experience at first because I remember arriving at the venue off a country lane and just sort of nipping through a gap in the hedge to get in. All of a sudden there was this different world behind that hedge. It felt like I'd stumbled upon an illegal cock fight or something.

I did a National Hot Rod race at Wimbledon in Ian McKellar's Toyota Starlet in 1995, the year he won the World Final. I'd done a Eurocar race the year before and had knocked Jason Hunn out of the way to get second place and then had gone on to win. Now, at this Hot Rod race, Jason's dad Ricky was taking part. There was revenge in the air. I made it as far as the second corner before Ricky Hunn put me hard into the post-and-rail fence. That was payback. Afterwards I got together with Paul Fearnley in the usual way to put the words together for the two-page article that was planned for the following week's edition. He had to work very hard to make my 300-yard event fill the space.

In 2000 there was stock car racing too, at Brafield in Northampton, where I raced Murray Harrison's BriSCA (British Stock Car Association) F1 car, a full V8-engined 800bhp thing. There was a test day beforehand and Antonio Pizzonia, the British Formula 3 Champion at the time, was there as well. He was having awful trouble with the car and thought it was terrible, with all the stagger and camber in its suspension. He said it was undriveable — until someone pointed out to him that he'd been going the wrong way around the track. In the race the throttle stuck open and I hit the fence but it was all great fun. Later I won a BriSCA F1 race at Coventry, when *Motorsport News* put some racing celebrities in a bunch of cars.

One other treasured thing about *Motorsport News* was receiving a 'Gerry' in 2005. Named after Gerry Marshall, who'd been nominated Britain's number-one motorsport hero in a reader poll and had died earlier that year, these were awards the newspaper gave out to celebrate its 50th anniversary. It was quite an accolade and I was very proud.

I thought the world of Gerry. My first-ever drive in a TVR Tuscan Challenge race came about because he hadn't been able to take part and had recommended me. Not long before, I'd finally been invited into the Gerry Marshall and Tony Lanfranchi drinking club, which I also considered to be a massive honour. I managed to keep up with them too. In 1993 I went to James Hunt's funeral in London with them and afterwards we all went back to Shepherd Market in Mayfair and did all of Tony's pubs in one afternoon. I don't remember the end of that session.

One of my early memories of the two of them was when I was racing in Formula 3 at Mallory Park. Dad was with me and at lunchtime we saw Gerry and Tony holding court in the bar. "Look at those two, knocking back the pints," dad said. "Let's go and watch them race to see what fools they make of themselves." Gerry was in a Ford Capri and Tony was in an Opel Commodore. They had the best battle for the lead, swapping places throughout and entertaining everyone. It was amazing. Afterwards, I turned around to dad, who always disapproved of drinking and smoking, and said: "Bloody hell, I think I need to start drinking more."

From time to time I also sampled some important historic cars as a test driver in my own right, so to speak, rather than for published articles. By far my most important association was with cars owned by Harry Leventis, for whom I'd raced the Ferrari 250 GTO at the inaugural Goodwood Revival in 1998. The guy who looked after these cars was Tim Samways and he obviously rated my abilities because I did occasional test sessions for him for over ten years.

One of my favourite Leventis cars was the Aston Martin DBR1/300 that Carroll Shelby and Roy Salvadori took to victory at Le Mans in 1959. I drove that car a lot and it was super, so sorted, because Leventis had spared no expense. For example, at one point it had needed a new engine block but there weren't any in existence, so he'd had to pay a fortune to have three new ones cast and machined from scratch.

When I had my last run in the DBR1/300, at Mallory Park on a Wednesday in August 2012, the purpose was to run in a new gearbox and differential. I did about 40 steady laps, a typical run for a test at Mallory, and then came into the pits for Tim Samways and his guys to check it over. Then he told me to go out again and do five fast laps. I'd done plenty of quick laps during previous tests and 48s was my usual benchmark for a good time in that car. I did five of those and came in again.

When I got out, Tim asked me if I'd enjoyed it. I wondered why he said that because I'd driven the car so often that it seemed an odd question and he'd never asked it before. When I asked why he'd bothered to enquire, he replied that there was something he hadn't mentioned beforehand. He told me that Leventis had sold the car a couple of days earlier — and that the buyer had paid $23 million. Then he said: "If I'd told you that, Fluxie, you wouldn't have been pulling such big angles at the Esses, would you?" Actually, I probably would have been.

At another Mallory Park session with Tim, I drove Aston Martin's Formula 1 car from 1959, the front-engined DBR4. Unlike the sports car of the same year, this hadn't achieved anything because it was an outdated front-engined design in a period when Cooper cleaned up with their rear-engined car driven by Jack Brabham. The car had no seat belts and because of that I really didn't want to drive it, but Tim had been let down and was stuck for a driver, so I agreed to help out. He said I could take it gently and didn't need to go above 4,000rpm.

It was an awful experience. Gerry Marshall had raced the

car a lot in earlier times and the big seat felt like it been made to suit someone of his bulk. I just wallowed around in this seat the moment I went into a corner and it scared the shit out of me. In any racing car, I like to be belted in as tightly as possible, so I found it very unnerving not to feel the slightest bit secure in the seat.

I also had one more race in a Leventis car, again at the Goodwood Revival in the RAC Tourist Trophy Celebration race, in 2004. This was a Ferrari 330 LMB, a derivative of the GTO, and this particular specimen raced at Sebring and Le Mans in 1963. Patrick Tambay was due to share it with Peter Hardman, Leventis's favoured driver, but had to drop out at the last minute due to illness, so I got the shout. It was another gorgeous car, and we finished third.

Another memorable day of testing with an historic car came that same year when Andy Mackie, whom I'd known since Formula Atlantic days, invited me to help sort a 1978 Formula 1 Ensign owned by David Crowthorne. I had a full day at Donington in the car and it was everything I enjoyed about testing: we were trying springs, dampers, roll bars, all of it. Because I knew Andy well, we just worked through his programme, we knew what the lap times should be, and it all turned out very well. I think by the end of the day we'd improved the car's lap times by something like 2.5s.

The worst historic car I ever tested was a Lotus 30 sports car with a 4.7-litre Ford V8. This brute's reputation preceded it because the great Jim Clark, who raced a Lotus 30 on the British scene in 1964, reckoned it was the most dangerous car he ever drove. The car belonged to Richard Drewitt, a hotshot TV producer who did things like the Clive James and Michael Parkinson chat shows, and he wanted me to test it at Goodwood.

On the first lap going down the Lavant Straight, I could feel it going like a boat with the front wanting to take off and the steering having less and less effect. I came straight into the pits and told Drewitt's people that it was a bit scary — and one of them turned round and said, "That's why we've got you down here!"

What was needed was to stop air getting under the front of the car. There was a fabrication shop based near the circuit so we went there. We managed to get something fashioned up from aluminium in a couple of hours and rivetted it under the nose. It didn't cure things completely but it certainly helped settle my heart rate a little bit. Wrestling that thing and passing the marshals' post where Bruce McLaren was killed in 1970 in his Can-Am McLaren M8D, a not dissimilar sort of car, I did start to wonder whether my £500 fee was worth it.

CHAPTER 18
A RADICAL REVOLUTION

After my wonderful period with TVR Tuscans faded away, at first I didn't have any regular racing on the horizon for the first year of the new millennium, although there was plenty of testing and driver coaching to keep me reasonably busy.

But one promising possibility came along when I got involved with Mike Millard. He and his brother Chris ran a jewellery business in Birmingham and had sponsored me from time to time. I'd also raced with Chris in his Porsche 911 Turbo in a two-driver British Porsche Cup event at Oulton Park in 1988 and we'd won, although there'd been a bit of chicanery that day because he had a secret lever under the dashboard to provide a temporary increase in turbo boost. You had to slacken your belts and lean forward to operate the lever but the effect was dramatic and it must have been worth a good 50bhp. There were a lot of decent drivers in that race and I remember just squirting past Tiff Needell and James Weaver.

Mike Millard's plan for 2000 was that he and I would take part in the SportsRacing World Cup, the FIA-sanctioned series of endurance races for open-cockpit sports prototypes run mainly in Europe. However, we only joined towards the end of the year because his car, a Rapier 6 powered by a Nissan 3-litre V6 engine, was delivered late and we had all kinds of problems with it. We only did two of the ten rounds, at Donington Park and Magny-Cours, and didn't finish either of them because the engine was unreliable.

At least in 2001, when the series was taken over by the FIA and renamed the FIA Sportscar Championship, we had the car ready to go from the start of the season but it still broke a lot. Third in our 3,000cc SR2 class and tenth overall at Donington was as good as it got. The whole thing was quite an eye-opener because the Rapier was so badly put together and just wasn't strong enough. At Magny-Cours that year, I went into the flat-out first corner, a left-hander, but when I turned in the car went straight on, hurtling towards a big wall. I had time to think to myself that this accident was going to hurt but somehow the car stopped just inches from the wall. Obviously something had broken but it was a bit more than 'something': the whole of the right-hand front suspension had pulled out of the monocoque. That's how shoddy the car was.

From time to time I got one-off drives. One came in the last round of the British GT Championship of 2000, at Silverstone, co-driving Stuart Bowler's Ferrari F40. Bowler had raced the car a lot and thought he was the bee's knees, but my first flying lap was four seconds quicker than he'd ever gone in his life. The car was great for the first few laps but then started to overheat because its intercooler was too small.

I'd hoped to return to the British GT Championship for 2001 but it didn't come to anything. In 2000, TVR had run a Cerbera Speed 12 in the championship for Ian McKellar and Bobby Verdon-Roe. The car was funded through McKellar's dad, also Ian, who had a haulage business. As I said earlier, I'd done a lot of mentoring for McKellar Junior and looked after him. As the drivers hadn't done that well in 2000 and only finished sixth in the championship, I hoped that McKellar Senior might put me in the car instead of Bobby, especially as my relationship with the family was much stronger than Bobby's.

I had a local mate, Cliff Peters, who ran a big building company. I pretended, on the off chance of getting the drive, that Cliff had a bit more cash than he really did and that he was happy to part with a chunk of it on my behalf. I got Jane to type a letter to McKellar Senior saying that I had this money behind me and that it would be coming along soon after the start of the season. Obviously, Jane knew this wasn't true — and remember that she, unbeknown to me, had been carrying on with McKellar Junior. So I suspect it came out that I was bullshitting. Anyway, I didn't get the drive.

My introduction to Radical Motorsport came early in 2001 when I attended a promotional day at Mallory Park as part of the press corps through my connections with *Motorsport News*. I drove ten different Radicals that day and totally loved them — great fun and quick.

When amateur racers Mike Hyde and Phil Abbott started Radical in 1997, their idea was to build a lightweight open sports car powered by a superbike engine, initially from Kawasaki. It all took off pretty quickly, helped by savvy marketing, and they created their first one-make race series for 1999. Soon they produced a bigger model, the Prosport, which in its more powerful form had a Suzuki Hayabusa powertrain.

One Prosport racer at the Mallory day was Bob Brooks. He needed someone to share his car with him in a two-driver race coming up at Snetterton and he asked me. He said he could pay me £250 and I accepted. Early in the race Bob ran third but then spun and gave me the car in 11th place. I managed to climb back to fourth.

Mick Hyde used to race TVR Tuscans, so I knew him very well, and Phil Abbott was the engineer behind the business. When they saw how much I liked their car, they hooked me up with another amateur driver, Roger Mayers, who'd been racing with a promising youngster, Robin Liddell, but needed someone to step in when Robin got a chance to compete in the USA. Roger and I raced at Pembrey, where we finished second, and also at Oulton Park and Snetterton.

After Robin came back from the States and reclaimed his seat, Tony Hancock asked me to share his car in a race at Donington. Getting together with Tony was certainly a blast from the past because we'd been in the same class at college back in 1973 when I'd been sent there by Ashby's garage. At that time Tony was an apprentice mechanic at Rolls-Royce in Weybridge and used to drive to college in a Ferrari Dino. Later he became a very successful restaurateur and took up racing. We won our Prosport race and it was a landmark for me because it was my 100th victory from my 500th race. Sharing that experience with Tony was really special.

I also used a Prosport to coach Matthew Gilmore, a young Formula 3 driver. It was a good training car for someone doing Formula 3 because it had the right levels of downforce and speed. One day I was chatting to Phil Abbott about this aspect when suddenly a penny dropped between us. If Radical built a two-seat version, then an instructor could sit in with a pupil and achieve so much more. The ability to lap together in a proper race car rather than some GT or saloon would take coaching to another level. That was the inspiration behind Radical's next venture, the SR3, which was launched at the *Autosport* International Show in Birmingham at the beginning of 2002.

For the show, Phil wanted to produce a big promotional poster featuring a photo of me and a quote under the headline 'Get Radical with Fluxie'. He said Radical would pay me for this and of course I bit their hands off — no one had ever asked to pay me to use my name before! In fact I'd never even heard of the phrase 'image rights', something that Formula 1 drivers get paid millions for these days. Anyway, I lost no time in posting my invoice for £2,000.

Besides that, all I had to do was attend the show and unveil the brand-new SR3 with fellow racer Michael Vergers. When we pulled the covers off that car, we couldn't have imagined that Radical would go on to make 1,100 examples over the next

12 years. Huge numbers of people have got into motorsport after starting off in a Radical and racing in the various Radical Challenge series that the company has supported in Britain, Europe and North America. Of course, the car is a great product and very reasonably priced, so that success is entirely deserved. And it's so good to drive: I've loved every Radical I've ever tried.

While at the show in Birmingham, I met a guy called Alan Jackson who asked me to race with him in that year's Radical Prosport championship. For some reason, he wanted to have a contract in place with me, even though I'd never had a contract in my life. I've always been entirely happy just confirming a deal with a handshake. Anyway, I went along with this and signed his contract — and that turned out to be a good thing.

We did the first round at Donington, where we didn't perform very well, and then he went off to Florida for a holiday. While there, he broke his leg water-skiing, so that was the end of any more racing with him. But I had that contract. So, for the second time in two years, I asked Ian Titchmarsh to get on a case for me and he obtained £1,500 for loss of earnings.

Then I became involved with the factory Radical team. I went to Spa-Francorchamps in Belgium to share with Charlie Hollings, whom I'd coached in 2001 in Formula Ford when he was part of the Zip Young Guns team. The deal with Charlie's dad was that they didn't bother with insurance but shook Phil Abbott's hand to guarantee £5,000 should the worst of the worst happen. Guess what?

I had a massive shunt at the Bus Stop on the last lap. I was in the lead but under pressure from Rob Garofall. Trying to block him going into the Bus Stop for the last time, I clipped the stack of tyres at the turn-in point. I didn't realise it, but this broke a track rod. When I accelerated towards the final part of the chicane, I went straight into the barrier and partially blocked the track. Marshals tried to push the car out of the way under yellows but, me being me, and knowing that the race would have to be red-flagged, I kept my foot on the brake so they couldn't move it. Sure enough, the results were given as the positions at the end of the previous lap — so I was the winner.

But Radical gave me the sack because repairing the car cost almost double the five grand that Charlie's dad paid them on the spot after the crash. So that was that with Radical.

Meanwhile, I was continuing with Mike Millard and the Rapier in the FIA Sportscar Championship and that carried on into 2003 as well. It was always a stop-start programme but there were a couple of bright spots. I qualified on the class pole in the wet at Barcelona for the first race of 2002 but we couldn't turn that into a decent result. Then in 2003 we finished third overall at the last round at Nogaro in France and finally won the SR2 class. But that wasn't as good as it sounds because by that time the series was on its knees, with only seven starters in that race and just four finishers.

I also had another dabble with the British GT Championship in 2002 when I got a last-minute ride at Donington for the final round. Steve O'Rourke had suffered a heart attack and couldn't do the race in his EMKA Racing Porsche 996 GT3 that he shared with Tim Sugden, his long-time driving partner. Tim was going for the championship in the GTO class so there was quite a lot of pressure attached to it — in fact, as it turned out, the most pressure I've ever felt at a race meeting.

To get used to the car, I only had five laps on the Friday before the race. Then they put me in for the start of the race so that Tim could take over for the all-important final laps. It was all on the line and all eyes were looking at me — but I drove like an old woman. There were worries about Jane on my mind and I was also too concerned about damaging the car. I think I was about fifth in class when I handed over to Tim and he was pretty pissed off that I hadn't done better. Tim tried as hard as he could but his rival, Jamie Davies in a Ferrari 360 Modena, pipped us in the end to win the class and take the title. Davies finished fifth overall and we were sixth.

Even if there wasn't too much racing in prospect, I was still doing testing and driver instruction. Two good opportunities to coach young Formula Ford drivers came along in 2001, with the Van Diemen works squad run by Jonathan Lewis and with Martin Hines's Young Guns team.

The Van Diemen role carried on into 2002 and that year we took the young guys — Wesley Barber, Mike Conway, Jan Heylen and Stuart Hall — to a Formula Ford round at Mondello Park in Ireland, so that was a big trip away for them. I told Jonathan that I felt we really ought to provide a memorable night out for these lads, so he and I took them to a place called Angels in Dublin. It was a lap dancing bar and we bought each of the boys a private dance. They'd never experienced anything like that and it was certainly an eye-opener for them. I shan't forget the looks on their faces.

Not long after that Porsche race with Tim Sugden, the Van Diemen drivers had a test day at Brands Hatch ahead of the Formula Ford Festival. I made an early start and got up long before Jane. While I was having a cup of tea in the kitchen, her phone was on the side and kept flashing with messages. I'd never looked at her phone before but on this occasion I picked it up. The messages were from a guy called Colin saying how nice it had been to see her and that they really should meet up again soon. I'd had an inkling that something might be going on and that confirmed it. I had to go to Brands with that in my head and do an honest day's work.

Jane left only a few weeks later to get together with this Colin, someone she'd known from long before and caught up with again on the Friends Reunited website. I didn't know him from Adam and, in a way, that made it a little more bearable for me. The only good thing was that Colin had a bit of money and so she didn't pursue the house until the kids were grown up.

When I say that Jane 'left', I mean that she left all of us. I found myself on my own looking after Coral and Wills, then aged 14 and 11.

Jane tried her best to be nice to the kids before she went. On her last afternoon, she took them to Leighton Buzzard and bought them a dog, a Shih Tzu with the unfortunate name of Randy. God, that dog was a pain. A few weeks later, Peter Morgan, the mechanic I'd known since Ehrlich days, rang up to ask how I was. I started moaning about Randy and how we were struggling to get it house-trained. Before going out anywhere, I'd have to lay newspaper down but somehow Randy would always manage to move it and shit straight on the carpet. I was always cleaning up after this damned dog and it just added to the stress on me at that time. Anyway, Peter said his mum's dog had just died and he thought she might like to take Randy on. So that's what happened. Very wisely, Peter's mum renamed it Lucky. The kids didn't mind it going off to a new home.

Life was bloody tough at that time. Normally I'd have turned to the pub for solace, but I had children to look after, a house to run and a career to keep afloat. I had to keep it all together. But you get through it because you have to, don't you?

I like to think I took my solo parenting responsibilities very seriously. One thing I did was to stop the kids eating junk food and make sure I cooked them proper fresh meals every evening. They were amazing and have never forgotten how much I stepped in for them.

CHAPTER 19
SHOULD I WEAR A BLAZER?

By this time, I had become very involved with the Rising Stars scheme run by the British Racing Drivers' Club, but before I tell you about that, let me rewind a bit.

The BRDC's circuit, Silverstone, has always been good for me, important to my career and a track I really enjoy, and winning the club's Silver Star in 1986 was an honour that I really treasure. So, when Tony Lanfranchi said to me in 1988 that I should go for a place on the board of the BRDC, I was quite taken by that surprising suggestion. He said, "We could do with someone young and on our side."

So I put my name forward and Sean Walker seconded me. In those days, when an election took place at a BRDC Annual General Meeting, only those members present could vote, whereas that changed soon afterwards so that the entire membership was polled. Tony and Sean were there on the day and I turned up with some other supporters like Colin Pool, Ian Walker and Chris Marshall. I thought it would be a doddle because there was no one serious amongst the other people going for it. I duly got voted on — but the other directors seemed not to like the idea of me on the board and somewhere along the way my appointment didn't get approved.

I was annoyed at the time but the experience served me well when the next opportunity came along three years later. Gerald Lascelles was retiring from his position as President and that meant a vacancy on the board. Jack Sears took over the Presidency and phoned me to say that the directors, at the suggestion of Tom Walkinshaw, who was now Chairman, were going to vote me on as a temporary member of the board. Then, when it came around to the next AGM about four months later, the membership would have their vote. If the membership didn't vote for me, that would be the end of it.

At my first board meeting, which was in the BRDC's old bungalow near the entrance to the circuit, most of the discussion was about an old honeysuckle hedge near the bungalow and what to do with it. I wondered what I'd let myself in for. The nicest thing about it was that we had a luxury five-course meal afterwards, something that happened at every board meeting.

Talk about extremes: at the second meeting, Tom Walkinshaw stood up and told us all that the BRDC really needed to diversify to expand its horizons. He said that the club needed to branch out from its focus on motor racing and add some other business interests. He said that buying into a car dealership business would be a good idea.

It was the first time that the idea had been floated. I wasn't party to subsequent meetings about this but what transpired was that Walkinshaw's plan was more for his personal benefit than the BRDC's. Walkinshaw was proposing that the club should invest £5.7 million into his own network of car dealerships.

There were two sets of due diligence done on the deal: one was honest, the other wasn't. The board of directors, me included, got the dishonest version. When we read it all through, though, it seemed to make sense. The directors would make the decision at the next board meeting.

I arrived early for the meeting, so I called into Roy Kennedy Racing's HQ, which was also near the entrance to the track. Roy said, "Oh, Fluxie, I know what the BRDC is discussing today." I wondered what he knew because this was meant to be totally secret. He told me that we were buying Tom Walkinshaw's garage group.

It turned out that the bloke who was supposed to deliver the due-diligence reports to the BRDC the previous afternoon had arrived too late, and so the first place he'd stopped was Roy Kennedy's workshop and he dropped them off there. Roy had obviously signed for them and opened one up himself to have a look. Nothing stays secret in motor racing for very long!

Anyway, one way or another, word did get out before the meeting. When it began, I remember Walkinshaw standing up and saying, "This board is like a bloody sieve."

Amongst those on the board were Derek Bell, John Watson, Richard Attwood, Barrie Williams, Paddy Hopkirk and David Piper. The one who gave Walkinshaw the hardest time about the whole deal was Piper. He was dead against it and Walkinshaw was trying to swat him down at any opportunity.

But the board, guided by the not-quite-so-true due-diligence report, voted for Walkinshaw's plan and invested £5.7 million of the BRDC's cash in a 50 per cent stake in his car dealership business.

The situation unravelled pretty quickly after that. The membership didn't like the deal and an Extraordinary General Meeting was called soon afterwards. The entire board got voted out. I think this probably means that I became the shortest-serving BRDC board member of all time as well as one of the youngest.

It ended up going legal. The BRDC sued the directors because the membership wanted their money back from the Walkinshaw deal. We all had to attend the High Court on three occasions. When I'd signed up to be a director, I was just hoping for a few extra Grand Prix tickets — I certainly didn't want to be liable for one-twelfth of 5.7 million quid.

Eventually it was proved that the accountants had committed fraud with the two separate reports on the situation. We directors were all exonerated because what we had voted on, even though we thought it was correct, turned out to be a lie. It was a narrow squeak for me personally: I thought I was going to lose my house. The experience taught me that I never again wanted to be a director of anything.

The way the BRDC operated back then was so old-fashioned. When I had my brief spell on the board, the new Luffield complex had just been built and I remember saying to Jack Sears that there was huge potential for hosting pop concerts. He looked at me like I was from another planet.

As the Tom Walkinshaw episode showed, there was plenty of money washing about the BRDC, but using any of it to support up-and-coming young drivers was still very much in the future. Although the annual *Autosport* BRDC Award for the most promising young driver already existed, a big step up came in 2000 when the BRDC's Rising Stars scheme began at the suggestion of Dave Brodie and Howden Ganley.

The following year I had a flash of inspiration. I felt that there could be better scrutiny of how the funding was being dished out, so I suggested a way that I could make a useful contribution. I knew a lot about the sorts of cars that were being raced by the supported young drivers — things like Formula 3, GTs and touring cars — so I proposed that I attend some test days and closely observe what was going on. I could see whether the teams knew what they were doing, what the engineers were like, and how the drivers themselves performed not just on the track but with their teams as well. I could make an all-round assessment of a team and a driver and give honest feedback to the BRDC board.

By this time Jackie Stewart was at the helm of the BRDC. I phoned him to explain my idea and offered my services for £300 a day. He agreed.

The Rising Stars scheme was all a bit arbitrary in those days. Someone would put a driver's name forward for support and the driver had to prove to the BRDC that he had two thirds of the necessary budget. If the BRDC decided to assist, it would put a maximum of the last third into the pot. The idea was that a driver who went on to bigger things would return the money, as David Coulthard did, but not everyone honoured that commitment. There was one guy, who should probably remain nameless, who received more money than the BRDC had ever previously handed over — £250,000 for a Formula 3 programme — and carried on in the category the following season with entirely independent funding but never gave a penny back.

When I observed things that left me unimpressed, I didn't pull any punches when reporting back to the board. Soon after starting my role, I went to a test at Oulton Park to assess Aaron Scott, who'd won the BRDC Formula Ford Championship in 1999 and then in 2001 was given some BRDC money for a season of Class B Formula 3 with Rowan Racing. In my view, Aaron wasn't performing very well when I watched him at Oulton Park and I knew I had to sort things out quickly to judge whether it was the car or the driver.

Martin O'Connell, who'd had a lot of Formula 3 success with Rowan Racing, happened to be there, so I asked Ray Rowan, the team owner, if he would put O'Connell in Scott's Dallara for a few laps. On his first lap, O'Connell was nine tenths quicker than Scott had managed all day. I wrote that in my report and told the board we were wasting the BRDC's money with Aaron. That caused some awkward moments, particularly as Aaron's dad, Dave, was very involved in the sport as an official and is now a renowned clerk of the course. He hated me for years as a result but I was just being an honest surveyor of it all. To be fair to Aaron, he went on to race competitively for many years, mainly in GTs, and nowadays has his own team.

At the end of that first year, I did an overall report giving my assessments of all the drivers who had received BRDC money and I sent this to the board. In my opinion there was only one who would ever make it. This was Andy Priaulx — and, yes, he went on to become a three-time world champion in touring cars.

I did actually have something to do with Andy getting into BMW, where he achieved all his touring car success. BMW UK motorsport boss Peter Walker phoned during 2002 to say that BMW was looking for a British driver for the European Touring Car Championship for the following season. He politely said that he couldn't offer me the drive because I was too old but he wanted advice about who to approach. Two people immediately came to mind: one was Ian McKellar, my former TVR Tuscan Challenge rival who'd messed around with my wife Jane although I didn't know that at this time, and the other was Andy Priaulx. I'd worked with BMW on track days so I knew the kind of thing they were after. I told Peter that the downside with McKellar was that he struggled with public speaking whereas Priaulx could do that perfectly as well as being very talented behind the wheel.

Peter asked me to make contact with Andy so I phoned him. It turned out he was in Australia at the time doing a couple of V8 Supercar races so I inadvertently woke him in the middle of the night. I apologised but told him I had a very serious reason for waking him because I had a manufacturer-backed drive for him for 2003. I didn't tell him who it was and said I wanted confirmation that I would get 10 per cent of his wages for the year in cash if it went ahead. If only I'd managed to make that arrangement for the whole of his BMW career!

Before long Andy faxed me to agree to my terms, so I gave him all the details of the deal with BMW and put him in touch with Peter Walker. They reached an agreement pretty quickly.

I was on my knees financially at the time. Andy was going to be getting £60,000, so my share was £6,000. I went to see Andy and his manager, Speedsport boss Mike O'Brien, at the team's Silverstone HQ. Mike wanted to write me a cheque but Andy of course knew that we'd agreed payment in cash and said we'd better pop into nearby Towcester to sort it out. While he headed off to a bank to get the money, I had a pint in the Saracen's Head Hotel over the road. That must be the most profitable trip to the pub I've ever had.

At the end of 2002, I was on the panel that interviewed the next batch of young drivers being considered for the BRDC scheme for the 2003 season. That year's intake included Lewis Hamilton, who'd just completed a season of the Formula Renault UK Championship with Manor Motorsport. He'd won a few races and finished third in the standings. Now he was going to do a second Formula Renault season with Manor and this time he intended to become champion.

I'd already had my own first-hand experience of Lewis's incredible talent, back in January 1996 at the *Autosport* International Show in Birmingham, just after his 11th birthday. He was such a prodigy in karting that he'd been invited to take part in a charity kart race at the show, racing against some seasoned old pros, me included. He beat all of us. I wished him the best of luck for his karting season ahead and kept him on my radar.

Lewis's BRDC interview at the end of 2002 was with Dave Brodie and me. He turned up with his dad — he was still only 17 and I'm not sure he'd passed his driving test — and he was wearing what looked like a hand-knitted white polo-neck jumper. We interviewed him on his own and he seemed so comfortable with the situation that I felt sure he'd benefitted from some interview training as part of McLaren's driver-development programme. He said all the right things.

When Dave and I chatted after the interview, only one thing bothered us. In nominating Lewis for the Rising Stars, we were putting forward the first black driver ever to be associated with the BRDC and we wondered how some of the older members might react. It was still a real old boys' club in many ways and we thought there might be a few shockwaves. Looking back, I realise it's disappointing that the topic even entered our minds, but I think it indicates what a different world we lived in even then, just 20 years ago.

Ever since, I've remained involved in the Rising Stars programme and it continues to be a very satisfying aspect of my life in racing. I've watched some of the young drivers I've instructed go on to proper success and that gives me enormous pride. I may have only worked with them for a couple of seasons, but I always hope that there were a few things I said that stuck with them and helped take them onwards.

CHAPTER 20
RACING PAST MY HALF CENTURY

The Ferrari Challenge played a big part in my life for the next few years and brought a string of very good coaching opportunities. It started in 2003 when Malcolm Swetman, whom I'd known for ages and was in charge of the Ferrari Challenge at that time, recommended me to Nick Hommerson, one of the drivers in the series. After I'd given Hommerson some tuition in his Ferrari 360 Modena at Donington, he promptly went on to win a race there, even though he'd done the series for three years and never won a thing.

That led to other Ferrari-owning amateurs wanting me to help them. Jason Hughes, who'd been chief mechanic on the Ferrari F40 that I'd raced once in 2000, set up his own team to run Phil Burton and Terry Coleman in the Ferrari Challenge in their 360 Modenas in 2004. They needed some guidance so Jason hired me to be Phil's coach and Eugene O'Brien to be Terry's. Jason offered £500 per day and that certainly helped keep the wolf from the door because we did quite a lot of days.

We went to Guadix in Spain for three days of pre-season running. On the first day it was all nice and gentle as Phil and Terry got to learn the circuit, with their coaches alongside them. But Phil was quicker and kept overtaking Terry. That evening, Terry, who was a very competitive character, told me he was getting fed up with this and wanted to know what I thought about it. I said I felt that he needed more time because Phil was more experienced. But Terry was convinced it was Eugene's fault.

Next day when we stopped for a mid-morning break, Phil and I had already lapped Terry and Eugene two or three times. Terry called me over and asked if I would do him a favour and sit with him for a few laps. I said I didn't want to do that without Eugene's agreement and he would have to consult him. Well, Eugene didn't mind.

I got in with Terry. Straight away he started talking himself around the lap. It was a non-stop commentary. I told him bluntly that he should stop prattling and listen to what I had to say about his driving. He was taken aback but it clicked. He started to improve and we hit it off.

The pressure really came on the third day, when Terry told me he'd arranged with the team for me to drive Eugene around and show him how it should be done. Well, that put both Eugene and me in a difficult position. It isn't easy in any case going round with a fellow racer next to you but this situation was just plain embarrassing. I tried to look as relaxed as possible, even though I was really tense, and made sure I hit every turn-in point and apex perfectly. Back in the pits,

Eugene sheepishly said "thanks for that" and got out of the car. After that, I became Terry's coach and Eugene was fired.

I coached both Phil and Terry throughout 2004 and then raced with them in turn for the next two years, always in Ferraris. In 2005, I was Phil's co-driver in British GT but that only lasted three rounds. After the Knockhill race, Phil phoned to say my services were no longer required because he now had a hungry youngster, Adam Wilcox, to partner him for free. Meanwhile, I continued to coach Terry, who was focused on Ferrari Challenge events around Europe.

Into 2006, Ferrari introduced the F430 as the 360 Modena's successor, so this model became eligible for the Ferrari Challenge. The European series was now being run by Loris Kessel and before the start of the season he organised a two-day test session at Mugello in Italy for people with their new cars. Besides being a super track, Mugello wasn't far from the Ferrari factory and the thinking was that plenty of expertise could be on hand to deal with teething problems.

That was a fantastic trip and at one point I remember wondering if life could possibly get any better. There I was on the roof of the pits, in warm sunshine after a nice lunch, taking a break from driving a Ferrari at a brilliant circuit and getting paid £600 a day for it. On top of that, Terry, who'd made his fortune from Scorpion car alarms, had flown us out there in his Learjet, just the two of us, and booked us into the super-swish Four Seasons Hotel in Florence. It was bliss. And a season of racing around Europe with Terry lay ahead.

There was one non-Ferrari outing in this period that didn't

go so well. John Griffiths, a journalist on the *Financial Times*, had a Porsche 935 and invited me to drive it with him at the Bahrain GT Festival in November 2004, six months after the first Bahrain Grand Prix. The car wasn't prepared too well and we had a lot of problems in practice, including the brake pedal going to the floor, which wasn't very helpful at a circuit with a first-gear hairpin at the end of the longest straight. Then in one of the races, at that very hairpin, I was hard on the brakes when I noticed a wheel rolling past me. At first I thought it belonged to someone else, but then I turned into the corner and the car fell on its side. The spokes had sheared through metal fatigue, so the rim and tyre had parted company. That rather summed up the trip.

A super opportunity presented itself for 2006. Another Ferrari Challenge driver, Kevin Riley, phoned at the end of 2005 and said he wanted to change direction and do the British GT Championship with me as his co-driver, even though I barely knew him. He planned to race a Mosler MT900, the American-made Chevy-powered muscle car, and asked who I thought should run it. I felt there was only one choice, Martin Short, my old TVR Tuscan rival who ran Rollcentre Racing and was now Mosler's importer. Shortie's connections with Mosler had begun in style when he campaigned one in British GT in 2003 with Tom Herridge and Tom became champion. I told Kevin that Martin would give him the best treatment and wouldn't rip him off budget-wise. He replied with those wonderful words: "We don't need to worry about budget."

Even though we only did five of the nine rounds because I had clashing Ferrari commitments with Terry Coleman, we finished third in the GT2 championship and *Autosport* rated me as the third best driver in the championship when it published its rankings at the end of the season. It was a great year. The Mosler was very reliable and a pleasure to drive, and Shortie ran a great team.

For 2007, Kevin wanted me full-time so I quit coaching and driving in Ferraris. We branched out into Europe in 2007 and did the first four rounds of the Spanish GT Championship as well as the last two rounds of the Dutch Supercar Challenge. In between, we did more British GT, now with a less powerful Chevy engine in the GT3 category, and a few Britcar GT events. It was all quite busy but our results weren't as good.

The first of those Spanish GT races was at Jarama. Before I went, my old friend Andy Mackie phoned and told me I'd love Jarama because there was a brothel called the Hotel Lovely only 500 metres from the paddock. I actually went there between practice and qualifying — just because I could.

Going into 2008, Kevin decided to run the Mosler with his own people, not Martin Short, and chose to focus on Dutch Supercar. There was a special category for Moslers and we did the whole series, racing at places like the Nürburgring and Hockenheim in Germany and Zandvoort and Assen in the Netherlands. We won at Assen but that was as good as it got. We also took in some more Britcar races, where it was easier to do well, and Kevin did like a trophy.

There were frustrations in racing with Kevin. One example

occurred at the Dutch Supercar round at Hockenheim. There was the normal pair of races, one on the Saturday and the other on the Sunday, and as usual we each started one of them. When it came to Sunday's race, which Kevin was due to start, his guys were warming up the car and he was still hanging around in his normal clothes. I told him he should get a move on as the race wasn't far away. When the lads drove the car to the assembly area, there was no sign of Kevin, presumably because he was at last getting changed into his race gear. When all the cars were pushed onto the grid, there was still no Kevin. When the rest of the field went off on their warm-up lap, he still hadn't shown up, so our Mosler had to be rolled back into the pitlane. Then, at last, Kevin appeared, as cool as a cucumber and in no hurry at all. He had to start the race from the pitlane and we'd gone from the front row of the grid to last place.

He paid me well enough, £500 a day, but sometimes I thought I was getting the money not just to drive the car but to listen to him talk. He used to tell me the same old racing stories week after week, most of all about his 1983 and '84 seasons sharing the amazing Chevy-powered BMW M1 that Mick Hill built around a Formula 5000 chassis for Thundersports. I used to wonder what it was like for his lovely wife Pauline listening to him go on and on every day.

Phil Abbott of Radical Motorsport called at the end of 2009, seven years after my sacking in the wake of the crash at Spa. His son James was about to turn 16 and wanted to race the following year, so Phil asked if I would coach him. We did that in a two-seat Radical SR3, of course, and went to pretty much every track in the country over the winter to get James up to speed, running at least once a week.

This got me back into the Radical family and I ended up competing in 2010 with Craig Currie, a motorcycle racer who'd won a competition that gave him five free Radical Challenge races in an SR3. At one of those races, at Castle Combe, I took a Japanese journalist round for a few laps with a camera mounted on the front of the car and showed him what it could do. He was absolutely blown away. Afterwards, he put a few minutes of footage up on YouTube called 'Ian Flux driving the Radical SR3 at Castle Combe' and added some tongue-in-cheek subtitles. Take a look: it's quite amusing — and the car looks impressively quick.

At Silverstone at the end of the year I raced the SR8, a model with Radical's own design of V8 engine, a 2.7-litre unit based on the Suzuki Hayabusa four-cylinder design. This was my first event in a V8 version and it was a Shell-backed car run by Slim Borgudd, my old Formula 3 rival and briefly a Formula 1 driver with Tyrrell. The entry was the biggest line-up of Radicals ever, with 52 cars, and I partnered Christian Droop, Radical's major shareholder. When Christian went out to qualify, something broke in the engine before I had a chance to set a time, so I had to start my race from the back of the grid. I eventually made it to eighth place.

Meanwhile, a guy called David Jacobs had arrived on the Radical scene and bought two cars for track days. One of them was an SR8 and he decided he wanted to go racing with it. He went mad spending money and he was also utterly mad as soon as he put on a crash helmet. He did that big Silverstone race in the car with Calum Lockie.

I'd become friendly with David and wanted to help when I saw things going the wrong way for him. Lockie had been advising him how to set up his car but frankly Calum didn't have much experience of Radicals and I felt he was leading David up the garden path. I had a word with the mechanics and got them to adjust the car to how it should have been. David liked the way it felt after that and asked me to race with him in 2011.

We did some testing over the winter and our first race together was at the Ascari track in Spain, where Radical had arranged an off-season event. Martin Brundle was in that race sharing a car with his son Alex, and they won. From that very first race with David it became pretty clear to me that in terms of temperament he was one of the worst drivers I've ever encountered. He'd get a red mist when he was on the track and just go crazy.

He was always in hot water and I got dragged in. In the six or seven races we did together, I had to go and see the clerk of the course every time because of something David had done and apologise for it.

At Spa he had an enormous shunt when he attempted a high-speed pass on the inside going into Eau Rouge and ended up in hospital. We missed a race while he recovered and came back at Brands Hatch. He was in the lead when someone went off at the bottom of Paddock Hill Bend and there were waved yellow flags all the way round the track. He didn't seem to notice the flags and when he got to the scene of the crash second time around it was as if he didn't even know the shunt had happened. He went off and hit the JCB that was dragging the damaged car out of the gravel. That got him banned — and left me out of a drive.

My renewed relationship with Radical lasted for five more years. I would jump into anyone's car and test and race whenever I got the chance. If one of the regular professionals couldn't make a meeting, I would step in. If someone was doing their first race, I would get put in alongside them to show them the ropes and to talk them through what they needed to be doing. There was no regular racing and I wasn't chasing a championship. I was just doing bit-part work but I liked it.

One of my pupils was Chris Hoy, the professional cyclist. After he decided to hang up his bicycle following the 2012 Olympics in London, he wanted to try his hand at motor racing, starting with a season in a Radical SR1 in 2013. To help him prepare, I spent a day sitting in with him at Cadwell Park after a very pleasant evening beforehand. When I took the wheel, this super-fit guy with six Olympic gold medals was amazed how quickly a 57-year-old who'd consumed too many pints and smoked too many fags the previous evening could make that Radical go round Cadwell.

Another time at Snetterton I gave some instruction to John Reynolds, the motorcycle racer who won the British Superbike Championship three times. He couldn't get his head round how quick and stable the Radical was through corners. Going into the fast right-hander after the pits, he wanted to change down about three gears. Mind you, I'd been no better when I tried one of Dr Ehrlich's 250cc grand prix bikes 30 years earlier.

A well-known novice I coached in a Radical was John Caudwell, the billionaire mobile phone mogul whose massive house in Mayfair featured on the TV programme *Britain's Most Expensive Home*. He came along for a day at Oulton Park and we had quite an amusing time. Afterwards, he also put up a video on YouTube, called 'Radical SR1 with instructor Ian Flux'. It was a totally new experience for him and in the video he described himself as "completely unskilled and inadequate".

I thought a session at Goodwood with Rowan Atkinson in a Radical would also be amusing — but it wasn't. I expected an afternoon of cracking jokes but soon realised that wasn't going to happen. He was very serious about his driving — and very careful.

Aside from the coaching, my main role with Radical was to do promotional days. There would be two or three professional drivers on hand and maybe nine or ten potential customers. If I sold a car on one of these days, I'd get £1,200 commission.

One of my biggest regrets in that period concerned Max Smith-Hilliard. He came up to Donington one day as a punter and after my sales patter he bought a Radical there and then. And he bought another one soon afterwards. When he got the taste for racing, he decided he'd like to buy an historic

Formula 1 car, and then another, and another. We became good friends and Max often says, "You've cost me a fortune." If he hadn't bought that first Radical, he reckons his life would have been very different.

My regret? Well, I felt that racing Radicals with him should have been my gig, but Max chose to team up with Nick Padmore. When he got into the Formula 1 cars, Nick drove them for him in the FIA Masters Historic Championship and won three titles in various cars, including a Williams FW07C. For me, that felt like a major missed opportunity.

CHAPTER 21
SOME ENDINGS, SOME BEGINNINGS

Other than my second time around with Radical, the only racing I've done in recent years has been in a few historic cars. Sure, the possibility of competing with old Formula 1 cars owned by Max Smith-Hilliard was a might-have-been, but I still drove some decent machinery from time to time.

In 2011 I raced with my old friend Sean Walker in his Lotus Elan 26R in the Guards Trophy GT and Sports Racing Championship. The highlight was going to Porto in Portugal to do the 90-minute street race there. Sean and I had never been to this track so we walked it and made a few notes about where we should be braking and turning in, all that kind of stuff. Then I stuck our little Lotus on overall pole position ahead of all sorts of much more powerful machinery, including E-type Jaguars. To cap it all, we won. The car ran perfectly all weekend and the only thing we had to do to it was fill it with fuel, bleed the brakes and polish it. We'd been paid €800 to go and do the race, and our air fares and hotel were covered, and on top of that there was generous prize money too and I came home with £1,800. It was the kind of racing weekend you dream about.

We had another season planned for 2012 but at the second race, at Brands Hatch, a Mustang went into the side of the Elan while Sean was steaming up the hill to Druids. The car had to be reshelled and he didn't get it back out until the Goodwood Revival in September and that was a race he did on his own anyway.

A good mate from Thundersports days was Colin Pool. Going into 2013, Sean, Colin and I went out for lunch, got a bit drunk, and worked out a deal that was going to be settled by the toss of a coin. Colin had a big box of bits for a late-1970s Osella PA3 sports car and Sean had a spare Formula 2 engine of the same period. Whoever lost the toss would have to put the Osella together and, depending which of them it was, buy the box of bits or the engine. Sean lost so the box of bits became his — and he completed the car by the end of the year. Into 2014, I had some good times driving that Osella.

I put the car on pole for the Martini Trophy at the Donington Historic Festival. I led the first of the weekend's two races until the rear bodywork started rubbing on a tyre when one of the mountings broke, but next day there were no such concerns and I won and took fastest lap. A couple of months later at Brands Hatch, I had one of those days of days when I won two races in different cars, not only in the Osella but also Mike Smith's Formula Atlantic March 79B. That was a very satisfying weekend.

The last race at which I got an overall podium was at Brands Hatch in July 2016 when I finished third in another of Sean's cars, his ex-Nigel Mansell Formula 3 March 783. A year earlier Sean had sold the Osella in a Silverstone auction for £142,000 then ten minutes later paid £56,000 for this March, the one that Mansell famously mortgaged his house for when he was on his uppers. After my near miss in getting the Unipart Formula 3 drive instead of Mansell all those years earlier, the irony of that outcome in that particular car wasn't lost on me. I'd just turned 60 and yet I could still get a podium in an ex-Mansell Formula 3 car!

I also had a chance to try an old touring car when I raced a Mazda 323F. It had been built up in 1994 for Slim Borgudd to run in the British Touring Car Championship but the money had fallen through and it had never actually raced. Allan Scott now owned the car and offered me several races in it. I won the class at the Silverstone Classic in 2017 and 2018, then a couple of weeks after that second Silverstone event I took another class win at Knockhill. I didn't know it at the time, but that race in Scotland, the David Leslie Trophy, was my last win.

M oney-wise, it began to get tricky after 2014. When my racing started to wind down in 2010, I'd gone back to working at Silverstone Racing School alongside everything I was doing with Radical, but by 2014 there were some dodgy goings-on at the Silverstone set-up and I suddenly found my income nosediving.

Sean Walker, who'd become such a good friend over the

years, took me on for two days a week in his FAI Auto Parts factory in Leighton Buzzard. I did parts picking, van driving — anything they wanted really. It made me appreciate just how lucky I'd been in my life because so many people do that kind of work five or six days a week, year in, year out, yet I only had to turn to it part-time during a period of difficulty.

I had quite a setback on 21st October 2020. That morning I'd driven Donny Kilcommons, the landlord of my local pub, The Dove, to Luton Airport as a favour. Back home, I was rushing around the place before going out to renew my driving licence. As I came downstairs — sober I might add — I missed the last two steps and snapped a tendon in my knee. Paramedics came round and off I went to hospital and stayed there for five days. Despite all my racing exploits, it was the longest I'd ever spent in hospital. It also meant I couldn't work — and I had less than £500 to my name at that point.

While I was stuck in hospital, my daughter Coral told me that Martin Short, my old TVR Tuscan rival, had set up a crowdfunding webpage to raise some money for me. I was truly grateful and will be forever in his debt. I couldn't believe everyone's generosity and even people I knew weren't on the best of wages were chipping in. One guy I'd coached chucked in £500. After a few days, the total was nearly £10,000.

About a year before I hurt myself, Shortie had kindly brought me back some duty-free fags from Spain and suggested I popped over to Silverstone to collect them. He was going to be testing a Mosler that day and said I should bring my race suit and helmet and have a go for old time's sake. So I did five laps. The car was totally familiar because I must have done thousands of laps in Kevin Riley's Mosler between 2006 and 2010. It all went fine, no problem... until a couple of minutes after I climbed out.

My heart was beating hard. I was breathing heavily. I was sweating. It dawned on me that suddenly, at the age of 63, I was past my sell-by date. I told Shortie and his guys that they were going to be the first to know — I was now officially a retired professional racing driver. In all honesty, I realised I could no longer ask people to pay me to race their cars if I couldn't give 100 per cent. Time to move over and make way for younger folk.

Another thing about Shortie. He'd rebuilt a Tuscan race car with the aim of getting it ready for the 30th anniversary of the TVR Tuscan Challenge. He took it along to a BRDC track day at Silverstone in March 2020 and gave me — now the retired racing driver — the chance to slip back into the cockpit. I didn't go crazy because it was his pride and joy, but immediately all the amazing memories came flooding back. There has never been another race series like it, before or since. Driving that car was like putting on a favourite pair of old shoes — and the shoes I wore to drive it certainly weren't the ones I'd been forced to wear when I made my Tuscan debut in Birmingham back in 1990!

That brief period of despair with my tendon injury was soon followed by a lovely development in my life. It all began when Andy Mackie, with whom I'd worked many a time, got in touch from his new home in Australia to say that a friend of his, David Button, was returning to racing after a 30-year lay-off and would welcome a bit of tuition at 'mates' rates'. We arranged this for Silverstone on 28th April 2021 in his Porsche Cayman GT4 and he agreed to my £250 fee.

With just a few days to go, David phoned to say that he couldn't make it but asked if I'd mind coaching Lucy Rogers instead. He wondered if I remembered her. I certainly did. He said he'd like her to take his place and he would pay.

Lucy and her older brother Pete had raced in Formula Ford in the eighties and that's how David knew her. During that time, Lucy took her one and only Formula Ford victory at Brands Hatch, on 18th May 1986, and oddly enough I was there that day, racing Mike Smith's Thundersaloons Chevette, although I didn't know her at the time. Very sadly, her brother Pete was killed the following year in a race at Donington and after that she stopped racing because her parents were so worried about it.

But Lucy did carry on doing some driver instruction and I first met her at one of Ian Taylor's BMW days in 1989. I thought she was lovely but by then I was married and she was about to get married too. We used to say good morning to each other at the briefings, polite as you like, but nothing more.

So, returning to 2021, Lucy just fancied driving a race car again. We got on well that afternoon, occasionally reminiscing while she did her laps in the Porsche, with some nerves after not driving around a track for so long and also because I was sitting next to her. I chose a moment to ask a leading question and she replied that she was in a "sort-of relationship".

I was hopeful. I messaged her a few times afterwards and eventually she succumbed and allowed me to take her out to lunch. We met for lunch a few more times and then began to see each more regularly.

I've never been so happy. It's lovely when I take Lucy to events now — and so many people still remember her.

My best walk down memory lane with Lucy was at the Goodwood Revival in 2021. That year was the 30th anniversary of the Jaguar XJR-15 race series and Valentine Lindsay, who owns one of the cars, organised a special celebration complete with demonstration runs. Two years before he'd already put together the biggest line up of XJR-15s ever assembled, 28 of them at a track day at Goodwood, and I'd helped out with that along with a few other people like John Watson and Tiff Needell. Like me, they'd raced an XJR-15 back in the day.

On the Friday evening at the Revival, we were invited to the ball in Goodwood House. There were about 300 guests there and it was incredible. The champagne just kept on flowing and I took full advantage. We went up the red carpet, had our picture taken, then went into the lobby to wait for dinner. After a while, security guards started pushing the assembled guests to one side, leaving us wondering who was about to arrive. A top VIP? All of a sudden, 20 historic grand prix motorcycles roared through the lobby along the red carpet. It was an incredible shock — and a terrific spectacle. A Giacomo Agostini MV Agusta, a Barry Sheene Suzuki, a Kenny Roberts

Yamaha — they kept on coming.

I was due to drive the XJR-15 that I'd raced back in 1991 but its owner had been called away on business and didn't want his car involved without him being present. So Val put me in his own car, which had been raced by American driver Andy Evans in the original championship. The car only arrived at the track on the Friday evening, while we were at the ball, because it hadn't been finished in time following £80,000 worth of repairs after a crash at the Festival of Speed a couple of months earlier. Because the car hadn't run and the track was damp, Val got a bit nervous and in the assembly area, just before I was about to go out, he came over, put his arm round me, and said he'd rather not run it without a shakedown.

But I did get to drive it for the demo on the Sunday. Everything about it — the power, the gearchange, the brakes, the sound — came flooding back during those five laps. Armin Hahne, whom I hadn't seen for 30 years, led the parade because he'd been the champion, then it was David Brabham and me. I ran right with David and we had a hoot. In fact all 12 of us put in a good effort for the crowd.

More memories came flooding back in March 2022. I'm quite active on social media and on Facebook there's a McLaren F1 GTR group that I belong to. After all, I did win a championship in one of those cars! Anyway, a guy called Greg Hurst messaged me and told me that his friend Chris Vassilopoulos's family now owned this car and wondered if I'd be interested to meet Chris and see it again. You may remember that Paul Lanzante had converted it into a road car for Jake Ulrich but now Dean Lanzante, Paul's son, had put it back to racing spec.

Greg and I went down to meet Chris at the incredible premises in Petersfield, West Sussex, where Dean Lanzante runs his business. What a place. It's like a quarter-scale version of the high-tech McLaren factory in Woking and inside it's full of stunning cars, including lots of McLarens. We sat down with Chris, a really nice guy in his 30s, and chatted about his F1 GTR. He had two dossiers about its entire history, all the way through from Ray Bellm's original ownership: the race record, restoration work, everything. It was very interesting, especially when I got to the photos of me back in 1996.

Then Chris showed me around the place. What started to get me really excited was an upstairs area where I could tell that a few of the shapes under their covers were Formula 1 cars. The first cover came off and I went starry-eyed. It was Ayrton Senna's 1988 championship-winning McLaren MP4/4. The next cover came off… Senna's 1991 title-winning MP4/6. They were parked next to each other, two icons of Formula 1 history just a few feet apart.

Then we went along some corridors and downstairs to the car I'd really come to see. When the cover was removed, it looked very different, the spitting image of the famous Le Mans winner of 1995, in black with Ueno Clinic branding. That in itself was a memory jogger. My old team-mate from Ehrlich days, Masanori Sekiya, had been one of the winning drivers, and he'd also brought the Japanese funding from Ueno Clinic. What the hell is Ueno Clinic, you may be wondering?

Well, it was a chain of private clinics in Japan catering for a procedure that was apparently all the rage with Japanese men — circumcising their penises for better sex.

Anyway, back to McLaren F1 GTR chassis #2R. What I didn't know was that in 1995, when it normally raced in Gulf colours, it had also been put into Ueno Clinic livery for one event. After winning Le Mans with chassis #1R, the Ueno Clinic boss wanted to have a stab at winning his home race, the Suzuka 1,000Km, and #2R did just that before being put back into its usual blue and orange. So, to honour that Suzuka victory in 1995, Chris had decided to present the car in that livery.

I sat in it and asked if I could start the engine. Chris said "yes". Muscle memory told me which buttons to push to get the V12 going. Click, click, click. The bark was amazing — and that's when the tears started. What a moment that was, real joy, a feeling almost of coming home.

When I look back, I realise that I've had an incredible journey. From those little acorns of racing a kart around a field at home, I found a career beyond anything I could have dreamed of.

I've been very lucky, and one thing has led to another, almost by chance. When I was racing, I always talked to a lot of people and tried to be friendly and approachable, and that had a big effect because all the chances I got were interconnected. With every car I ever drove, somewhere the seed had been planted earlier in my journey by a friend or a contact.

My testing ability stood me in good stead and I think this has probably been the best aspect of my career. I absolutely adored getting a car to the point where it was a race winner. When you know your car is better tuned than anyone else's on the grid, that's a pretty worthwhile feeling. You then know that as long as you don't make a mistake, you should win.

Having some background as a mechanic helped me develop these skills. It really took off when I got to the Ehrlich team in Formula Atlantic because I was then in charge of my destiny. I prepared my own car, properly hands-on. I knew what to look for, what bits were wearing out, what made a difference. Those three years at Ehrlich taught me the skills I needed to take me forward. When we changed things on the car, I could always feel it straight away.

Lister boss Laurence Pearce once said to me that I should have made far more of this skill — and charged more for my services. He pointed out that what I could bring to sorting a car could save so much money, time and effort for drivers and teams who didn't know how to do it. He was right. Just as an example, I remember one team in Formula Ford 2000 that had been chasing wheelspin for a couple of meetings and eventually they put me in the car to try and get to the bottom of it. After two corners, I knew it was the clutch slipping, not wheelspin.

Laurence was always so good to me. He now lives in Portugal and looks after cars belonging to oil and gas entrepreneur Larry Kinch. When restoration work has been done on one of Larry's cars, Laurence likes to make sure it's running properly.

He could pick any one of numerous drivers he knows to undertake this kind of shakedown work but he likes me to do it. I once asked him over a beer why he picked me. He said, "Fluxie, it's because when you go out of the pitlane, you're fucking on it from the word go."

I did that for three years until Covid came along and ruined things. It was a shame because I loved flying out to Porto and running those cars around the Boavista circuit, things like a Formula Junior Lola from the sixties, and a Formula 3 Martini and Formula 2 March from the seventies.

I've kept count of all the competition cars I've driven and the total is nearly 600. Of course, many of them I tested rather than raced, but my total number of races is also pretty amazing... 754 of them.

I dread to think how many pints I've consumed in that time. I know I've had the reputation of being a pisshead and there were certainly times I didn't get a drive because of that. I've already mentioned a couple of instances. I think the one that really made a massive difference was not getting the Unipart Formula 3 drive in 1979. Looking back, I can see that team boss Dave Price made the right decision to choose Nigel Mansell over me, but at the time I hated Mansell for beating me to that. Still, imagine me doing sponsor duties with Unipart, talking to their customers about air filters or suspension bushes. I'd have been a liability.

All the same, I was able to make my living from racing for nearly four more decades after that. I can't think of any other driver like me in this respect who simply had to make a living this way, all the way through to about the age of 60. When I think around all my contemporaries in racing, they've all been able to draw on money from elsewhere, whether a garage business, a restaurant, whatever. I've had nothing else apart from racing. I certainly haven't made a fortune but I've made a lifetime of memories.

In the middle of it all, I also had those years as a single parent. I'm so proud of Coral and Wills — and the grandchildren they've given me. Coral's son George came first, on 21st April 2012. Then Wills also became a dad when Arthur arrived on 26th July 2021. Coral longed for another child and after years of IVF she finally got pregnant again and gave birth to Primrose on 26th March 2022. When I went around there to see Primrose, George came out to greet me wearing a T-shirt emblazoned with 'I used to be an only child and now I'm gonna be a brother'. Lovely.

I don't think there's a 17-year-old around today who could go on to do what I did. It just wouldn't be possible. I guess that makes me the last of a generation.

PHOTO CREDITS

Author's collection: pages 65, 66, 67, 68, 69, 70, 71, 72, 73, 74, 75, 76 top, 78, 79 bottom, 80 bottom, 145 bottom, 147 top, 148, 149, 150 top, 151, 152 bottom, 153 bottom, 155 bottom, 159 bottom, 160 bottom, 225, 226 top, 227, 228, 229, 230, 231, 233, 234, 235 top, 238 top, 239 top and 240.

Jim Bamber: page 226 bottom.

Paul Boothroyd: page 146 top.

Denis Briot: front cover.

John Brooks: pages 235 bottom and 236 bottom, back cover.

Chris Davies: pages 76 bottom, 77 and 80 top.

Jakob Ebrey: pages 159 top, 238 bottom and 239 bottom.

John Gaisford: pages 150 bottom, 158 bottom and 160 top.

Malcolm Griffiths: page 237 top.

Gary Haggaty: page 232.

Duncan Hands: pages 154 bottom and 155 top.

Russell Hobman: page 145 top.

Pascal Huit: page 236 top.

Gary Kimber: page 147 bottom.

Motorsport Images: pages 152 top, 154 top, 156–157, 158 top and 237 bottom.

Doug Rees: page 153 top.

Fred Scatley: page 146 bottom.

Peter Tempest: page 79 top.

INDEX

ABBA 43
Abbott, James 277–278
Abbott, Lionel 144, 152, 161, 169, 170
Abbott, Phil 238, 256, 257, 258, 277–278
ADA Engineering 139–141
Adams, Tony 131
Agostini, Giacomo 77, 86–88, 289
Aintree 105
Aitken, Matt 181–182
Alcock, Tony 56
Allam, Jeff 167, 178, 188
Amstrad 120
Apollo Race & Rally Wear 116
Aquila 120, 121, 122, 130, 139, 147
RO83S 119
Argo 88
JM19 165, 166
Armes, Ray 187
Arrows 98
Arsenal Football Club 132
Ascari (circuit) 279
Ashby's Garage 32, 40–41, 256
Ashley, Ian 44–45, 46, 130
Asquith Autosport 143
Assen 276
Aston Martin
DBR1/300 249–250
DBR4 250–251
Atkinson, Rowan 281
Attwood, Richard 265
Audi 97
A4 221–222, 225
Austin 89
Austrian Grand Prix
1974 (Osterreichring) 44, 45
Autosport 42, 64, 111, 129, 220, 227, 257, 267, 270, 276

Bahrain 236, 275
Bailey, Julian 210, 211, 214

Bain, Duncan 105, 106, 109–110, 111–112, 113–114, 145
Baird, Gil 122, 124
Baker, George (grandson) 240, 295
Bamber, Jim 226
Barber, Wesley 260
BARC (British Automobile Racing Club) 64
Barcelona 259
Barclays Bank 216, 217
Barnard (kart) 30, 68, 69
Barrichello, Rubens 245
Baypark Raceway 91, 113
BBC (British Broadcasting Corporation)
Grandstand 120, 186
Top Gear 11, 209
Beaujolais Run
1986 132–133
Beeches, Steve 168, 212
Beecroft, Dave 192
Belgian Grand Prix
1974 (Nivelles) 43
1991 (Spa) 155, 179, 181–183
Bell, Derek 222, 265
Bell, Justin 222
Bellm, Ray 110, 204–205, 291
Benetton
B194 243, 244, 245
Bennetts, Dick 92
Bernasconi, Paul 63
Biela, Frank 221
Birmingham Superprix
1986 130
1990 155, 170–173, 193, 287
Birrane, Martin 84
Blackbushe 27, 28
Blakeney, Pat 175
Blanchet, Mike 77
Blower, Colin 194, 195, 218, 226
BMW 128–129, 144, 174, 176, 186, 188, 269, 270, 288

3 Series 185
320i 176, 177
M1 102, 277
M3 128, 158, 178, 185
Boavista 294
Bond-Smith, John 134
Borgudd, Slim 83, 278, 285
Bowler, Stuart 254
Brabham 41, 59
Brabham, David 181, 290
Brabham, Geoff 64, 76, 135
Brabham, Jack 21, 59, 250
Bracey, Ian 79, 100–101
Bradley, Frank 108, 119, 121
Bragg, David 19, 20
Brands Hatch 13, 14, 20, 21, 25, 39, 40, 44, 52, 55, 63, 68, 71, 79, 82, 95–96, 99, 100, 110, 116, 121, 123, 126, 130, 135, 137, 141, 142, 144, 149, 150, 151, 162, 170, 206, 209, 233, 261, 279–280, 284, 285, 288
Brawn, Ernie 45–46, 98
Brawn, Ross 98–99
BRDC (British Racing Drivers' Club) 64, 85, 133, 136, 142, 143, 162, 165, 263–271, 287
Chris Bristow Trophy 136, 149
Rising Stars 263, 267–271
Silver Star 133, 263
Young Driver of the Year 136, 267
Briggs & Stratton engine 27
Brimble, Ray 48, 50, 51, 52, 53, 56
Brindley, John 115, 123, 124, 135, 142
Brise, Tony 52, 53, 56, 127
BriSCA (British Stock Car Association) 248
Britcar GT Series 237, 276
British Grand Prix
1965 (Silverstone) 21
1974 (Brands Hatch) 44

1975 (Silverstone) 53
1978 (Brands Hatch) 81, 82
1980 (Brands Hatch) 96
1984 (Brands Hatch) 117
1991 (Silverstone) 155, 156–157, 158, 179, 181, 189
1992 (Silverstone) 186
1999 (Silverstone) 219
British GT Championship 197, 204–211, 214, 216, 222, 227, 237, 254–255, 259–260, 274, 275–276
British Touring Car Championship (BTCC) 143–144, 154, 158, 159, 161, 166, 170, 171, 173, 178, 185–186, 187–190, 198, 220, 241, 285
BRM 119
Broadley, Andrew 138
Broadley, Eric 138
Brodie, Dave 116, 267, 271
Brooks, Bob 256
Brown, Neil 127
BRR Motorsport — see 'Burke Ratcliffe Racing'
Brundle, Alex 279
Brundle, Martin 245, 279
BS Fabrications 52
Buckmore Park 68
Burke, Nigel 135, 137
Burke Ratcliffe Racing (BRR) 135, 136, 141–142, 149, 165, 178
Burton, Phil 272–273, 274
Button, David 288

Cadwell Park 40, 86, 199, 280
Campbell-Walter, Jamie 199–201, 218
Can-Am 115, 116, 123, 135
Candy, Vivian 101
Castle Combe 104, 121, 195, 217–218, 278
Caudwell, John 281
Chapman, Colin 242
Cheever, Eddie 140
Chevrolet
  V8 engine 135, 165, 275, 277
Chevron
  B8 116, 117, 146
  B23 45

B47 86
B56 104
Childs, Frank 98, 99
Chrysler
  Viper 219
Citroën
  2CV 160, 195
Clark, David 219
Clark, Jeremy 233
Clark, Jim 20, 21, 242, 251
Clarke, Peter 191–192
Cleland, Bill 166, 167
Cleland, John 166–167, 178, 186, 188
Clinton engine 15
Cloud Engineering 64, 81, 84
Cole, Steve 197, 201
Coleman, Terry 272–274, 276
Computer Consortium Racing 119, 120, 127
Connaught 40, 60
Conway, Mike 260
Cook, Dave 131, 137, 166, 167
Coombs, Bill 174
Cooper 13, 250
Corbett, Gerry 126
Cornock, Alan 121
Cosworth 42, 101, 139
  BDA 91
  BDG 84
  DFV 43, 110, 242
Coulthard, David 268
Countdown Developments 216
Crawford, Chris 139
Croft 40, 45, 70, 215, 222–223
Crowther, Leslie 133
Crowthorne, David 251
Crystal Palace 21
Currie, Craig 278
Currie, Norman 15
Cutner, Lewis 50
Cygnus 117

Daewoo 192
Dallara 268
  F394 221
Dance, Bob 242
Darrian 205
Dave Cook Racing Services 131
Davenport Vernon 131–132

David Price Racing 89
Davies, Jamie 260
Daytona 104, 139–141
de Angelis, Elio 242
de Cesaris, Andrea 88, 93
de Dryver, Bernard 86
De Havilland 89, 90
Deayton, Angus 29
Dennis, Ron 41–42, 48, 222
Dent, Stuart 111
Dickins, Stanley 139
Dijon 244
Dinnage, Chris 242
Dire Straits 93
Donington Park 64, 76, 82, 83, 87, 110, 116, 117, 130, 143, 144, 146, 159, 166–167, 170, 176, 178, 185, 188, 190, 193–195, 197, 198, 205, 209, 213, 215, 217, 221, 225, 231, 242–243, 245–246, 251, 254, 256, 258, 259 260, 272, 281, 284, 288
Dorset Racing 84
Dougall, Rad 59
Down, Richard 84–85
Dowsett, Phil 100
Dowson, Roger 191
Drewitt, Richard 252
Dron, Tony 80, 214
Droop, Christian 278
Duez, Marc 224
Duffy, Gil 185
Dunn, John 166
Dutch Supercar Challenge 237, 276–277
Duxbury, Graham 107–108, 119
Duxbury, Jill 108–109
Dyer, Ian 77

Ecclestone, Bernie 59
Eddie Jordan Racing 171
Edwards, Guy 86
Ehrlich 78–80, 89–100, 104–105, 108, 113, 115, 240, 261, 291, 293
  RP4 96, 101
  RP5 79, 90, 104
  RP5B 104, 105
Ehrlich, Dr Josef 78, 79, 89, 90, 91, 93, 94, 95, 96, 97, 98, 99, 103–104, 105, 163, 179, 281

Ehrlich, Geoffrey 93
Eisner, Alan 116, 117, 146
Embassy Hill — see 'Hill'
EMC (Ehrlich Motor
  Company) 89
EMKA Racing 102, 210,
  259
Enderby, David 190
Ensign 251
Esso 53, 96, 97
European Grand Prix
  1985 (Brands Hatch) 124
European Touring Car
  Championship (ETCC)
  144, 152, 269
Euser, Cor 181, 182–183
Evans, Andy 290
Evans, Bob 84, 85
Eyre, Richard 243

Fabi, Teo 92
Fagan, Ricky 153, 167,
  168
FAI Auto Parts 286
Fangio, Juan Manuel III
  181
Fearnley, Paul 220–221,
  247
Ferrari 203
  250 GTO 214, 233, 249
  330 LMB 251
  360 Modena 260, 272,
    274
  Dino 256
  F2004 245–246
  F40 254, 272
  F430 274
Ferrari Challenge 272, 274,
  275, 276,
FIA GT Championship 208
FIA Historic Formula 1
  Championship 242
FIA Masters Historic
  Championship 282
FIA Sportscar
  Championship 236, 254,
  259
FIA Touring Car World
  Cup 221
FIA World Sports-
  Prototype Championship
  162
Fiat
  126 72
Fiedler, Klaus 244
Financial Times 275

Fittipaldi 64, 86
  F8 109, 110, 115
Flux, Arthur (grandson) 295
Flux, Carolyn (sister) 12,
  71, 206–207
Flux, Coral (daughter) 96,
  138, 143, 170, 206, 213,
  240, 243–244, 261, 286,
  295
Flux, Eileen (mother) 11,
  12, 13, 14, 17, 18, 21,
  22, 29, 30, 32, 44, 46,
  71, 72, 100
Flux, Harold (grandfather)
  12, 17, 18, 33, 64
Flux, Jane (ex-wife) (née
  White) 105, 111, 112,
  113, 114, 116, 118, 122,
  132, 133, 138, 139, 140,
  148, 170, 171, 180, 181,
  192, 206, 213, 214, 255,
  261, 269
Flux, John (father) 11, 12,
  13, 14, 15, 16, 18, 20, 21,
  22, 27, 28, 29, 30, 32,
  33, 34, 37, 38, 64, 71,
  95, 96, 100, 249
Flux, Mervyn (uncle) 13, 14
Flux, William (son) 96, 170,
  178, 181, 206, 213, 240,
  243, 261, 295
Flux-Heath, Primrose
  (granddaughter) 295
Ford
  Capri 249
  Cortina 28, 34, 44
  Escort
    Mk 1 223–224
    Van 33
    RS Cosworth 191
  Mondeo 193, 232
  Mustang 21, 284
  Sierra
    RS500 Cosworth 143,
    144, 152, 154, 161,
    166, 169, 170, 171,
    183
  Sapphire RS Cosworth
    183–184
  Transit 49, 51, 72, 105
  V8 engine 251
Formula 1 41–46, 48–58,
  64, 70, 77, 83, 87, 98,
  109, 130, 135, 164, 165,
  193, 219, 242–244, 251,
  257, 278, 282, 283, 291

Formula 2 107, 131
Formula 3 8, 38, 58–62,
  63–64, 72–76, 77, 81,
  84, 85, 86, 88, 89, 90,
  91, 96, 99, 105, 117, 118,
  122, 125, 127, 128, 139,
  147, 164, 221, 242, 249,
  257, 267, 268, 278, 285,
  294
Formula 6 (karting) 27–28,
  30, 32, 33–34, 36, 37,
  39, 68, 69, 206
Formula 3000 124, 125,
  171
Formula 5000 38, 277
Formula Atlantic 78–79,
  80, 85, 90, 94–100,
  104–106, 109, 114, 115,
  120, 130, 145, 240, 251,
  284, 293
Formula Ford 7, 37, 38, 97,
  175, 258, 260, 288
  Formula Ford Festival
    126, 141, 151, 261
  Formula Ford 2000 105,
    107, 119, 120, 293
Formule Libre 119
Formula Pacific 90–94,
  112–113, 145
Formula Palmer Audi
  246
Formula Renault UK 270
Formula Vauxhall Lotus
  161
Formula Vee 7, 37–40, 42,
  45, 46, 51, 53, 54, 55,
  58, 60, 69, 70, 71, 94,
  127, 164, 209, 233
Foster, Len 120
Foulston, John 123, 124,
  135, 141
Freeman, Hugh 97
French Grand Prix
  1975 (Paul Ricard) 52,
  53

GAC (car) 209
Ganley, Howden 267
Garofall, Rob 259
German Grand Prix
  1974 (Nürburgring)
  44–45
Giacomelli, Bruno 60, 61
Gilmore, Matthew 257
Gollop, Will 222–223
Goode, Graham 166

Goodwood 7, 13, 20, 43,
  49–50, 54, 59, 61, 62,
  70, 73, 84, 85, 203, 215,
  252, 281, 289
  Festival of Speed 87
  Revival 214–215, 233,
    249, 251, 284, 289
Gravett, Robb 187, 188,
  189
Gray, Kenny 59
Greasley, John 208, 210
Greaves, Jonathan 44
Greene, Keith 185
Greenhalgh, Clive 193,
  195, 199
Griffiths, John 236, 275
Griffiths, Malcolm 224, 241
Grob, Ian 45
Grob, Ken 41, 45
Grolsch 190, 192
Group C2 139, 142, 143,
  162, 165
Group N 144, 152, 191
Grundy, Ken 183, 184
Guadix 273
Guards Trophy GT
  and Sports Racing
  Championship 283
Guerrero, Roberto 88
Gulf 204, 205, 292
Gustavsson, Rob 117, 125

Haas, Carl 139
Hahne, Armin 182–183,
  290
Hailwood, Mike 90
Hales, Mark 162, 194, 195,
  196
Halfords 158, 185, 186, 189
Hall, Adrian 81
Hall, Stuart 260
Hamilton, Lewis 270–271
Hancock, Tony 256–257
Hanson, James 216
Hardman, Peter 161, 191,
  251
Harrison, Ian 187
Harrison, Murray 248
Harrods 87, 222
Harrower, Ian 139
Hart engine 131
Harvey, Tim 186, 188
Hawkwind 36
Hay, Richard 218
Henton, Brian 38
Herd, Robin 64

Herridge, Tom 275
Hesketh 44, 100
Heylen, Jan 260
Higgins, Mark 223
Hill 48–58, 72
  GH1 48, 49, 50, 56, 244
  GH2 56, 237, 244
Hill, Bette 61, 74
Hill, Damon 166
Hill, Graham 48, 49–52,
  53–54, 55–56, 57, 58,
  59, 61, 64, 72, 96, 237,
  242, 244
Hill, Mick 277
Hillman
  Imp 33
Hines, Martin 260
Hi-Tech Motorsport 127
Historic Formula 1
  Championship 242
Hobbs, David 140
Hockenheim 276, 277
Hodgetts, Chris 173, 196
Hogarth, Paul 185
Holbay 59
Holden
  Commodore 144
Hollamby, Olly 39
Hollings, Charlie 258
Holmes, Colin 107
Homer, Len 104
Hommerson, Nick 272
Honda
  Prelude 137
Hopkirk, Paddy 265
Horn, Gordon 100
Horn, Rosie 100
Hotels
  Four Seasons, Florence,
    Italy 274
  Loews, Monaco 97, 181
  Lovely, Jarama, Spain
    276
  Saracen's Head,
    Towcester,
    Northamptonshire
    270
  Sintra, Macau 105–106
  Vacation Hotel,
    Christchurch,
    New Zealand 92–93
Howell, Alan 49, 64, 81,
  82, 83, 84, 86
Hoy, Chris 280
Hughes, Jason 272
Humphries, Marvin 124

Hunn, Jason 247
Hunn, Ricky 247
Hunt, James 248
Hurst, Greg 290–291
Hyde, Alan 199
Hyde, Mike 256
Hyde, Steve 216

Ibec 79, 100, 101, 102
Ingliston 128
Ingram-Monk, Peter 36–37
Ireland, Innes 215
Ives, Carol 56

Jackson, Alan 258
Jacobs, David 278–279
Jaguar 167, 182
  E-type 283
  XJR-9 140
  XJR-15 155, 156–157,
    158, 179–183, 185,
    289, 290
Jaguar Intercontinental
  Challenge 179
James, Clive 252
James, Matt 220
Janspeed 169
Jarama 276
Jessop, Ray 41, 42, 48
John Player Special 242
Jonathan Lewis Racing
  215
Jones, Alan 52, 53
Jones, Bev 53
Jones, Brian 55
Jones, Davy 145
Jones, Karl 143, 144, 152,
  175
Jordan, Eddie 102, 171
Jordan, Nick 59

Kawasaki 256
Keegan, Rupert 60, 61
Kennedy, Roy 135, 158,
  159, 178, 185, 186, 189,
  265
Kent, John 173, 197, 198,
  226
Kessel, Loris 274
Kilcommons, Donny 286
Killarney 108
Kinch, Larry 293
King, James 64
Kirby, Keith 46
Knapp, Steve 139
Knight, Richard 115

Knockhill 177, 197, 274, 285
KVG Racing 45
Kyalami 108

Lanfranchi, Tony 248–249, 263
Lanzante, Dean 291
Lanzante, Paul 204, 207, 290, 291
Lascelles, Gerald 264
Lawler, Alo 100, 105, 110
Le Mans 97, 139
 1959 249
 1963 251
 1981 79, 84, 100–102
 1995 80, 204, 205, 208, 222, 229, 291, 292
Lee, Vic 143, 144, 150, 178
Lee-Davey, Tim 102–103
Lees, Geoff 60, 208
Lep International 112, 145
Leslie, David 79, 95, 96, 142, 179, 182, 188, 285
Level 42 160, 195
Leventis, Harry 214, 249, 250, 251
Lewis, Chris 42
Lewis, Jonathan 215, 260
Liddell, Robin 256
Lindsay, Valentine 289, 290
Lindup, Mike 160, 195
Linford, Mick 187, 188, 189
Lipizzaner horses 109
Lister
 Storm 208–211, 214
Live Aid 121
Llandow 39
Llewellin, John 178
Llewellyn-Davies, Anthony 121
Lockie, Calum 279
Lola 48, 52, 77, 84, 121, 138–139, 141, 151, 164, 165, 294
 T89/90
 T294 84, 85
 T530 123, 124, 135, 136, 141, 149, 150
 T594 118, 123, 130, 146
Lotus 242
 Elan 26R 283, 284
 Lotus Cortina 21
 Type 7 15
 Type 30 251
 Type 87B 242–243

Loudon, Dave 200
Lovett, Peter 118
Lydden Hill 38
Lyon, John 195

Macau Grand Prix
 1982 105–106, 107
Macdonald Race Engineering 115
MacDonald, John 86
MacDonald, Phil 86
Mackie, Andy 251, 276, 287
Magnussen, Jan 221
Magny-Cours 235, 254
Mallock, Ray 100, 109
Mallory Park 39, 90, 98, 219, 249, 250, 255, 256
MAN 212
Manfeild 92, 113
Manor Motorsport 270
Mansell, Nigel 77, 85, 86, 88, 90, 123, 158, 175, 181, 193, 194, 203, 285, 294
March 81, 93, 96, 117, 294
 743 43
 753 82
 763 60
 773 64, 81, 82
 781 115
 782 92, 111
 78B 105
 793 77, 88, 285
 79B 284
 822 107
Maries, Chris 172
Marshall, Chris 263
Marshall, Gerry 129, 170, 195, 196–197, 248–249, 250–251
Martini (car) 294
Mass, Jochen 162
Mazda
 323F 239, 240, 285
 Rotary engine 118, 123, 130, 146
Mayers, Roger 256
McKellar, Ian (Jr) 200, 211, 214, 247, 255, 269
McKellar, Ian (Sr) 255
McLaren 91, 271, 291
 F1 GTR 204–205, 207, 210, 211, 222, 227, 229, 290–292

M6 115
M8D 252
MP4/4 291
MP4/6 291
McLaren, Bruce 252
McMillan, Dave 92
McRae, Graham 38
McRae, Jimmy 173
Meek, Chris 43, 45
Melling, Al 197
Menu, Alain 187
Mercedes 177, 212
 190E 153, 167
MG
 Maestro 126
 Turbo 176
 MGA Twin-Cam 13
Middlebridge Racing 169
Mikkola, Hannu 223–224
Millard, Chris 253
Millard, Mike 235, 236, 253–254, 259
Millbrook 174
Millen, Steve 92, 94
Miller, Andy 221
Minitec 144, 152, 161, 169, 170
Mitsubishi
 Starion 218
Mobberley, Mick 127, 129
Modus 59, 74
Monaco Grand Prix
 1974 43
 1975 52
 1976 61, 74
 1977 63–64
 1980 96–98, 101
 1991 155, 179, 180–181
Mondello Park 95, 105, 201–202, 260
Monza 53
Morgan, Peter 97, 101, 105, 106, 112, 120, 261–262
Moroso 139, 164
Morris
 Marina TC 87
Morris, Mel 169
Morrison, Andy 179
Mosler 237, 275–277, 286–287
 MT900 275
Moss, Stirling 20, 133, 215
Motor Racing Stables 13
Motoring News 220, 221, 223, 225, 232, 234, 246, 247

Motorsport News 221, 231, 238, 243, 248, 255
Motor Sport 221, 237, 243
Motul 41
Mountune Engines 183
Mugello 274
Murphy, Rob 152, 161
Musguin, Andrew 33, 34
MV Agusta 87, 289

Needell, Patsy 8
Needell, Tiff 7–9, 38, 59, 60, 81, 96, 100, 101, 108, 120, 128, 129, 148, 156–157, 176, 181–182, 185, 208, 209, 210, 214, 232, 253, 289
Neill, Terry 132
Neve, Patrick 59, 73
Nevitt, Roger 183
New Zealand Grand Prix 1980 (Pukekohe) 91 1984 (Pukekohe) 113
Newman, Paul 135
Nicol, John 173
Nielsen, John 180
Nissan
Skyline GT-R 169
V6 engine 254
Nissen, Kris 187
Nivelles 43
Nogaro 236, 259
Nürburgring 44, 45, 276
Nursey, Dennis 169

O'Brien, Eugene 126, 189, 190, 272, 273–274
O'Brien, Mike 119, 120, 147, 270
O'Connell, Martin 268
O'dor, Kieth 162, 169
O'Rourke, Steve 102, 210, 211, 259
Ockley 46, 58, 60, 61, 64, 74, 81, 85
Offord, Sid 82
Olympic Games
London 2012 280
Opel
Commodore 249
Orgee, Roger 96
Osborn, Paul 245
Osella
PA3 239, 284, 285
Osterreichring 45, 53

Oulton Park 88, 110, 119, 131, 134, 135, 142, 175–176, 192, 197, 198, 213, 217, 253, 256, 268, 281
Owen, Richard 119, 122, 127, 130, 139, 141
Oxton, Dave 92, 93

Padmore, Nick 282
Palm, Gunnar 223
Parkinson, Michael 252
Paul Ricard 52, 56, 244
Paul Stewart Racing 221
Pearce, Laurence 208, 209, 211, 293–294
Pembrey 160, 161, 195, 208, 256
Penthouse 28
Percy, Win 182
Perkins, Larry 59, 92
Peterborough Motor Club 135–136, 149
Peters, Cliff 255
Peugeot 187, 188, 189, 198
306 (rallycross) 222–223
405 Mi 16 159, 187, 242
Phillips, Ian 171
Pierpoint, Roy 21
Pilbeam 120
Piper, David 265
Piquet, Nelson 81, 82
Pizzonia, Antonio 216, 248
Playboy 28
Pool, Colin 142, 204, 263, 284
Porsche 182
Cayman GT4 288
911 Turbo 253
924 182
935 236, 275
956 203
962 165
993 GT1 208, 210
996 GT3 259–260
Port Elizabeth 108
Porter, Les 28, 54
Porto 283
Prater, Don 117, 118, 123, 125, 127, 130, 146
Pratt, John 126
Priaulx, Andy 269, 270
Price, David 77, 81, 85, 86, 87, 294
Prodrive 178, 185, 187
Prosport 190–191
Pryce, Tom 42, 43, 54, 57–58

Pubs and bars
Angels, Dublin, Ireland 260
The Dove, Newport Pagnell, Buckinghamshire 118, 286
The Greyhound, Croydon, Surrey 36
The Horse and Jockey, Dunstable, Surrey 111
The Kentagon, Brands Hatch, Kent 121, 124
The Surrey, Caterham, Surrey 31
Pukekohe 91–92, 93, 113
Pullen, Bert 39–40, 60
Purley, David 44, 244
Pye, Marcus 129

Queen 56

R&D Motorsport 183
Race of Champions 1975 52
Radbourne Racing 100
Radical 235, 238, 245, 255–259, 277–282, 285
Prosport 256, 257, 258
SR1 280
SR2 259
SR3 257–258, 278
SR8 278, 279
V8 engine 278
Ralt 59, 63, 64, 81, 83, 92, 94, 163
RT1 59, 61, 62, 74, 76
RT4 95, 105
RT4/81 109, 110, 111, 112, 113, 145
RAM Racing 86
Rapier 235, 236, 254, 259
Ratcliffe, Andrew 135
Ratzenberger, Roland 195
Reid, Anthony 103, 126, 211
Reid, John 194
Renault
4 241
16 94
19 159
Laguna 241–242
Reynard
SF80 107
Reynolds, John 280–281
Richards, Terry 56

Riley, Brett 88, 89, 90, 91, 92
Riley, Kevin 237, 275–277, 287
Riley, Pauline 277
Road Atlanta 164–165
Roberts, Kenny 289
Roberts, Steve 176–177
Rochester Motor Club 36
Roe, Michael 86
Rogers, Lucy 288–289
Rogers, Pete 288
Rollcentre Racing 275
Rolls-Royce 90, 256
Rondel Racing 41, 48
Roni 117, 118, 122–123, 125, 126, 147, 191, 221
Rosberg, Keke 243
Rossiter, Jeremy 85
Rotax engine 95, 103
Rouse, Andy 143, 170, 188
Rover 129, 168, 174, 175, 185, 186, 187
    216 GTi 160, 186
    Metro 175
    SD1 175
    V8 engine 196, 197
Rowan, Ray 268
Roy Kennedy Racing 158, 265
Royale 39, 119, 121
    RP38 121
    RP42 129
Rufforth 40
Rush, Mervyn 26
Ryan, Tom 167

Saab 170
Safir 7, 59, 73
Saints Transport 212
Salvadori, Roy 249
Samuelson, Ben 199
Samways, Tim 249, 250
Sanada, Matsuaki 104, 109, 110, 178, 179, 180, 183
Sauber-Mercedes 162
Saunders, Dave 91, 94, 112
Scania 212
Scarab 37, 38, 39, 40, 46, 69, 70, 209
Scheckter, Ian 107, 108
Scheckter, Jody 107
Schools
    Moleside, Cobham, Surrey 17, 21

Belmont, Dorking, Surrey 22–27, 67
Caterham, Surrey 29–31, 32, 35–36
Schirle, Chris 172, 173
Schumacher, Michael 243, 245
Scott, Aaron 268
Scott, Allan 285
Scott, Dave 123, 268
Sears, Jack 264
Sebring 139, 164, 251
Sekiya, Masanori 80, 104, 105, 115, 291
Senna, Ayrton 105, 134, 172, 195, 242, 291
Serra, Chico 81
Shadow 43–44, 48, 119
Sharp, Ian 88
Shaw, Jeremy 97
Sheene, Barry 289
Shelby, Carroll 249
Sheldon, John 183
Shell 58, 278
Shelton, Dave 243
Short, Martin 197–198, 213, 275, 276, 286–287
Shrike 129, 130, 139, 147, 148
    P15 122, 127, 134
Silentnight 192
Silkolene 189
Silverstone 21, 38, 40, 43, 53, 59, 63, 64, 74, 82, 86, 88, 101, 104, 110, 117, 120, 121, 122, 128, 136, 141, 142, 144, 147, 149, 152, 155, 156–157, 158, 178, 179–180, 181, 185, 186, 187, 188, 191, 196, 197, 200, 205, 207, 208, 219, 222, 239, 254, 263, 270, 278, 279, 285, 286–287, 288
Silverstone, Phil 81, 82
Silverstone Racing School 126, 285
Smallman, Andy 49, 56
Smith, Chris 194, 203
Smith, Kenny 92
Smith, Mike 130–131, 192, 284, 288
Smith-Hilliard, Max 281–282, 283

Snetterton 38–39, 95, 121, 122, 129, 141, 142, 146, 147, 148, 153, 161, 165, 167–168, 171, 221, 256, 280–281
Sonny and Cher 23
Soper, Steve 188
South, Stephen 60
South African Grand Prix 1977 (Kyalami) 57
Spa 24 Hours 1991 183–184
Spa-Francorchamps 155, 160, 179, 181–184, 186, 210–211, 258–259, 277, 279
Sparrow, Will 223
SportsRacing World Cup 254
Sports 2000 81, 116, 119, 120–122, 127, 129–130, 133–134, 138–139, 141, 142, 147, 148, 151, 162, 163, 164, 215, 231
Sports Car Club of America (SCCA) 164
Stevens, John 175
Stevenson, James 203
Stewart, Jackie 61, 74, 267
Stewart, Rod 109
Stock Aitken Waterman 181–182
Stott, Paul 162
Streber Motorsport 194, 197, 199, 203
Stuck, Hans 221, 222, 225
Sugar, Alan 120
Sugden, Tim 210, 211, 260, 261
Surtees, John 98
Sutton, David 223
Suzuka 292
Suzuki 289
    Hayabusa 256, 278
Swetnam, Malcolm 183, 184
Swift 165
Swindon Racing Engines 104
Syscom 127
Sytner, Frank 178

Tambay, Patrick 135, 251
Tauranac, Ron 59, 61, 62, 63, 163
Taylor, Bert 216, 217
Taylor, Chris 190–191

Taylor, Ian 81, 118, 127–129, 130, 142, 143, 150, 153, 160, 167, 168–169, 174, 176–177, 186, 187, 288
Taylor, Mark 215, 216
Taylor, Mike 'Fulmar' 129–130, 134–135, 148, 215, 231
Taylor, Moya 128, 186
Taylor, Wayne 139
TC Prototypes 49, 52
Team Central 193, 197
Team Sovereign 235, 236
Tech-Speed 122
Templeton, Trevor 105
Thatcher, Margaret 99
Thatcher, Mark 99
The Bee Gees 24
The Rolling Stones 23
Thompson, John 49
Thomson, James 119
Thruxton 63, 76, 86, 88, 121, 122, 133, 158, 161–162, 170, 175, 195, 240
Thundersaloons 130–132, 137, 166, 192, 288
Thundersports 116–117, 118, 123, 127, 130, 135, 141–142, 146, 149, 150, 204, 277, 284
Thyrring, Thorkild 191
Tiga 139
  TS86 142, 204
  GC287 162
Titchmarsh, Ian 219, 258
TOCA Shootout
  1992 188
  1993 193–195
Token 41–45, 48, 49, 52, 59, 70, 100, 130
  RJ02 42
Tourist Trophy
  1962 (Goodwood) 215
  1988 (Silverstone) 144, 152
  1996 (Donington Park) 198–199
Toyota 224, 241
  Celica
    2000 GT 223
    GT-Four 224, 241
  Starlet 247
  Supra Turbo 144, 150
Tredaire 108
Triggs, Barry 39, 40

Trimmer, Tony 101, 109, 115
Triumph
  Dolomite Sprint 88
  TR7 85
Trojan 15
Tro-kart 15
Trundle, Neil 41, 42, 43, 44, 45, 48
Turner, Alan 49, 57, 58, 59, 64, 223
TVR 196, 199, 200, 203, 213, 217
  AJP V8 engine 197
  Cerbera Speed 12 255
  Tuscan 155, 170–173, 193–202, 203, 204, 206, 212–213, 214, 215, 216–219, 222, 226, 229, 230, 231, 253, 256, 275, 286, 287
TVR Tuscan Challenge 170–173, 193–202, 205, 212–213, 216–218, 226, 227, 229, 231, 248, 269, 287
TWR (Tom Walkinshaw Racing) 179, 181, 182
Tyrrell 44, 278

Ueno Clinic 291–292
Ulrich, Jake 204–205, 207, 208–211, 212–213, 216, 222, 227, 291
Unipart 77, 81, 85, 88, 128, 285, 294

Van Diemen 105, 126, 216, 260, 261
  RF78 108
Vassilopoulos, Chris 290–291, 292
Vauxhall 131, 132, 133, 166
  Astra GTE 132–133, 166
  Cavalier 167, 178
  Chevette 131–132, 137, 166, 223, 288
Venn, Bruce 39
Verdon-Roe, Bobby 187–188, 198–199, 200–201, 202, 231, 255
Vergers, Michael 257
Vic Lee Motorsport 185
Villiers engine 15, 28
Vincent, Paul 115, 116, 117

Vincent, Sue 116
Vlassopulos, Tony 41, 43
Volkspares 39
Volkswagen
  Beetle 14, 37, 39
  Caravanette 33

Walker, Ian 263
Walker, Murray 120, 189
Walker, Peter 269, 270
Walker, Sean 119, 120, 122, 141, 143, 154, 162, 166, 170, 171, 242, 263, 283, 284, 285–286
Walkinshaw, Tom 144, 167, 179, 182, 264, 265, 266, 267
Wallace, Andy 222
Wallinder, Magnus 210
Warnock, David 185
Warwick, Derek 76, 81, 82, 179, 181
Wasyliw, Nick 117
Watson, John 265, 289
Weaver, James 129, 164, 253
Webb, John 116, 130, 142
Welkom 108, 109
West Oxfordshire Motor Auctions 134
West Surrey Racing 92
Wheeler, Peter 196, 197, 217
Wigram 92, 93, 113, 145
Wilcox, Adam 274
Wilds, Mike 129, 135–137, 142, 149
Willhire
  24 Hours (1988) 167
  25 Hours (1989) 153, 167–168
Williams 119, 123, 175, 181, 241
  FW06 77, 87, 88
  FW07C 282
Williams, Barrie 265
Winks, Des 137
Wollek, Bob 181
Woodfield, Brian 41
World Rally Championship 241

Yeomans, Jason 199

Zandvoort 195–196, 276
Zolder 87
Zwolsman, Charles 182